The Age of Jackson

The Age of Jackson

Edited by
ROBERT V. REMINI

UNIVERSITY OF SOUTH CAROLINA PRESS
Columbia, South Carolina

THE AGE OF JACKSON

Copyright © 1972 by *Robert V. Remini*.

All rights reserved. Printed in the United States of America.
No part of this book may be used or reproduced in any manner without written
permission except in the case of brief quotations embodied in critical articles and
reviews. For information address Harper & Row, Publishers, Inc., 10 East 53rd Street,
New York, N. Y. 10022.

First HARPER PAPERBACK edition published 1972.

This edition published by the UNIVERSITY OF SOUTH CAROLINA PRESS, *Columbia, S. C.*,
1972, by arrangement with HARPER PAPERBACKS, from whom a paperback edition is
available.

International Standard Book Number: 0-87249-274-5
Library of Congress Catalog Card Number: 72-5337

Suggested Library of Congress classification furnished by McKissick Memorial Library
of the University of South Carolina:
E381.R

Manufactured in the United States of America

For Joseph R. Frese, S. J.

Contents

Introduction

THE AGE of Jackson opened and closed with a bang! To be sure the explosions at either end of the period were different. The age commenced in 1828 with the raucous shouts of politicians and their "hurra boys" proclaiming the election of Andrew Jackson to the presidency and in the process nearly wrecking the White House in their exuberance to honor him upon his inauguration.[1] And the age closed with the crackle of gunfire that started the Mexican War in 1846. What followed was a long, tragic drift into secession and civil war, developing almost inexorably out of the Mexican conflict.[2]

Not every historian would agree to these precise events in marking the perimeters of the age. Surely one must go back into the early decade of the 1820s, they argue, or even before, to find the genesis of many important developments of the 1830s and 1840s.[3] And some historians are frankly offended by the title, "Age of Jackson." They prefer other designations, such as the "Age of Egalitarianism," the "Age of Materialism," the "Age of Opportunism," or the "Age of Innovation," to name just a few.[4] Unquestionably, these titles have merit since they catch significant characteristics of the period, yet there is something to be said for maintaining the older designation. For one thing Jackson's overwhelming presence pervades the entire era. The age was actually informed by his presence. Although some students slight his importance and find Henry Clay, Daniel Webster and John C. Calhoun more attractive for study, nevertheless any close investigation reaffirms Jackson's central role in the major events of the

1. Document # 4.
2. After everything that has been said about the causes of the Civil War it should be clear that many of the events leading to that tragedy were set in motion as a consequence of the adventure into Mexico.
3. See Richard H. Brown, "The Missouri Crisis, Slavery and the Politics of Jacksonianism," *South Atlantic Quarterly* LXV (Winter, 1966): 55–72.
4. Lee Benson, *The Concept of Jacksonian Democracy: New York as a Test Case* (Princeton, 1961); Edward Pessen, *Jacksonian America: Society, Personality, and Politics* (Homewood, Illinois, 1969); Douglas T. Miller, *The Birth of Modern America, 1820–1850* (New York, 1970).

period.[5] For another, Jackson personally symbolized the entire era, even developments and currents of thought over which he had absolutely no connection, interest or knowledge. He "shared and possessed all the creative ideas of his country and his time," claimed George Bancroft; "he expressed them with dauntless intrepidity; he enforced them with an immovable will; he executed them with an electric power that attracted and swayed the American people."[6] The judgment is extravagantly partisan, nevertheless it is still true that the meaning Jackson held for his contemporaries encompassed an enormous range on many levels, and swung from the most philosophic, idealistic and elegant to the most pragmatic, sordid and vulgar.[7] For those who admired him he was the Hero of the Battle of New Orleans, the self-made man who rose from cabin to the executive mansion all on his own. For those who despised him he was a savage frontiersman, a violent, grasping, immoral ruffian whose administration disgraced the nation by turning the government over to the lowest classes in society.[8] And, finally, as

5. It is significant that at present there are major publishing projects under-way to make available the collected works of Clay, Webster and Calhoun, each sponsored by a University with support from the National Historical Publications Commission. At this writing no similar project is yet contemplated for the Jackson papers. The Ladies Hermitage Association, which maintains Jackson's home in Tennessee, would like to initiate such a project and have already made a financial commitment to it. However, no University has yet agreed to undertake professional responsibility for editing and publishing the papers. Hopefully, this situation will change in the immediate future.

6. Bancroft, *Literary and Historical Miscellanies* (New York, 1855), p. 479.

7. For an excellent analysis of how Jackson was cast in the image of his own age see John William Ward, *Andrew Jackson: Symbol of an Age* (New York, 1955).

8. Admiring biographies of Jackson include Marquis James, *The Life of Andrew Jackson* (Indianapolis and New York, 1938) and Robert V. Remini, *Andrew Jackson* (New York, 1966). Arthur M. Schlesinger, Jr., *The Age of Jackson* (Boston, 1946) is also sympathetic. John S. Bassett, *The Life of Andrew Jackson* (New York, 1928) is a critical, scholarly but unexciting account of Old Hickory's life that ends with a favorable interpretation of Jackson; and James Parton's *The Life of Andrew Jackson* (New York, 1861) is critical and well written and ends with a slightly unfavorable interpretation of Jackson. Glyndon G. Van Deusen, *The Jacksonian Era 1828–1848* (New York, 1959) is a useful survey of the period. Perhaps the most recent and most critical study of the age and the man is Edward Pessen's *Jacksonian America.*

the Chicago *Democrat* indicated in its issue of January 21, 1834, there were some Americans—perhaps many—who lived during the period and themselves recognized that theirs was the "Age of Jackson." "In coming time," read the newspaper, "when history shall have recorded his glory it will be mentioned with pride, by those whose youthfulness have prevented them from yet figuring on the stage of action, that 'I was born in the Age of Jackson.'"

Another concept that troubles some historians is the notion that the Jacksonian age witnessed the so-called Rise of the Common Man. The phrase can be misunderstood, of course, particularly if applied to the elective field where the common man had been rising for decades. Nor can it be accurately used to describe the sudden appearance of a rude majority who seized control of the government through the election of their "idol" and dismissed those whose claims to federal office were based on intellect, education, family and long public service. Rather, the phrase needs to be understood in terms of the sudden outpouring of sentiment preached in newspapers and the public forums praising ordinary citizens for their virtue and wisdom. There was an upsurge of admiration and respect for "the people." There was a vocal affirmation of the merits of the mass electorate. There was the emergence of a democratic spirit that repudiated traditional notions of deference, position and place. The reason for this can best be explained by the fact that this was a romantic era, strongly influenced by the preceding revolutionary age, which affirmed the rights of all men, not just those of wealth and social standing.[9]

With respect to government, the phrase "Rise of the Common Man" can be appreciated when applied to Jackson's own attitude toward those who served the people through appointed office. Just prior to his election to the presidency, he supposedly told Amos Kendall, one of his staunchest supporters in Kentucky and later his postmaster general, that he intended to remove from office all men who opposed his election, were appointed for political reasons "or against the will of the people, and all who are incompetent."[10] Of course he did not carry out his threat and his removals were rela-

9. Carl Russel Fish, *The Rise of the Common Man, 1830–1850* (New York, 1927).
10. Kendall to Francis Blair, March 7, 1829, Blair-Lee Papers, Princeton University Library.

tively modest.[11] Nevertheless, in his first message to Congress in December, 1829, he declared his intention of establishing the principle of rotation in office. He believed that all intelligent men could serve the government on a regularly rotating basis. He argued that no one had an intrinsic right to office and that long tenure invited corruption and inefficiency.[12] His public embrace of the spoils system earned Jackson devastating criticism. He was charged with deliberately driving the best qualified and experienced from government service and replacing them with political hacks.[13] But in *theory* his policy represented a way in which the central government could be made to respond immediately to the changing demands of the American people as expressed in the ballot box. Furthermore, it would obviously open government service to a much larger number of people than had previously been the case. Thus, the old cliché about the "Rise of the Common Man" does indeed contain a considerable measure of truth.

There is still another term that can elicit critical notice—the phrase "Jacksonian Democracy." There is question whether the designation has any precise meaning in view of the long evolution of the democratization of American institutions. Actually the term is more the invention of historians who devised it to explain a very broad movement during the second quarter of the nineteenth

11. It has been estimated that Jackson removed only 919 persons out of 10,093 during the first eighteen months of his administration. For the entire eight years of his presidency he dismissed a little more than ten per cent of all officeholders, which is certainly not the record of a spoilsman when these figures are considered in the light of normal replacements due to death and resignations plus those removed for incompetence and dishonesty. See Leonard D. White, *The Jacksonians: A Study in Administrative History, 1829–1861* (New York, 1954). Sidney H. Aronson in his *Status and Kinship in the Higher Civil Service: Standards of Selection in the Administrations of John Adams, Thomas Jefferson and Andrew Jackson* (Cambridge, 1964) demonstrates how little difference existed between the men chosen for federal office by these three presidents.

12. Document # 9.

13. James Parton's biography of Jackson is one long moan about the misfortunes visited upon the country because of the spoils system. "General Jackson's appointment-and-removal policy," Parton wrote, "I consider an evil so great and so difficult to remedy, that if all his other public acts had been perfectly wise and right, this single feature of his administration would suffice to render it deplorable rather than admirable." Parton, *Jackson*, III: 692.

century involving major political, social and economic changes.[14] These changes, and the activating forces behind them, were quite complex and often contradictory. They were to be found on different levels—local, state, regional and national—and frequently they had nothing to do with Jackson himself or his political party.

Over the years Jacksonian Democracy has meant different things to different historians. For some it represented a frontier democracy seeking equality with the rest of the nation; for others it was the urban masses demanding social and economic improvements; for many it was the classic conflict between the rich and poor, the workers versus the capitalists; for still others it was the struggle of incipient entrepreneurs anxious for personal profit; while another group modified this entrepreneurial thesis and argued that although Jacksonians had their eye "on the main chance" they also sought the restoration of "old republicanism" with its virtues of simplicity, integrity and morality. And there are other interpretations, some of which emerged even before the age had run its course.[15]

Jackson himself has not been especially helpful in providing clues to an understanding of the movement that bears his name because he was so contradictory. His fundamental caution was

14. Contemporaries spoke of "Jacksonism," which was defined by the *Boston Daily Advertiser and Patriot* (October 22, 1832) as an appeal "to the worst passions of the least informed portion of the people."

15. It is not possible to list all the interpretations and those cited in the text are given a very rudimentary presentation. The following works include most of the major statements about Jacksonian Democracy: Frederick Jackson Turner, *The United States, 1830–1850* (New York, 1935); Arthur Schlesinger, *Age of Jackson*; Algie M. Simons, *Social Forces in American History* (New York, 1911); Louis Hacker, *The Triumph of American Capitalism* (New York, 1940); Bray Hammond, *Banks and Politics in America from the Revolution to the Civil War* (Princeton, 1957); Richard Hofstadter, *The American Political Tradition* (New York, 1948); Marvin Meyers, *The Jacksonian Persuasion: Politics and Belief* (Stanford, 1957); Joseph Dorfman, *The Economic Mind in American Civilization*, Volume II (New York, 1946); Louis Hartz, *The Liberal Tradition in America* (New York, 1955); Thomas P. Abernethy, *From Frontier to Plantation in Tennessee* (Chapel Hill, North Carolina, 1932); Lee Benson, *The Concept of Jacksonian Democracy*; Edward Pessen, *Jacksonian America*; Vernon L. Parrington, *Main Currents in American Thought*, Volume II (New York, 1954); Alexis de Tocqueville, *Democracy in America* (London, 1835); M. Ostrogorski, *Democracy and Party System in the United States* (New York, 1902).

obscured by regular impetuousness; his periodic outbursts of violence masked a characteristic gentleness; and his exasperating tendency to reduce issues to a personal contest conflicted with his natural inclination to study details of a problem. One early biographer labelled him a "democratic autocrat. An urbane savage. An atrocious saint."[16] His life style corroborated these contradictions, for he was a frontiersman who lived on a large plantation and enjoyed the privileges of upper class society in Tennessee. He claimed to represent the will of the people, but as Michael Chevalier, the French traveler, noted, his tactics in politics was not so much to respond to the popular will as it was to "throw himself forward with the cry of, 'Comrades, follow me!' "[17]

In order to understand Jacksonian Democracy many historians have attempted to identify the social classes and laboring groups which supported Jackson. Agreement is still remote. Yet it seems clear from the electoral statistics of 1828 and 1832 that Jackson himself enjoyed widespread support that ranged across all classes and sections of the country. He attracted farmers, mechanics, laborers, professionals and even businessmen. And all this without Jackson being clearly pro- or antilabor, pro- or antibusiness, pro- or antilower, middle or upper class. It has been demonstrated that he was a strikebreaker, yet at different times—although not on any regular basis—he and the Democrats received the backing of organized labor.[18] Perhaps the best that can be said in any general way

16. Parton, *Jackson*, I: vii.
17. Michael Chevalier, *Society, Manners and Politics in the United States* (Boston, 1839), p. 181.
18. This is my own view based on studies of New York and Pennsylvania for the 1828 and 1832 elections. Robert V. Remini, *The Election of Andrew Jackson* (New York, 1963), *Andrew Jackson*, and *Andrew Jackson and the Bank War* (New York, 1967). However, most labor historians probably take an opposite view. The question of labor's support has been intensively debated by historians over the last twenty-five years. See Schlesinger, *Age of Jackson*; Joseph Dorfman, "The Jackson Wage-Earner Thesis," *American Historical Review* LIV (January, 1947): 296–306; Richard B. Morris, "Andrew Jackson, Strikebreaker," *American Historical Review* LV (October, 1949): 54–68; Edward Pessen, "The Workingmen's Movement of the Jacksonian Era," *Mississippi Valley Historical Review* XLIII (December, 1956): 428–443, and "The Working Men's Party Revisited," *Labor History* IV (Fall, 1963): 203–226; Walter Hugins, *Jacksonian Democracy and the Working Class* (Stanford, 1960); Donald B. Cole, *Jacksonian Democracy in New Hampshire* (Cambridge, 1970); William A. Sullivan, "Did Labor

about the great numbers of Americans who flocked behind Jackson and the Democratic party is that they were more nearly the popular party of the less affluent in society than their opposition, the National Republican and Whig parties.[19] In other words the older interpretation of the Democrats as the egalitarian party— with some exceptions to be noted later on—still makes more sense than any other interpretation that has since been advanced to explain the composition of the Jacksonian movement.[20]

Furthermore, the Democrats had a fairly clear idea of what they were attempting to accomplish with their numerical majority. Simply stated, their rhetoric—and it must be remembered that their rhetoric was bombastic in the extreme—pulsed with a determination to eliminate economic and political privilege. They in-

---

Support Andrew Jackson?", *Political Science Quarterly* LXII (December, 1947): 569–580; Edward Pessen, "Did Labor Support Jackson?: The Boston Story," *Political Science Quarterly* LXIV (June, 1949): 262–274; Robert T. Bower, "Note on 'Did Labor Support Jackson?: The Boston Story,' " *Political Science Quarterly* LXV (September, 1950): 441–444, and Edward Pessen, *Most Uncommon Jacksonians, The Radical Leaders of the Early Labor Movement* (Albany, 1967).

19. In *The Concept of Jacksonian Democracy*, Lee Benson argued that New York's men of wealth were equally divided between the Democratic and Whig parties because the leaders of the major parties enjoyed the same wealth and status. This thesis has been successfully refuted, I think, by Frank Otto Gatell in his article, "Money and Party in Jacksonian America: A Quantitative Look at New York City's Men of Quality," *Political Science Quarterly* LXXXII (June, 1967): 235–252. Gatell shows that New York's men of wealth were predominantly Whig. See also Edward Pessen, "The Wealthiest New Yorkers of the Jacksonian Era: A New List," *The New York Historical Society Quarterly* LIV (April, 1970): 145–172, and "Moses Beach Revisited: A Critical Examination of His *Wealthy Citizens* Pamphlets," *The Journal of American History* LVIII (September, 1971): 415– 426.

20. The older interpretation is delineated in such works as Dixon Ryan Fox, *Decline of Aristocracy in the Politics of New York, 1801–1840* (New York, 1919); Frederick J. Turner, *The United States*; Frederick A. Ogg, *The Reign of Andrew Jackson* (New York, 1919); William McDonald, *Jacksonian Democracy* (New York, 1907); Edward Channing, *A History of the United States*, Volume V (New York, 1926); William O. Lynch, *Fifty Years of Party Warfare, 1789–1837* (Indianapolis and New York, 1931). This general interpretation is given a modern and more sophisticated reading in Schlesinger's *Age of Jackson* and more recently in Donald Cole's *Jacksonian Democracy in New Hampshire*.

sisted they were defending public rights against private advantage. In his farewell address, Jackson warned Americans that unless they checked the "spirit of monopoly and thirst for exclusive privileges you will in the end find that the most important powers of the Government have been given or bartered away. . . ."[21] The warning was constantly reiterated by other Democrats. "Following the destruction of the Bank," wrote one, "must come that of all monopolies, of all PRIVILEGE."[22] Jacksonians excoriated monopolies because they enjoyed special favors denied to others. They attacked them because their advantages institutionalized inequality. In fact the editor of the New York *Evening Post* defined liberty as "nothing more than the total absence of all MONOPOLIES of all kinds, whether of rank, wealth or privilege."[23] It may be naïve to say so, in view of the historical revisionism of recent years, yet nothing seems more obvious than that the Jacksonians believed what they preached— however emotional their language—and that they actually stood for certain political and economic principles which were fundamentally democratic in nature.[24]

They also expected the federal government to serve as an honest broker between different laboring classes and to refrain from exercising powers which might provide one group an advantage over the others. As Jackson declared in his veto of the Bank Bill, "when the laws undertake to add . . . exclusive privileges, to make the rich richer and the potent more powerful, the humble members of society—the farmer, mechanics, and laborers— . . . have a right to complain of the injustice of their Government."[25] Although Democrats advocated limited government and tended to espouse the rights of the states, this did not mean they were committed to laissez-faire as an absolute doctrine. They were quite prepared to use regulatory powers to ensure economic equality when occasion demanded, particularly on the state level.[26]

21. James D. Richardson, *Messages and Papers of the Presidents*, Volume II (Washington, 1897), p. 1525.
22. *Boston Quarterly Review* III (July, 1840): 394.
23. May 22, 1834.
24. This position is well documented in a recent study on *Jacksonian Democracy in New Hampshire* by Donald Cole.
25. Document # 14.
26. They were also ready to encourage economic development by such measures as promoting canal and road building within the states.

To most Jacksonians the term "privilege" was synonymous with "aristocracy." Removed from the American Revolution by a generation and looking back on it with reverence, they equated all democratic advances achieved in the country in terms of a struggle against aristocracy—a struggle that still went on. "The Aristocracy and the Democracy of the country are arrayed against each other," was the verdict of one Jacksonian, and while the language was overwrought and the interpretation simplistic, his impression genuinely represented the fundamental belief of most Democrats.[27] Similarly, Jackson's impressive presidential victory in 1828 was interpreted by contemporaries as the "triumph of numbers" wherein the "Democracy" exercised its elective might and voted him into office. The interpretation has since been sharply criticized by historians who find Jackson's triumph hardly a "popular revolution"; yet a "popular revolution" was precisely now most Americans at the time understood what had happened; and this applies to those who opposed Jackson's election as well as those who favored it.[28]

Thus, if Jacksonian Democracy means anything at all, the definition must begin with what the Democrats believed was a crusade against political and economic privilege. The principle—and Jacksonians were committed to it as principle—was incessantly repeated, sometimes in the most unlikely places. For example, Catherine E. Beecher published a book in 1847 entitled *Treatise on Domestic Economy for the Use of Young Ladies at Home and at School* and touched on it in an offhanded way. "Every man may aim at riches," she wrote, "unimpeded by any law or institution

27. Michael Hoffman to Azariah C. Flagg, November 8, 1828, Flagg Papers, New York Public Library.
28. Edward P. Gaines to Jackson, n.d., Jackson Papers, Library of Congress; Isaac Munroe to John Bailey, December 26, 1828, Bailey Papers, New York Historical Society; Robert Wickliffe to Henry Clay, October 7, 1828, H. Shaw to Clay, January 9, 1829, Clay Papers, Library of Congress; *Niles Weekly Register*, December 6, 1828, Edward Everett to A. H. Everett, December 2, 1828, Everett Papers, Massachusetts Historical Society. For a penetrating criticism of the "popular revolution" thesis see Richard P. McCormick, "New Perspectives on Jacksonian Politics," *American Historical Review* LXV (January, 1960): 288–301. See also McCormick's *The Second American Party System: Party Formation in the Jacksonian Era* (Chapel Hill, North Carolina, 1966) and Chilton Williamson, *American Suffrage from Property to Democracy, 1760–1860* (Princeton, 1960).

which secures privileges to a favored class, at the expense of another. Every law, and every institution, is tested by examining whether it secures equal advantages to all; and, if the people become convinced that any regulation sacrifices the good of the majority to the interests of the smaller number, they have the power to abolish it."[29]

As Miss Beecher said, "every man may aim at riches," and indeed a considerable number of Americans in the Age of Jackson were feverishly caught up in the pursuit of money. Many of them were grasping, conniving, avaricious men on the make whose concern about the privilege of others only masked their own selfish interests. These men were driven by the acquisitive spirit. They wanted more than they had. "There are no bounds among us to the restless desire to be better off," editorialized the *American Review*, "and this is the ambition of all classes."[30] So blatant and vulgar was this scramble for wealth that some students of the period have interpreted it as the fundamental cause of the War against the Second Bank. They do not see the War as a struggle between the democracy and the money power; rather they regard it as the outward reach of a new entrepreneurial middle class attempting to share what established businessmen already possessed. They see it as an attack upon an older set of capitalists by a newer, more numerous set. This interpretation flatly denies any idealistic or democratic content to the War.[31]

No one can question the argument that many, if not most, men actively engaged in annihilating the Second Bank were anxious for material gain,[32] but to interpret the War in such a limited and cynical way distorts the political realities of the Jacksonian age. Granted Democrats were men on the make; granted they wanted to improve their economic status; nevertheless, they were also committed to the principle that no class or chartered monopoly deserved special rights that set them apart. If the Jacksonians wanted to get ahead themselves they also wanted it for everybody

29. Beecher, *Treatise on Domestic Economy* (New York, 1847), p. 27.
30. Document # 33.
31. The spokesmen for this interpretation are Bray Hammond, *Banks and Politics in America*, pp. 286–548, and Richard Hofstadter, *The American Political Tradition*, Chapter 3.
32. It should also be said that many of these men acted out of ignorance of the Bank's functions and usefulness to the national interest.

else. The Bank War does not express the ambition of small capitalists so much as it represents a commitment by many different classes of people to the democratic principle that there should be economic opportunity for all.

Americans generally—not simply Jacksonians—openly and gleefully acknowledged their concern for the almighty dollar. It was reflected in their value system, their attitudes toward people, even the stories and jokes they told about themselves. To them it was all very natural and normal. But they denied that wealth was more valued in America than Europe. They simply insisted that the pursuit of money in other countries was necessarily confined to a very small group of people—the privileged class, the elite, the aristocracy—while in America it was open to all.

Yet, with all their talk about providing opportunity for the largest number and eliminating restrictions blocking the economic and political progress of the American people, the Jacksonians were virtually indifferent to social inequalities. In an age of reform when there was so much ferment for improving the conditions of American life, the Jacksonians were singularly unresponsive towards women's rights, prison reform, educational improvements, protection of minors and other forms of social betterment. Their treatment of the Indians, in removing them west of the Mississippi River, constitutes one of the most frightful examples of bigotry and greed in American history.[33] Although it has been argued that the policy of removal was intended, among other things, to preserve the Indian from certain extinction, still that policy was executed with calculated contempt for Indian life and property.[34] Furthermore, the Jacksonian record on slavery was abysmal. Not only did they disregard the rights—let alone the torment—of the black man but they allied themselves with the Southern power structure to protect and perpetuate the institution of slavery. Speaking generally, there would appear to be no direct relationship between the Jacksonians and the reform impulse of the period. Their political opponents, the Whigs, had a much better record on social legisla-

33. Document # 12.
34. A very able defense of the removal policy as policy is F. P. Prucha, "Andrew Jackson's Indian Policy: A Reassessment," *The Journal of American History* LVI (December, 1969): 527–539. See also Mary E. Young, "Indian Removal and Land Allotment: The Civilized Tribes and Jacksonian Justice," *American Historical Review* LXIV (October, 1958): 31–45.

tion. Voting patterns in a number of northern legislatures seem to demonstrate two interesting phenomena: Whig consciousness of social wrongs and Democrat concern for political and economic reform.[35]

There are other distinguishing features of Jackson's America. To begin with, the age marked a dramatic change in the style and content of the political process. Little of it had much to do with the struggle for the suffrage since elective rights for white male adults had already been attained throughout the country with relative ease. True there were pockets of disenfranchised, but in most instances these were eventually eradicated with a minimum of conflict or resistance. Compared to the European scene the American experience was a model of orderly and democratic advance.

The noise and nonsense so characteristic of American electioneering came into vogue during the Jacksonian period. A wildly extravagant campaigning style developed, offering such things as parades, barbecues, songs, tree plantings, buttons and other paraphernalia in the belief that such hoopla appealed to the great mass of voters and encouraged them to vote. Popular personalities were nominated and identified as representatives of the democracy. In addition, the convention system was introduced in the selection of national candidates; committees were developed in a highly structured pyramid from local groups on up through county and state organizations.[36] Indeed, the period was marked by intense political organization that saw the final evolution of most American electoral forms. The mania for organization reached beyond the political sphere, however, and was adopted by many reformers who were agitating for the abolition of slavery, abolition of imprisonment for debt, improvement of prisons and asylums, temperance, women's rights and world peace. Much of the success of these reform efforts was directly attributable to the sophistication of their organizational structure and operation.

35. Herbert Ershkowitz and William G. Shade, "Consensus or Conflict? Political Behavior in the State Legislatures during the Jacksonian Era," *The Journal of American History* LVIII: 591–621. An excellent statement on the Whig position is Glyndon Van Deusen, "Some Aspects of Whig Thought and Theory in the Jacksonian Period," *American Historical Review* LXIII (January, 1958): 305–322.
36. Documents # 2, 3.

But as curious and fascinating as these changes were in altering the form of American politics they were not nearly as important as the radical transformation that occurred in the political *thinking* of professional politicians. In the past political leaders condemned parties as cankers on the body politic. In his Farewell Address, George Washington warned the nation against the disruptiveness of political parties, insisting they were factions concocted by artful men intent on subverting the will and needs of the American people. John Adams echoed Washington's sentiments by labelling parties the greatest political evil operating within the country. This attitude, generally shared by many Founding Fathers, slowly changed during the first decades of the nineteenth century, but underwent a drastic shift during the Age of Jackson. Now a new breed of politician emerged: the professional, of which Martin Van Buren of New York was the prototype, who argued that a highly organized two party system openly engaged in a fair contest for public office was the only way to ensure a free and representative government. These politicians detested the single party structure of the Era of Good Feelings and attributed all the bad feelings of that period to the lack of a two party system. Modern government, they contended, demanded well functioning political parties openly arrayed against each other. Van Buren claimed that democratic principles in government were impossible without party politics; others declared that parties not only preserved liberty by allowing for opposition but also inhibited governmental corruption by providing the means for periodic reexamination of the conduct of public business.[37]

For all their pious preaching about liberty and integrity in government, politicians were probably more convinced of the need for parties because of their belief that the party system would produce stability—stability in government and in society. Political organizations were essential for a stable, orderly government since only a well defined two party system could effect a balance of power between opposing forces. And balance of power was crucial

37. See Richard Hofstadter, *The Idea of a Party System: The Rise of Legitimate Opposition in the United States, 1780–1840* (Berkeley, 1969); Robert V. Remini, *Martin Van Buren and the Making of the Democratic Party* (New York, 1959); and Michael Wallace, "Changing Concepts of Party in the United States: New York, 1815–1828," *American Historical Review* LXXIV (April, 1969): 453–491.

to the elimination of civil strife. As Van Buren argued in his letter to Thomas Ritchie, the reestablishment of the party system was the best, perhaps the only, way of resolving differences between the major sections of the country, and indeed of quieting the mounting agitation over slavery. Otherwise, he declared, prejudices between the free and slave states were certain to get worse.[38]

Like Metternich, who was seeking to thwart revolutionary discontent in Europe, Van Buren, and similar politicians, were attempting to banish political disorder from the United States by a balance of power achieved through two well organized and active parties. Political stability was what these men desired, and they reckoned that party structure was the only way to obtain it.[39] The party would be the bulwark of the constitutional system; it would reinforce the established order of society; it would preserve domestic tranquility.

Obviously such a political system was profoundly conservative, yet it mirrored the mood and desire of most Americans. As Alexis de Tocqueville remarked in *Democracy in America*, most Americans were essentially conservative in their politics; they demanded change but they abhorred revolution. And change could be achieved through the regular shifts in administration from one party to the other, all reached through nonviolent conflict. As several politicians of the Jacksonian age repeatedly asserted, neither a one-party nor a tri-party system could produce these happy results.[40] For the United States there must be two parties, each nearly equal to the other in numerical strength. As it turned out, acceptance of these ideas provided the country with stability and legitimacy for more than a century, interrupted only briefly by the Civil War.

Despite the system's conservative bent, it nonetheless realized some innovative, creative and democratic changes in the political

38. Document # 1.
39. The "very discord" generated by contending parties, wrote Van Buren, "may in a government like ours, be conducive to the public good." Quoted in Richard Hofstadter, *The Idea of a Party System*, pp. 251–252. For a statement about parties controlling civil disorder see George Bancroft, *Literary and Historical Miscellanies*, pp. 485–487.
40. Jabez D. Hammond, *The History of Political Parties in the State of New York* (Cooperstown, New York, 1845) II: 308–309; Hofstadter, *The Idea of a Party System*, p. 262.

process. Splendid campaigning efforts were inaugurated—however gross and nonsensical some of them were—to interest the electorate in party affairs and encourage greater mass participation in the operation of government. The right to hold federal office was thrown open to all on the theory that rotation advanced democratic attitudes among all classes of people. Then, when Jackson challenged the Second Bank and vetoed its recharter, he took the issue to the people for decision in the presidential election of 1832. For the first, and one of the few, times in American history the electorate was invited to decide a major issue. And the choice was clear: Henry Clay and the Bank or Andrew Jackson and no Bank. When they responded with overwhelming approval for the President's action, Jackson interpreted their vote as a mandate to proceed further and remove the government's deposits from the Bank, thus hastening the institution's ultimate demise. Thereafter he regarded himself as the representative of all the people, implying that only he, as President, enjoyed this distinction. Moreover, he said he was directly responsible to the people, a notion so novel and daring that constitutionalists, like Daniel Webster, denounced him for violating the letter and spirit of the written Constitution.[41]

Indeed, this age witnessed the marked alteration in the relationships between the several branches of government, most particularly in the relationship between the President and the Congress.[42] Under Jackson the powers of the presidential office were vastly expanded. Where, in the past, the chief executive functioned somewhat like a prime minister, acting with scrupulous care toward the Congress and sometimes merely responding to its direction, now under Jackson that office was converted into one of genuine leadership, one that could shape national policy and command action from the legislature. For example, Jackson exercised the veto as no other President had before him. Previously the power had

41. Documents # 19–22.
42. Much has been made of Jackson's contempt for John Marshall because of his remark to the effect that Marshall had made his decision, "now let him enforce it." It is doubtful that Jackson ever made the statement, however characteristic and however much it expressed his opinion. In any event the attitudes between the two men did not affect the constitutional relationship between the executive and judicial offices. Not even the Bank veto which questioned the constitutional argument in the McCulloch case disturbed the relationship.

been used to negate legislation whose constitutionality was questionable; Jackson, on the other hand, vetoed bills for a variety of reasons—political, social, economic, constitutional, or simply practical reasons. In effect, this meant that Congress was forced to consider presidential wishes *before* enacting any legislation, otherwise it risked a veto. Hereafter, the President exercised considerable influence over the legislative process and markedly strengthened his ability to lead the country and dictate national policy. As Webster recognized, Jackson claimed for the President "not the power of approval, but the primary power, the power of originating laws."[43]

Thus, the history of dynamic and aggressive executive leadership in the United States begins with Andrew Jackson. Because of its intrinsically conservative, balance-of-power structure, the American government requires periodic jolts of strong executive action if it is to avoid becoming static and thereby, like the Metternichian system, risk total breakdown. Jackson not only provided bold presidential strokes but in the process he created national issues and national politics,[44] something missing from the American scene for more than a decade. He accomplished this feat because of his phenomenal hold on the affections of the American people. The "less informed—'the unsophisticated classes' of people," wrote one old line Whig, "believed him honest and patriotic; that he was the friend of the *people*, battling for them against corruption and extravagance and opposed by dishonest politicians. They loved him as their friend. . . ."[45] James Parton, one of Jackson's earliest biographers, agreed with this evaluation. During the last thirty years of his life, wrote Parton, "he was the idol of the American people," honored "before all other living men."[46]

Jackson's most successful and popular action as President involved his handling of the crisis over nullification with South Carolina.[47] In meeting the emergency he proceeded cautiously, attempting to be conciliatory. He did not explode in a succession of

43. Document # 17.
44. Such national issues as rotation, Indian removal, destruction of the national bank, and the French Spoliation controversy, to name a few.
45. Nathan Sargent, *Public Men and Events*, Volume I (Philadelphia, 1875): 347.
46. Parton, *Jackson*, III: 684–5.
47. Documents # 25–32.

rash and hasty actions, as some expected. Instead, he alternated between the gesture of conciliation and the menace of retaliation, and by his adroit maneuvering ultimately prevented bloodshed and the disruption of the Union. He succeeded because he not only recognized that the Union would be tested by the support he received from the American people but because he knew intuitively how to marshal his enormous popularity to provide that support.

In turning aside the threat of secession, Jackson exploited one of the most powerful political impulses then operating within the United States—the impulse of union. While, at the same time, there was much theorizing about nullification, secession and states rights, still it was the idea of union that really held the affections of the American people. Even among those who were philosophically committed to preserving the prerogatives of the states, such as Jackson himself, there was intense devotion to the larger concept of a unified whole, segments bound together to form a single nation. Jackson's most famous quotation was his strong pronouncement that the Union must be preserved. Daniel Webster in his Senate debate with Robert Y. Hayne encapsulated the idea in glowing rhetoric, concluding that without union there could be no liberty. There were critics, of course, men capable of trifling with secession to achieve their political purposes, but neither their logic nor eloquence could diminish the strong impulse toward union, and it was this impulse that Jackson skillfully mobilized to terminate the crisis with South Carolina.[48]

This uncommon devotion to the sense of union was one expression of a strong nationalistic sentiment that had been swelling within the country since the War of 1812. But there were other expressions of that sentiment, such as the aggressive territorial expansion of the nation during the 1840s. The desire for Texas, California and Oregon was simultaneously explained and pardoned as the natural evolvement of the nation's destiny, manifestly ordained by providence.[49] There was nothing new about the west-

48. On the nullification crisis see William W. Freehling, *Prelude to Civil War: The Nullification Controversy in South Carolina, 1816–1836* (New York, 1965); Major L. Wilson, " 'Liberty and Union': An Analysis of Three Concepts Involved in the Nullification Controversy," *Journal of Southern History* XXXIII (August, 1967): 331–355 and "Andrew Jackson: The Great Compromiser," *Tennessee Historical Quarterly* XVIII (Winter, 1966): 615–636.
49. Documents # 37–39.

ward movement. That was part of a larger American experience. What was special to the Jacksonian era was the rationalization applied to it by spokesmen of the Democratic party. John L. O'Sullivan's phrase about "Manifest Destiny" was quickly adopted by most expansionists who blithely insisted that the country had some sort of divine right to lands presently claimed by Indians, Mexicans and British. This was yet another expression of a romantic age that could easily dismiss "foreign" rights in the exalted vision of an expanded empire stretching from ocean to ocean.

Manifest Destiny was also a subtle way of convincing Northerners that expansionism was not a conspiracy by Southerners to make additional territory available for slavery. There was absolutely no foundation, declared O'Sullivan, to the charge that the annexation of Texas was "a great pro-slavery measure—calculated to increase and perpetuate that institution. Slavery had nothing to do with it," he insisted. "Opinions were and are greatly divided, both at the North and South, as to the influence to be exerted by it on Slavery and the Slave States. That it will tend to facilitate and hasten the disappearance of Slavery from all the northern tier of the present Slave States, cannot surely admit of serious question."[50] Northerners were hardly taken in by this dubious argument and many of them recognized that expansion only heightened sectional tensions and threatened serious dissension between the North and South.

By the time the Age of Jackson had begun a new cultural and intellectual force from Europe had already swept across the United States. Although the old commitment to the ideas of the Enlightenment, such as the efficacy of reason and order, continued to persist, the romantic ideas of a new age started to take hold. The poetry and essays of Coleridge and Wordsworth coupled with the ruminations of such German philosophers as Kant and Fichte perfumed the intellectual atmosphere with a heady endorsement of the sensate in man. The mind no longer ruled as the sole perceiver of truth and beauty; the emotions were ackowledged as a partner. No longer were human feelings suspect; now they were to be enjoyed and obeyed. Romantics glorified nature as perceived through the senses; they stressed man's intuitive powers; they reemphasized the importance of the individual.

50. Document # 38.

In America the most obvious expression of the romantic age was the transcendental movement.[51] This was a New England phenomenon which proclaimed not simply the goodness of man but his divinity. Transcendentalists were mystics in their approach to knowledge, for they believed man could "transcend" experience and reason to discover the wonders of the universe. And since man was capable of unlimited perfectability, he was capable of governing himself. Government must be founded on good will. It must never coerce the individual against the sovereign dictates of his independent conscience. Transcendentalists believed in the doctrine of the minimized state concerned for social justice and committed against social regimentation.

Besides these cultural and intellectual forces there were other influences contributing to the dynamic changes of the Jacksonian era. After the War of 1812 the country slowly freed itself from its economic dependence upon Europe and began to build a viable domestic economy, not one based exclusively on international trade. The standard of living rose sharply, something that had remained relatively stable during the entire colonial and early national periods of American history. This was especially true in the cities where population rocketed from something less than a million in 1790 to over 11 million in 1840. Cities like Philadelphia, Baltimore and Boston doubled in population, while New York exploded from 130,000 in 1820 to over a million by 1860. In the west new cities were founded, such as Chicago, Cincinnati and St. Louis, all of which soon had populations exceeding 100,000.[52] Into these cities poured a restless—an ever restless—populace along with the immigrants from Europe seeking a new start. During the 1830s and 1840s Irish, German and Scandinavian immigrants were added to the steady stream still coming from Great Britain.

Of major significance in understanding the Age of Jackson was the Transportation Revolution, itself a manifestation of American enterprise and nationalism. The Revolution antedated the Jacksonian period by a decade or more, marked by the extensive construction of canals and turnpikes. The success of the Erie Canal in New York, which linked the midwest with the east coast, excited

51. Documents relating to transcendentalism and the reform movement of the Jacksonian era can be found in Walter Hugins, *The Reform Impulse, 1828–1847* (New York, 1972).
52. Document # 41.

Americans to the possibility of an immense network of interconnecting passageways stretching across the country and binding the nation together. With the Jacksonian era came the start of railroading; and toward the close of the period the Communications Revolution was inaugurated with the invention and application of the telegraph.[53] These revolutions galvanized the economy, especially in attracting prodigious amounts of capital, both home and abroad. By the beginning of the forties, despite the Panic of 1837, the country had reached the "take-off stage" of economic development that ultimately transformed the country into a powerful industrial, as well as agricultural, nation.[54]

Such was the Age of Jackson, a fantastic period of change and ferment, of men searching and experimenting and altering the tone and style of American society. The cultural quickening that produced such towering figures as Emerson, Thoreau, Hawthorne, Lowell, Cooper and Melville, the social reforms that harnessed the humanitarianism of a generation, the communitarian experiments that dared attack rampant materialism, the religious innovations that added a spiritual dimension to social utopianism—all shaped this age of hope and promise.

But there were serious failures. Slavery strengthened its fearful grip on the nation, despite the challenge of abolitionists. Although Jacksonian Democracy represented a commitment to free the common man from the restrictions that cramped his life, the black man was not included in this bright vision. Thus, by the close of the age, sectional controversy generated by slavery fissured the country. As the controversy became more intense, as one political crisis followed another, as more and more men began to question the value of the Union, Jacksonian Democracy collapsed and disappeared in the turmoil that marked the coming of the Civil War.

53. Document # 34.
54. See George R. Taylor, *The Transportation Revolution* (New York, 1951); Douglass C. North, *The Economic Growth of the United States, 1790–1860* (New York, 1965); Robert W. Fogel, *Railroads and American Economic Growth* (Baltimore, 1964) and Albert Fishlow, *American Railroads and the Transformation of Ante-Bellum Society* (New York, 1965).

The Age of Jackson

I

The New Political Age

1. "We Must Always Have Party Distinctions"

THE FOLLOWING *letter written by Martin Van Buren, then U.S. Senator from New York and leader of a political machine known as the Albany Regency, to Thomas Ritchie, editor of the* Richmond Enquirer *and leader of a Virginia machine called the Richmond Junto, is one of the most important documents in American political history and is therefore printed in its entirety. Not only does it list the arguments for summoning a national nominating convention to support Jackson for the presidency but it outlines Van Buren's plan to revive the Republican party through an alliance between Northern Republicans and Southern planters, an alliance which ultimately produced the Democratic party. The letter is also significant because of its discussion of the necessity and importance of political parties in American life.*

Washington Jan 13th, 1827

Dear Sir,

You will have observed an article in the Argus upon the subject of a national convention. That matter will soon be brought under discussion here and I sincerely wish you would bestow upon it some portion of your attention. It was first suggested to me by the Vice-President[1] and Mr. Ingham of Penn.[2] are the only persons with whom I have as yet conversed. They think it essential. It will be an important movement and should be fully and deeply considered. The two papers in the city of N. York devoted to Mr. Clinton's[3] views, the *Statesman* and the *Enquirer*, are you see out

SOURCE: Martin Van Buren to Thomas Ritchie, January 13, 1827, Van Buren Papers, Library of Congress.
1. John C. Calhoun.
2. Samuel D. Ingham, appointed Secretary of the Treasury by Jackson in 1829.
3. De Witt Clinton, governor of New York. He died the following year.

against it. Their motive is obvious. It would interfere with Mr. Clinton's object which (*however appearances may at some times indicate*) depend upon it, is the Presidency at the next election. I have no political intercourse with him, but this I know confidently, altho I do not wish to be quoted for it. The most of his friends think his chance a bad one and would prefer that he should give it up. But they cannot persuade him to do or at least will not succeed in doing it, till it is too late to make a successful retreat. When I speak of Noah[4] as the friend of C, I presume I tell you nothing new; an intelligent and constant observer of his movements cannot be in doubt upon that subject. His entanglement with Mr. Clinton, produced by his embarrassments and a belief that our defeat in 1824 was permanent has destroyed his influence at home altogether. Had he frankly stated that he could not oppose Mr. Clinton for any reason, the circumstances would have been over-looked. But the course he has seen fit to adopt has produced a very general impression upon the Republicans of the State, that he has been treacherous to them which it will take a long time to efface; this has been a source of great regret to me, he has some excellent points and I sincerely hope he may get over it. His paper as well as those few others in the state exclusively devoted to him (that not being the case with most of the old Federal papers) will exhibit for a long time to come the impress of his politics, viz lamentable and extreme variableness. On the part of the Republican papers you will witness a mild but steady and firm trend leading constantly to the great object in view. For myself I am not tenacious whether we have a congressional caucus or a general convention, so that we have either; the latter would remove the embarrassment of those who have or profess to have scruples as to the former, would be fresher and perhaps more in unison with the spirit of the times, especially at the seat of the war Pennsylvania and New York. The following may, I think, justly be ranked among its probable advantages. First, it is the best and probably the only practicable mode of concentrating the entire vote of the opposition and of effecting what is of still greater importance, the substantial reorganization of the old Republican Party. 2nd its first result cannot be doubtful. Mr. Adams[5] occupying the seat and being determined not to surrender it except "in extremis" will not submit his pretension to

4. Mordecai M. Noah, editor of the New York *Courier and Enquirer.*
5. President John Quincy Adams.

the convention. Noah's real or affected apprehension upon that subject is idle. I have long been satisfied that we can only get rid of the present, and restore a better state of things, by combining Genl. Jackson's personal popularity with the portion of old party feeling yet remaining. This sentiment is spreading, and would be sufficient to nominate him at the Convention. 3rd the call of such a convention, its exclusive Republican character, and the refusal of Mr. Adams and his friends to become parties to it, would draw anew the old Party lines and the subsequent contest would reestablish them; State nominations alone would fall far short of that object. 4th it would greatly improve the condition of the Republicans of the North and Middle States by substituting *party principle* for *personal preference* as one of the leading points in the contest. The location of the candidates would in a great degree be merged in its consideration. Instead of the question being between a northern and Southern man, it would be whether or not the ties, which have heretofore bound together a great political party should be severed. The difference between the two questions would be found to be immense in the elective field. Altho' this is a mere party consideration, it is not on that account less likely to be effectual. Considerations of this character not infrequently operate as efficiently as those which bear upon the most important questions of constitutional doctrine. Indeed Genl. Jackson has been so little in public life, that it will be not a little difficult to contrast his opinions on great questions with those of Mr. Adams. His letter to Mr. Monroe operates agt him in N. York by placing him in one respect on the same footing with the present incumbent. Hence the importance, if not necessity of collateral matter to secure him a support there. 5th it would place our Republican friends in New England on new and strong grounds. They would have to decide between an indulgence in sectional and personal feelings with an entire separation from their old political friends, on the one hand or acquiescence in the fairly expressed will of the party, on the other. In all the states the divisions between Republicans and Federalists is still kept up and cannot be laid aside whatever the leaders of the two parties may desire. Such a question would greatly disturb the democracy of the East. In New Hampshire I think it would give us the victory; in all New England it would give them trouble, keep them employed at home and check the hopes of their friends elsewhere. 6th its effects would be highly salutary on your section of the union by the revival of old party distinctions.

We must always have party distinctions and the old ones are the best of which the nation of the case admits. Political combinations between the inhabitants of the different states are unavoidable and the most natural and beneficial to the country is that between the planters of the South and the plain Republicans of the North. The country has once flourished under a party thus constituted and may again. It would take longer than our lives (even if it were practicable) to create new party feelings to keep those masses together. If the old ones are suppressed, geographical divisions founded on local interests, or what is worse prejudices between free and slave holding states will inevitably take their place. Party attachment in former times furnished a complete antidote for sectional prejudices by producing counteracting feelings. It was not until that defence had been broken down that the clamour agt Southern Influence and African Slavery could be made effectual in the North. Those in the South who assisted in producing the change are, I am satisfied, now deeply sensible of their error. Every honest Federalist of the South therefore should (and would if he duly reflected upon the subject) prefer the revival of old party feelings to any other state of things he has a right to expect. Formerly, attacks upon Southern Republicans were regarded by those of the North as assaults upon their political brethren and resented accordingly. This all powerful sympathy has been much weakened, if not, destroyed by the amalgamating policy of Mr. Monroe. It can and ought to be revived and the proposed convention would be eminently serviceable in effecting that object. The failure of the last caucus furnished no argument agt a convention nor would it against another caucus. The condition of things is essentially different. Then the South was divided, now it is united. Then we had several parties, now we have in substance but two and for many other reasons. Lastly the effect of such a nomination on Genl. Jackson could not fail to be considerable. His election, as the result of his military services without reference to party and so far as he alone is concerned scarcely to principle would be one thing. His election as the result of a combined and concerted effort of a political party, holding in the main, to certain tenets and opposed to certain prevailing principles, might be another and a far different thing.

But I forebear, I have already spun out this letter to an unconscionable length. The little acquaintance I have with you scarcely justified me in making this communication. But I write to you in strict confidence—a confidence inspired altogether by your public course. You will not be so unjust as to suspect me of the small design of wishing only to be civil, when I say that there is not another man in the union can render as much service to the cause in which we are engaged as yourself. The lamentable state of the press, must have occurred to you more frequently than to myself. If I were to ask you to name me another editor who fully understands and duly appreciates the importance of the great principles we contend for, without the establishment of which our success would dwindle into insignificance—where would you find him? And yet the press is the great lever by which all great movements in the political world must be sustained. Let me then repeat my request, that you will bestow upon this point all the attention you can afford. If it is successfully carried through, there is no limit to the advantages that would result from it. The principal opposition is to be apprehended from the friends of Genl. Jackson's erroneously supposing that there is no danger of the nomination's falling upon another. This can and must be obviated.

2. The Committee System

ONE IMPORTANT characteristic of this new political age was the high degree of party organization which occurred to create mass support for a particular candidate. Although there was nothing new about the committee system, the intensity and range of committee organization to link the party to the largest number of people was certainly novel. And it was not so much the popular groundswell in Jackson's favor that is significant in understanding the political alterations that occurred at this time as it is the skill and determination of the new breed of politician, such as Allan Campbell, author of the following letter, to construct an apparatus which would determine the electoral outcome.

Louisville/Kentucky/February 4th, 1827

Dear Gen'l:

I have given you the annexed list, for the purpose of enabling you, if you should think proper, to write to certain men in this

SOURCE: Major Allan Campbell to Andrew Jackson, February 4, 1827, Andrew Jackson Papers, Library of Congress.

state, and at the same time, to give you the best data now at command, from which to estimate your present strength in Kentucky.

To defeat, or check the purposes of the aristocracy, it became indispensibly necessary for the Republicans, to have recourse to extraordinary means and exertions—I therefore originated, and with the cooperation of about half a dozen, intelligent and zealous friends, carried into full and successful operation last year, a plan or System of Committees, from a Principle or Central Committee at Louisville, down to Sub-Committees into every ward of the town, and Captains Company in the country—In the execution of which, our Sub-Committees not only kept the secret so well, that our adversaries remained entirely ignorent and secure, until over-whelmed in disgraceful /ruin/ but likewise went so far in detail, in their /regu/lar reports, as to give the names of each voter, how each would vote, both on the local and national questions. By which I find, that in Jefferson and Oldham Counties (which vote together) seven eighths of the New Court, and three eighths of the Old Court voters, will at this time support you for the next U.S. Presidency.

The organization of this Committee Plan, so as to embrace the whole state, has already been commenced by your friends, and it is expected to be in full and successful operation, before the next August elections, with a view not only to your elevation, but like-wise to the resuscitation and success, of our local Republican cause or question.

3. The Convention System

THE DEVELOPMENT of the convention system—both state and national—completed the process of organizing and disciplining this new political age. The convention system became the easy process by which the party structure was engrafted on the state and by which state politics was joined to national politics behind the leadership of the presidential candidate. It furthered the importance and control of politicians who could manage their states through county and local committees that were cre-

SOURCE: Thomas Ford, A History of Illinois (New York, 1854), I: 313–5, 316–22.

*ated by the convention or were responsible to it. The role of the politi-
cian was therefore enhanced during the Jacksonian era and his usefulness
to the governmental process was accepted and defended. But Americans
have always been ambivalent about professional politicians. Somehow
they can not seem to do without them, yet they are convinced that the
worst aspects of political life are directly attributable to them. Thomas
Ford, who understood the purpose and value of the convention system,
tried to place it into historical perspective in his study of Illinois history.*

After party spirit arose so as to require candidates to come out on
party grounds there was for a time no mode of concentrating the
action of a party. A number of candidates would come out for the
same office, on the same side. Their party would be split up and
divided between them. In such a case the minority party was
almost sure of success, this being the only case in which one is
stronger than many. As party spirit increased more and more, the
necessity of some mode of concentrating the party strength became
more and more apparent. The large emigration from the old States,
bringing with it the zeal and party organization in which it had
been trained from infancy gave a new impulse to the consolidation
of the strength of party. An attempt at this was early made by the
New England and New York people living in the north part of the
State, by introducing the convention system of nominating
candidates.

This system was first tried in counties and districts in the north;
but on account of the frauds and irregularities which first attended
it, small progress was made in it from 1832, when its introduction
was first attempted, until 1840, the people generally preferring the
election of independent candidates. . . . At first the system encountered the furious opposition of the whigs, who, being in the
minority, were vitally interested to prevent the concentration of
the democratic strength. The western democrats looked upon it
with a good deal of suspicion. It was considered a Yankee contrivance, intended to abridge the liberties of the people by depriving
individuals, on their own mere motion, of the privilege of becoming candidates, and depriving each man of the right to vote for a
candidate of his own selection and choice. . . .

The system has some advantages and disadvantages in this
country. Those in favor of it say that it furnishes the only mode of
concentrating the action of a party and giving effect to the will of
the majority. They justly urge that since the organization of parties

the old system of electing from personal preference is carried into each party in the mere selection of candidates, which distracts the harmony of a party by introducing competition amongst distinguished men for the mere privilege of becoming candidates, without any means of deciding between them except at the polls. Accordingly it is strictly true that where two or more men of the same party are candidates without a nomination they are apt to hate each other ten times as intensely as they do the prominent men of the opposition party. A whig is to be elected by whigs, a democrat by democrats. The success of either depends upon the number and strength of their respective parties; but an aspiring whig or democrat has still to seek support in his own party in opposition to his own prominent political friends by a canvass of his merits as a man. Such being the case it is not likely that the ambitious men of the same party who are excited against each other by mere personal contests will decline in favor of others so as to have but a single candidate for the same office in the same party. Without a nomination, a party may be greatly in the majority, but by being divided on men the minority may succeed in the elections and actually govern the majority. To remedy this evil it was proposed by conventions of delegates, previously elected by the people, to provide but a single set of candidates for the same party. It was also urged by some that these bodies would be composed of the best-informed and principal men of a party, and would be more competent than the people at large to select good men for candidates. This body to the people would like a grand jury to a circuit court. As the court would have no power to try any one for crime without a previous indictment by the grand jury, so the people would have no right to elect any one to office without a nomination by a convention. In the one case innocent men could not be publicly accused and tried for crime without a private examination of their guilt and establishing a probability of its existence; so the people would be restrained from electing any one to office without a previous nomination of a body more fitted to judge of his qualifications. The convention system was said to be a salutary restraint upon universal suffrage, compelling the people to elect men of standing who alone could be nominated by conventions.

On the other side it was urged that the whole convention system was a fraud on the people; that it was a mere fungus growth engrafted upon the constitution; that conventions themselves were got up and packed by cunning, active, intriguing politicians to suit the wishes of a few. The mode of getting them up was for some active man to procure a few friends in each precinct of a county to hold primary meetings where delegates were elected to county conventions, who met at the county seats and nominated candidates for the legislature and for county offices; and appointed other delegates to district and State conventions to nominate candidates for Congress and for governor. The great difficulty was in the primary meetings in the precincts. In the Eastern States, where conventions originated, they had township governments, little democracies, where the whole people met in person at least once a year to lay taxes for roads and for the support of schools and the poor. This called the whole people of a township together, enlightened their minds, and accustomed them to take a lively interest in their government; and whilst assembled they could and did elect their delegates to conventions. In this mode a convention reflected the will of a party as much as the legislature reflected the will of the whole people. But how is it in Illinois? We had no township governments, no occasions for a general meeting of the people, except at the elections themselves; the people did not attend the primary meetings; a few only assembled who were nearest the places of meeting, and these were too often mere professional politicians, the loafers about the town, who having but little business of their own were ever ready to attend to the affairs of the public. This threw the political power out of the hands of the people, merely because they would not exercise it, into the hands of idlers—of a few active men who controlled them. If any one desired an office he never thought of applying to the people for it; but passed them by and applied himself to conciliate the managers and idlers about the towns, many of whom could only be conciliated at an immense sacrifice of the public interest. It is true that a party had the reserved right of rebellion against all this machinery; no one could be punished for treason in so doing otherwise than by losing the favor of his party and being denounced as a traitor; which was almost as efficacious in restraining the refractory as the pains and penalties of treason, the hanging and disembowelling of former times. . . .

By means of the convention system and many exciting contests the two parties of whigs and democrats were thoroughly organized and disciplined by the year 1840. No regular army could have excelled them in discipline. They were organized upon the principles of national politics only, and not in any degree upon those of the

State. The first effect of this seemed to be that all ideas of State rights, State sovereignty, State policy and interests, as party questions, were abolished out of men's minds. Our ancestors had greatly relied upon the organization of State sovereignties as checks to anti-republican tendencies and national consolidations. For this purpose all the State constitutions, Illinois amongst the rest, had declared that no person holding an office under the United States should hold an office under the State government. The object of this was to sever all dependence of the State upon the national government. It was not permitted the President to appoint the officers of the State governments for this would at once lay the State governments at the feet of the President. But if the State officers were not appointed by the President they were elected upon a principle which made them, if belonging to his political friends, as subservient to his will as if he had appointed them. The President was the leader of his party in the nation and there was no principle of party in the State but this. Men were elected to office upon the popularity of the President and upon the principles which the President put forth; and they were thus compelled in self-defence to support and defend him through good and evil, right or wrong, as much as if they owed their offices to his gift. Besides this their parties absolutely required them to do so. It may be remarked here as a curious fact that the politicians all over the nation pretending to be most in favor of State rights and State sovereignty have contributed most to overthrow them by forever insisting upon the organization of parties upon national questions.

4. Jackson's Inauguration

THE AGE OF JACKSON is dominated by a raucous exuberance which was best described by Mrs. Margaret Bayard Smith, the wife of the Maryland Senator, who recounted in detail the inauguration of Jackson on March 4, 1829. The scene she depicts throbs with the noise, presence and pleasure of ordinary citizens, roaming the streets of Washington and the public rooms of the White House, who somehow identified with the President and believed that he represented their will. As the

SOURCE: Gaillard Hunt, ed., *The First Forty Years of Washington Society Portrayed by the Family Letters of Mrs. Samuel Harrison Smith* ... (New York, 1906), pp. 290–297.

United States Telegraph *reported on March 5:* "For ourselves, it was the proudest moment of our existence. When we saw the President seated by the side of the representatives of other nations—he habited in a suit of plain black cloth, manufactured by his enterprising fellow citizens of Baltimore—they with the embroidered coats, glittering with gold and ornamented with stars and ribbands—he the representative of the supremacy of the will of the people—they wearing the badges of hereditary power—we were impelled to contrast the plain citizen, whose confidence is placed in the virtue, the intelligence and the affections of a great people, with the tawdry pageant of hereditary power, who on such occasions, would look to the bayonet and the strong arm of military force, to protect him against the violence of a people, whom he considers himself born to oppress. Where lives the American who does not rejoice in the contrast?"

TO MRS. KIRKPATRICK

Washington, March 11th, Sunday, 1829

. . . Thursday morning. I left the rest of this sheet for an account of the inauguration. It was not a thing of detail of a succession of small incidents. No, it was one grand whole, an imposing and majestic spectacle and to a reflective mind one of moral sublimity. Thousands and thousands of people, without distinction of rank, collected in an immense mass round the Capitol, silent, orderly and tranquil, with their eyes fixed on the front of that edifice, waiting the appearance of the President in the portico. The door from the Rotunda opens, preceded by the marshals, surrounded by the Judges of the Supreme Court, the old man with his grey locks, that crown of glory, advances, bows to the people, who greet him with a shout that rends the air, the Cannons, from the heights around, from Alexandria and Fort Warburton proclaim the oath he has taken and all the hills reverberate the sound. It was grand,—it was sublime! An almost breathless silence, succeeded and the multitude was still,—listening to catch the sound of his voice, tho' it was so low, as to be heard only by those nearest to him. After reading his speech, the oath was administered to him by the Chief Justice. The Marshal presented the Bible. The President took it from his hands, pressed his lips to it, laid it reverently down, then bowed again to the people—Yes, to the people in all their majesty. And had the spectacle closed here, even Europeans must have acknowledged that a free people, collected in their might, silent and tranquil, restrained solely by a moral power, without a shadow around of military force, was majesty, rising to sublimity, and far surpassing the majesty of Kings and Princes, surrounded with armies and glittering in gold. But I will not anticipate, but will give you an account of the inauguration in more detail. The whole of the preceding day, immense crowds were coming into the city from all parts, lodgings could not be obtained, and the new-comers had to go to George Town, which soon overflowed and others had to go to Alexandria. I was told the Avenue and adjoin-ing streets were so crowded on Tuesday afternoon that it was difficult to pass.

A national salute was fired early in the morning, and ushered in the 4th of March. By ten oclock the Avenue was crowded with carriages of every description, from the splendid Barronet and coach, down to waggons and carts, filled with women and children, some in finery and some in rags, for it was the people's President, and all would see him; the men all walked. Julia, Anna Maria and I, (the other girls would not adventure) accompanied by Mr. Wood, set off before 11, and followed the living stream that was pouring along to the Capitol. The terraces, the Balconies, the Porticos, seemed as we approached already filled. We rode round the whole square, taking a view of the animated scene. Then leaving the carriage outside the palisades, we entered the enclosed grounds, where we were soon joined by John Cranet and another gentleman, which offered each of us a protector. We walked round the terrace several times, every turn meeting new groups of ladies and gentlemen whom we knew. All with smiling faces. The day was warm and delightful, from the South Terrace we had a view of Pennsylvania and Louisiana Avenues, crowded with people hurry-ing towards the Capitol. It was a most exhilarating scene! Most of the ladies preferred being inside of the Capitol and the eastern portico, damp and cold as it was, had been filled from 9 in the morning by ladies who wished to be near the General when he spoke. Every room was filled and the windows crowded. But as so confined a situation allowed no general view, we would not coop ourselves up, and certainly enjoyed a much finer view of the spectacle, both in its whole and in its details, than those within the walls. We stood on the South steps of the terrace; when the ap-pointed hour came saw the General and his company advancing up the Avenue, slow, very slow, so impeded was his march by the crowds thronging around him. Even from a distance, he could be discerned from those who accompanied him, for he only was uncovered, (the Servant in presence of his Sovereign, the People). The south side of the Capitol hill was literally alive with the multitude, who stood ready to receive the hero and the multitude who attended him. "There, there, that is he," exclaimed different voices. "Which?" asked others. "He with the white head," was the reply. "Ah," exclaimed others, "there is the old man and his gray hair, there is the old veteran, there is Jackson." At last he enters the gate at the foot of the hill and turns to the road that leads round to the front of the Capitol. In a moment every one who until then had stood like statues gazing on the scene below them, rushed onward, to right, to left, to be ready to receive him in the front. Our party, of course, were more deliberate, we waited until the multitude had rushed past us and then left the terrace and walked round to the furthest side of the square, where there were no carriages to impede us, and entered it by the gate fronting the Capitol. Here was a clear space, and stationing ourselves on the central gravel walk we stood so as to have a clear, full view of the whole scene. The Capitol in all its grandeur and beauty. The Portico and grand steps leading to it, were filled with ladies. Scarlet, purple, blue, yellow, white draperies and waving plumes of every kind and colour, among the white marble pillars, had a fine effect. In the centre of the portico was a table covered with scarlet, behind it the closed door leading into the rotunda, below the Capitol, and all around, a mass of living beings, not a ragged mob, but well dressed and well behaved respectable and worthy citizens. Mr. Frank Key, whose arm I had, and an old and frequent witness of great spectacles, often exclaimed, as well as myself, a mere novice, "It is beautiful, it is sublime!" The sun had been obscured through the morning by a mist, or haziness. But the concussion in the air, produced by the discharge of the cannon, dispersed it and the sun shone forth in all his brightness. At the moment the General entered the Portico and advanced to the table, the shout that rent the air, still resounds in my ears. When the speech was over, and the President made his parting bow, the barrier that had separated the people from him was broken down and they rushed up the steps all eager to shake hands with him. It was with difficulty he made his way through the Capitol and down the hill to the gateway that opens on the avenue. Here for a moment he was stopped. The living mass was impenetrable. After a while a passage was opened, and he mounted his horse which had been provided for his return (for he had walked to the Capitol) then such a cortege as followed him! Country men, farmers, gentlemen, mounted and dismounted, boys, women and children, black and white. Carriages, wagons and carts all pursuing him to the President's house,—this I only heard of for our party went out at the opposite side of the square and went to Col. Benton's lodgings, to visit Mrs. Benton and Mrs. Gilmore. Here was a perfect levee, at least a hundred ladies and gentlemen, all happy and rejoicing,—wine and cake was handed in profusion. We sat with this company and stopped on the summit of the hill until the avenue was comparatively clear, tho' at any other time we should have thought it terribly crowded. Streams of people on foot and of carriages of all kinds, still pouring towards the President's house. We went Home, found your papa and sisters at the Bank,[6] standing at the upper windows, where they had been seen by the President, who took off his hat to them, which they insisted was better than all we had seen. From the Bank to the President's house for a long while, the crowd rendered a passage for us impossible. Some went into the Cashier's parlour, where we found a number of ladies and gentlemen and had cake and wine in abundance. In about an hour, the pavement was clear enough for us to walk. Your father, Mr. Wood, Mr. Ward, Mr. Lyon, with us, we set off to the President's House, but on a nearer approach found an entrance impossible, the yard and avenue was compact with living matter. The day was delightful, the scene animating, so we walked backward and forward at every turn meeting some new acquaintance and stopping to talk and shake hands. Among others we met Zavr. Dickinson with Mr. Frelinghuysen and Dr. Elmendorf, and Mr. Saml Bradford. We continued promenading here, until near three, returned home unable to stand and threw ourselves on the sopha. Some one came and informed us the crowd before the President's house, was so far lessen'd, that they thought we might enter. This time we effected our purpose. But what a scene did we witness! The *Majesty of the People* had disappeared, and a rabble, a mob, of boys, negros, women, children, scrambling, fighting, romping. What a pity what a pity! No arrangements had been made no police officers placed on duty and the whole house had been inundated by the rabble mob. We came too late. The President, after having been *literally* nearly pressed to death and almost suffocated and torn to pieces by the people in their eagerness to shake hands with Old Hickory, had retreated through the back way or south front and had escaped to

6. Branch Bank of the United States of which Mr. Smith was president. It stood at the corner of 15th Street and Pennsylvania Avenue.

his lodgings at Gadsby's. Cut glass and china to the amount of several thousand dollars had been broken in the struggle to get the refreshments, punch and other articles had been carried out in tubs and buckets, but had it been in hogsheads it would have been insufficient, ice-creams, and cake and lemonade, for 20,000 people, for it is said that number were there, tho' I think the estimate exaggerated. Ladies fainted, men were seen with bloody noses and such a scene of confusion took place as is impossible to describe,— those who got in could not get out by the door again, but had to scramble out of windows. At one time, the President who had retreated and retreated until he was pressed against the wall, could only be secured by a number of gentlemen forming round him and making a kind of barrier of their own bodies, and the pressure was so great that Col Bomford who was one said that at one time he was afraid they should have been pushed down, or on the President. It was then the windows were thrown open, and the torrent found an outlet, which otherwise might have proved fatal.

This concourse had not been anticipated and therefore not provided against. Ladies and gentlemen, only had been expected at this Levee, not the people en masse. But it was the People's day, and the People's President and the People would rule. God grant that one day or other, the People, do not put down all rule and rulers. I fear, enlightened Freemen as they are, they will be found, as they have been found in all ages and countries where they get the Power in their hands, that of all tyrants, they are the most ferocious, cruel and despotic. The noisy and disorderly rabble in the President's House brought to my mind descriptions I had read, of the mobs in the Tuileries and at Versailles, I expect to hear the carpets and furniture are ruined, the streets were muddy, and these guests all went thither on foot.

5. "The Procession Was Nearly a Mile Long"

POLITICIANS of the Jacksonian era developed some of the worst barbarisms of American electioneering. They invented much of the nonsense of modern presidential campaigns. The purpose of these excesses was

SOURCE: Michael Chevalier, *Society, Manners, and Politics in the United States* (Boston, 1839), pp. 306–8.

to create mass enthusiasm for the party and its candidate and nothing enthused the electorate more than parades, rallies, tree plantings, barbecues, jokes, cartoons, slogans and campaign buttons and songs. The climax of this absurdity was reached in the celebrated Log Cabin campaign of 1840 when "Tippecanoe and Tyler Too" triumphed over the "Little Magician," Martin Van Buren. However, the following selection, written by a touring and perceptive Frenchman, Michael Chevalier, describes some of the hoopla of the 1832 campaign when Jackson won an imposing victory over Henry Clay and the friends of the Second National Bank.

Already democracy, especially in the Western States, is beginning to have its festivals which thrill its fibers and stir it with agreeable emotions. There are religious festivals, the Methodist camp meetings, where the people go with delight, despite the philosophical objections of other more middle-class sects who find fault with their heated zeal and noisy ranting, and despite, or rather in consequence of, the convulsive and hysterical scenes of the *anxious bench*. In the older States of the North there are political processions, pure party demonstrations for the most part, but which are interesting in that the democracy has a share in them; for it is the Democratic party that gets up the most brilliant and animated. Besides the camp meetings, the political processions are the only things in this country which bear any resemblance to festivals. The party dinners with their speeches and deluge of toasts are frigid, if not repulsive; for example, I have never seen a more miserable affair than the dinner given by the Opposition, that is to say, by the middle class, at Powelton, in the neighborhood of Philadelphia. But I stopped involuntarily at the sight of the gigantic hickory poles which made their solemn entry on eight wheels for the purpose of being planted by the democracy on the eve of the election. I remember one of these poles, its top still crowned with green foliage, which came on to the sound of fife and drums and was preceded by ranks of Democrats, bearing no other badge than a twig of the sacred tree in their hats. It was drawn by eight horses, decorated with ribbons and mottoes. Astride the tree itself were a dozen Jackson men of the first water, waving flags with an air of anticipated triumph and shouting, *Hurrah for Jackson!*

But this parade of the hickory tree was but a by-matter compared with the procession I witnessed in New York. It was the night after the closing of the polls when victory had gone to the Democratic party. The procession was nearly a mile long; the Democrats marched in good order to the glare of torches; the banners were more numerous than I had ever seen in any religious festival; all were transparencies on account of the darkness. On some were inscribed the names of the Democratic societies or sections; *Democratic young men of the ninth or eleventh ward*; others bore imprecations against the Bank of the United States; *Nick Biddle* and *Old Nick* were shown, more or less ingeniously, doing business together; it was their form of our banner with the prayer, "Deliver us from evil." Then came portraits of General Jackson afoot and on horseback; there was one in the uniform of a general and another in the person of the Tennessee farmer with the famous hickory cane in his hand. Portraits of Washington and Jefferson, surrounded with Democratic mottoes, were mingled with emblems in all designs and colors. Among these figured an eagle—not a painting, but a real live eagle—tied by the legs, surrounded by a wreath of leaves and hoisted upon a pole, after the manner of the Roman standards. The imperial bird was carried by a stout sailor, more pleased than was ever any city magistrate permitted to hold one of the cords of the canopy in a Catholic ceremony. Farther than the eye could reach the Democrats came marching on. I was struck with the resemblance of their air to the train that escorts the Eucharist in Mexico or Puebla. The American standard-bearers were as grave as the Mexican Indians who bore the sacred candles. The Democratic procession, also like the Catholic procession, had its halting places; it stopped before the houses of Jackson men to fill the air with cheers and before the doors of the leaders of the Opposition to give three, six, or nine groans. If these scenes were to find a painter, they would be admired at some distant day no less than the triumphs and sacrificial pomps which the ancients have left us in marble and brass. For this is something more than the grotesque fashion of scenes immortalized by Rembrandt; this belongs to history, it belongs to the sublime; these are episodes of a wondrous epic which will bequeath a lasting memory to posterity, the memory of the coming of democracy.

II

Battles of the Jackson Administration

6. Andrew Jackson, Martin Van Buren, John C. Calhoun, Daniel Webster and Henry Clay: Five Personalities

MUCH OF THE color and excitement of the Jacksonian period is attributable to the principal characters of the period, many of whom were larger than life. And they were not to be found exclusively in one party or one society. Indeed much of American life in the 1830s and 1840s was dominated by extraordinarily vital and unusual people. Although the political leaders of this period were different from the giants of the preceding generation who founded the republic, they were nonetheless major figures in American history. Harriet Martineau, a British traveler who had entré into the highest political circles, recorded her impressions of the five most active and interesting personalities of the age. Although she was partial to the Whigs she tried to be objective in her assessment of the Democrats.

At the President's I met a very large party, among whom there was more stiffness than I witnessed in any other society in America. It was not the fault of the President or his family, but of the way in which the company was unavoidably brought together. With the exception of my party, the name of every body present began with J, K, or L: that is to say, it consisted of members of Congress, who are invited alphabetically, to ensure none being left out. This principle of selection is not perhaps the best for the promotion of ease and sociability; and, well as I liked the day, I doubt whether many

SOURCE: Harriet Martineau, *Retrospect of Western Travel*, Volume I (London, 1838): 111–13, 243–45, 252–55, 288–92.

others could say they enjoyed it. When we went in, the President was standing in the middle of the room to receive his guests. After speaking a few words with me, he gave me into the charge of Major Donelson, his secretary, who seated me, and brought up for introduction each guest as he passed from before the President. . . . At dinner, the President was quite disposed for conversation. Indeed, he did nothing but talk. His health is poor, and his diet of the sparest. We both talked freely of the governments of England and France; I, novice in American politics as I was, entirely forgetting that the great French question was pending, and that the President and the King of the French were then bandying very hard words. I was most struck and surprised with the President's complaints of the American Senate, in which there was at that time a small majority against the administration. He told me that I must not judge of the body by what I saw it then; and that after the 4th of March I should behold a Senate more worthy of the country. After the 4th of March there was, if I remember rightly, a majority of two in favour of the Government. The ground of his complaint was, that the senators had sacrificed their dignity by disregarding the wishes of their constituents. The other side of the question is, that the dignity of the Senate is best consulted by its members following their own convictions, declining instructions for the term for which they are elected. It is a serious difficulty, originating in the very construction of the body, and not to be settled by dispute.

The President offered me bonbons for a child belonging to our party at home, and told me how many children (of his nephew's and his adopted son's) he had about him, with a mildness and kindliness which contrasted well with his tone upon some public occasions. He did the honours of his house with gentleness and politeness to myself, and, as far as I saw, to every one else. About an hour after dinner, he rose, and we led the way into the drawing-room, where the whole company, gentlemen as well as ladies, followed to take coffee; after which, every one departed; some homewards, some to make evening calls, and others, among whom were ourselves, to a splendid ball, at the other extremity of the city.

General Jackson is extremely tall and thin, with a slight stoop, betokening more weakness than naturally belongs to his years. He has a profusion of stiff grey hair, which gives to his appearance whatever there is of formidable in it. His countenance bears commonly an expression of melancholy gravity; though when roused, the fire of passion flashes from his eyes, and his whole person looks then formidable enough. His mode of speech is slow and quiet; and his phraseology sufficiently betokens that his time has not been passed among books. . . .

Mr. Van Buren and his son happened to be in Albany, and called on me this afternoon. There is nothing remarkable in the appearance of this gentleman, whom I afterwards saw frequently at Washington. He is small in person, with light hair, and blue eyes. I was often asked whether I did not think his manners gentlemanly. There is much friendliness in his manners, for he is a kindhearted man: he is also rich in information, and lets it come out on subjects in which he cannot contrive to see any danger in speaking. But his manners want the frankness and confidence which are essential to good breeding. He questions closely without giving anything in return. Moreover, he flatters to a degree which so cautious a man should long ago have found out to be disagreeable: and his flattery is not merely praise of the person he is speaking to, but a worse kind still,—a scepticism and ridicule of objects and persons supposed to be distasteful to the one he is conversing with. I fully believe that he is an amiable and indulgent domestic man, and a reasonable political master, a good scholar, and a shrewd man of business: but he has the scepticism which marks the lower orders of politicians. His public career exhibits no one exercise of that faith in men, and preference of principle to petty expediency by which a statesman shows himself to be great.

The consequence is that, with all his opportunities, no great deed has ever been put to his account, and his shrewdness has been at fault in some of the most trying crises of his career. The man who so little trusts others, and so intensely regards self as to make it the study of his life not to commit himself, is liable to a more than ordinary danger of judging wrong when compelled, by the pressure of circumstances, to act a decided part. It has already been so with Mr. Van Buren, more than once; and now that he is placed in a position where he must sometimes visibly lead, and cannot always appear to follow, it will be seen whether a due reverence of men and a forgetfulness of self would not have furnished him with more practical wisdom than all his "sounding on his dim and perilous way." . . .

Mr. Calhoun, the cast-iron man, who looks as if he had never

been born, and never could be extinguished, would come in sometimes to keep our understandings upon a painful stretch for a short
while, and leave us to take to pieces his close, rapid, theoretical,
illustrated talk, and see what we could make of it. We found it
usually more worth retaining as a curiosity than as either very just
or useful. His speech abounds in figures, truly illustrative, if that
which they illustrate were but true also. But his theories of government, (almost the only subject on which his thoughts are employed,) the squarest and compactest theories that ever were
made, are composed out of limited elements, and are not therefore
likely to stand service very well. It is at first extremely interesting to
hear Mr. Calhoun talk; and there is a never-failing evidence of
power in all he says and does, which commands intellectual reverence: but the admiration is too soon turned into regret,—into
absolute melancholy. It is impossible to resist the conviction that
all this force can be at best but useless, and is but too likely to be
very mischievous. His mind has long lost all power of communicat-
ing with any other. I know no man who lives in such utter intellectual solitude. He meets men and harangues them, by the fire-side,
as in the Senate: he is wrought, like a piece of machinery, set a-
going vehemently by a weight, and stops while you answer: he
either passes by what you say, or twists it into a suitability with
what is in his head, and begins to lecture again. Of course, a mind
like this can have little influence in the Senate, except by virtue,
perpetually wearing out, of what it did in its less eccentric days:
but its influence at home is to be dreaded. There is no hope that an
intellect so cast in narrow theories will accommodate itself to
varying circumstances: and there is every danger that it will break
up all that it can, in order to remould the materials in its own way.
Mr. Calhoun is as full as ever of his Nullification doctrines; and
those who know the force that is in him, and his utter incapacity of
modification by other minds, (after having gone through as remarkable a revolution of political opinion as perhaps any man ever
experienced,) will no more expect repose and self-retention from
him than from a volcano in full force. Relaxation is no longer in
the power of his will. I never saw any one who so completely gave
me the idea of possession. Half an hour's conversation with him is
enough to make a necessarian of any body. Accordingly, he is more
complained of than blamed by his enemies. His moments of soft-
ness, in his family, and when recurring to old college days, are

hailed by all as a relief to the vehement working of the intellectual machine; a relief equally to himself and others. Those moments are as touching to the observer as tears on the face of a soldier. . . .

Mr. Webster owes his rise to the institutions under which he lives,—institutions which open the race to the swift, and the battle to the strong; but there is little in him that is congenial with them. He is aristocratic in his tastes and habits: and but little republican simplicity is to be recognized in him. Neither his private conversation nor his public transactions usually convey an impression that he is in earnest. When he is so, his power is majestic, irresistible; but his ambition for office, and for the good opinion of those who surround him, is seen too often in alternation with his love of ease and luxury, to allow of his being confided in as he is admired. If it had been otherwise, if his moral had equalled his intellectual supremacy, if his aims had been as single as his reason is unclouded, he would long ago have carried all before him, and been the virtual monarch of the United States. But to have expected this would have been unreasonable. The very best men of any society are rarely or never to be found among its eminent statesmen; and it is not fair to look for them in offices which, in the present condition of human affairs, would yield to such no other choice than of speedy failure or protracted martyrdom. Taking great politicians as they are, Mr. Webster's general consistency may be found not to have fallen below the average, though it has not been so remarkable as to ensure on his behalf a confidence at all to be compared with the universal admiration of his talents.

Mr. Webster speaks seldom in the Senate. When he does, it is generally on some constitutional question, where his reasoning powers and knowledge are brought into play, and where his authority is considered so high, that he has the glorious satisfaction of knowing that he is listened to as an oracle by an assemblage of the first men in the country. Previous to such an exercise, he may be seen leaning back in his chair, not, as usual, biting the top of his pen, or twirling his thumbs, or bursting into sudden and transient laughter at Colonel Benton's oratorical absurdities, but absent and thoughtful, making notes, and seeing nothing that is before his eyes. When he rises, his voice is moderate, and his manner quiet, with the slightest possible mixture of embarrassment; his right hand rests upon his desk, and the left hangs by his side. Before his first head is finished, however, his voice has risen so as to fill the chamber and ring again, and he has fallen into his favourite attitude, with his left hand under his coat-tail, and the right in full action. At this moment, the eye rests upon him as upon one under the true inspiration of seeing the invisible, and grasping the impalpable. When the vision has passed away, the change is astonishing. He sits at his desk, writing letters or dreaming, so that he does not always discover when the Senate is going to a division. Some one of his party has not seldom to jog his elbow, and tell him that his vote is wanted.

There can scarcely be a stronger contrast than between the eloquence of Webster and that of Clay. Mr. Clay is now my personal friend; but I have a distinct recollection of my impressions of his speaking, while he was yet merely an acquaintance. His appearance is plain in the extreme, being that of a mere west-country farmer. He is tall and thin, with a weather-beaten complexion, small grey eyes, which convey an idea of something more than his well-known sagacity,—even of slyness. It is only after much intercourse that Mr. Clay's personal appearance can be discovered to do him any justice at all. All attempts to take his likeness have been in vain, though upwards of thirty portraits of him, by different artists, were in existence when I was in America. No one has succeeded in catching the subtle expression of placid kindness, mingled with astuteness, which becomes visible to the eyes of those who are in daily intercourse with him. His mode of talking, deliberate and somewhat formal, including sometimes a grave humour, and sometimes a gentle sentiment, very touching from the lips of a sagacious man of ambition, has but one fault,— its obvious adaptation to the supposed state of mind of the person to whom it is addressed. Mr. Clay is a man of an irritable and impetuous nature, over which he has obtained a truly noble mastery. His moderation is now his most striking characteristic; obtained, no doubt, at the cost of prodigious self-denial, on his own part, and on that of his friends, of some of the ease, naturalness, and self-forgetfulness of his manners and discourse. But his conversation is rich in information, and full charged with the spirit of justice and kindliness, rising, on occasion, to a moving magnanimity. By chances, of some of which he was totally unaware, I became acquainted with several acts of his life, political and private, which prove that his moderation is not the mere diffusion of oil upon the waves, but the true stilling of the storm of passion and selfishness. The time may come when these acts may be told; but it has not yet arrived.

7. The Eaton Affair

No sooner did the first Jackson administration begin than it was embroiled in a bruising power struggle between the Vice President, John C. Calhoun, and the Secretary of State, Martin Van Buren. Each hoped to succeed Jackson as President and each stooped to political intrigue to further his designs. The first open conflict involved the unfortunate social furor over Margaret (Peggy) Eaton, the wife of the Secretary of War. The wives of the other cabinet members, including Ingham, Branch and Berrien as well as Calhoun, refused to socialize with Peggy because of her reputation as a promiscuous woman. Jackson exploded over this affront to the Eatons, seeing in Peggy much of his late wife, Rachel, who also suffered public abuse because of her divorce from her first husband and the unusual circumstances surrounding her marriage to Jackson. Eventually Jackson dissolved his cabinet and formed another, whereupon Ingham, Berrien and Branch issued a statement in the newspapers justifying their position and repeating their slander against Peggy. In his published reply, Eaton traced the entire history of the affair, accusing Calhoun of masterminding a plot against himself and his wife. Naturally it is an intensely partisan statement and must be treated with caution, but it does reflect the furious emotional turmoil generated at the start of Jackson's administration, and it exposes the political rivalry that arose very quickly between Calhoun and Van Buren.

A place in General Jackson's cabinet, by me, was never desired. My ambition was satisfied with a seat which thrice had been kindly bestowed upon me by my fellow-citizens of Tennessee. Distrust in my competency to discharge the duties of one of the departments, and a reluctance to encounter its labors, induced me to prefer my situation in the senate. About to enter upon untried scenes, with a limited knowledge of the characters and feelings of those by whom he was to be surrounded, the president felt anxious to have near him some of his long tried personal friends, in whom he had entire confidence. He desired that judge White, my colleague in the

Source: Niles Weekly Register, September 17, 24, 1831.

senate, or myself should accept one of the departments. I urged it upon judge White, because I consider him better qualified, and better adapted to the station, than myself. He declined it. I then felt it my duty to accept the offer of the president. He had just lost the partner of his bosom, and was solitary and disconsolate. As in his kindness he seemed to think I could be serviceable to him, it did not seem consistent with the friendly relations which had long subsisted between us, to leave him at such a moment.

Mr. Van Buren was appointed, because the president had confidence in his talents and integrity, and because he appeared to be the expectation of the country. Mr. Ingham was selected, for the reason that the president was *induced* to believe that the democracy of Pennsylvania desired it. Mr. Barry, from a confidence reposed in him by the president, derived from his personal knowledge of his worth and merits. Between the first and last named gentlemen and myself, the most cordial friendship has always subsisted: nothing has ever arisen to interrupt in the least our friendly relations.

Mr. Branch and myself were born and reared in the same county of North Carolina, educated at the same college, and had been associates and friends, in early, and in more advanced life. I solicited his appointment as a member of the cabinet, and at the president's request informed him of the selection. He made no objection—not the least, save on the score of a modest distrust of his competency, and expressed at the time much gratitude towards the president, and exhibited much good feeling towards myself.

With Mr. Berrien I had been on terms of intimacy, and supposing him to be a man of talents and honor, was pleased that he was selected. The president requested me to confer with him in relation to his acceptance. At that time we were in habits of the kindest intercourse. He seemed highly flattered by this manifestation of the president's confidence, and offered no objection to an acceptance, except intimating a possible interference with his private business. The next day he informed me that he would accept, which reply I communicated to the president.

I met all the members of the cabinet as friends, personal and political, to whom was assigned the highest destiny, by harmony of feeling among themselves, of giving unity of design and vigor of action to the administration of general Jackson. In the same light I am sure, did he consider us. In the singleness of his heart and the ardour of his patriotism, he suspected not that there was amongst us, any other object, than by our cordial support, to enable him in the cabinet, as he had done in the field, "to fill the measure of his country's glory." Far otherwise were the feelings and purposes of Messrs. Ingham, Branch and Berrien. . . .

Without the president's knowledge, and without mine, this cabal of "personal, political and long tried friends," were thus endeavoring to control all the cabinet arrangements, and secretly to place around the president men of their selection and stamp. It was not for him to select his own counsellors, or decide who were his "personal, political and long tried friends"—men who had supported him only when they had lost all hope of Mr. Calhoun—who had joined his standard only when their favorite candidate had disappeared from the contest, and who had supported him as a secondary choice—your Inghams, Berriens, and others, were now arrogating to become his exclusive counsellors, and to thrust from his presence as unworthy of his trust and confidence, those who had supported him for his own sake—whose attachment was cemented by years of confidential intercourse—whose faith and energies were pledged to his support, and whose hopes were all concentrated in the success and prosperity of his administration.

Mr. Branch was made the instrument of abler heads, and attempted to become a manager in this business. In his recent letter, he mentions a call which he made on the president previous to my nomination to the senate, at which he arrogantly represented that my selection would be improper and unfortunate, and gave his reasons, which appeared to have related solely to my family. He also states he then came to advise me against accepting a place in the cabinet, admitting that the charges made against my family were false, but representing "what use the opposition would make of it," and that "the enemies of the president would not fail to make a handle of it." He says that he placed Mrs. Jackson and Mrs. Eaton on the same footing, and desired to save the president "from recollections which would be painful and distressing." Mr. Branch has a treacherous recollection. He kept no note book, or, like his co-partner, Mr. Ingham, he has accommodated his notes to emergencies. I can put him right in this affair, not doubting his admission of the truth of the narration I offer, if honor be left him, although he may deny the motive which I feel persuaded influenced him at the time.

Failing in the attempt to prevent my appointment, and to dissuade or rather to deter me from accepting, Mr. Branch was next made the instrument of a piece of secret management, having in view the same result. . . .

Not a doubt is left on my mind, that before the nomination of the cabinet to the senate, the means of operating on public opinion, and forcing the president to exclude me, were devised, arranged and fixed upon, by and with the knowledge and approbation of Messrs. Ingham and Berrien, if not of Mr. Branch; and the means to be employed under their boasted sense of honor—an honor which in their bosoms inspired an earnest desire to transmit to their children, "an unsullied, good name" were the abuse and slander of a mother, with two innocent daughters, whose good name was blended with hers, and in attacks upon my integrity and honor. Did they reason themselves into the belief, that the inheritance of a parent's good name, was of no value, only as it regarded their children; and that whether others lived or perished, was not material, if they and theirs were safe.

Did I merit such course of treatment from Mr. Berrien? We had served together for several years in the senate of the United States. He was invited to, and was present at my marriage, six or eight weeks before. We were in habits of daily friendly intercourse; on my part, free and unrestrained, and, as I supposed, equally so on his. He professed to be my friend, and such I thought him. . . .

The question so gravely raised and discussed in the public newspapers about visiting—leaving a card, and invitations to "large parties" or small ones, in this city, cannot but appear matters of derision to the American people. Who calls upon his neighbor, or invites him to eat and drink with him, and who does not, is a matter of no concern to the people; and to them it must appear ridiculous, that statesmen and cabinet counsellors, have thought it necessary to disturb them with matters so trifling. But even these have been rendered of some importance, as developing the motives of men, and accounting for events of higher importance. And in this view is it, that I am about to introduce such a topic, and beg to be pardoned for doing so.

After my marriage in January 1829, my wife and myself visited Philadelphia, and were absent from Washington two weeks. Amongst those who had called in our absence to visit and pay us the customary congratulations, were Mr. and Mrs. Calhoun—their cards had been left. In cities, leaving at a neighbor's house, a card—a small piece of pasteboard with the name upon it, is called a visit. Not long afterwards, we called at Mr. Calhoun's lodging to return the civility. After sending in our names, we were invited up to the vice president's parlor, where Mrs. Calhoun was alone, and received us with much politeness.—We spent a short time, quite agreeably, and took our leave. Afterwards, these calls were not repeated on either side. This was a short time before it was understood who would compose the cabinet of general Jackson.

Soon after the cabinet was organised, indications of those secret views, which Mr. Berrien now openly avows, began to manifest themselves. The motive was not apparent, yet was it sufficiently evident, that there was a settled design to put a ban on my family, and render my position at Washington disagreeable to me. This was to be promoted by all the influence and importance which high station conferred on some of my colleagues. Confederacies were formed, and efforts made to awaken prejudices. To give countenance to the confederates, and to aid their efforts, old slanders were revived, and new ones circulated.

In the autumn of 1829, new attacks began to be made, in whispers, on my integrity. It was said I had conspired with my wife's first husband, Mr. Timberlake, to defraud the government of large sums of money. Other attempts to get rid of me, having failed, I was now to be presented as being in default to the government, through fraud practised on it. Mr. Timberlake had been a purser in the navy, and this charge was based upon a reported deficiency in his accounts with the public; and on a *private letter* of mine, detained in the 4th auditor's office, showing that on my suggestion, he had remitted money to me. Copies of my *private confidential letters* to him, had been taken from the office, that I might not escape through *apprehended indulgence and favor*, on the part of Mr. Kendall. Matters were considered well arranged, and the proof complete to show, that this delinquency was wholly occasioned by remittances of money to me, and which was yet in my possession. Such were the whispers circulated through the society of this place. But a close investigation, which occupied some time, showed that Mr. Timberlake's account had been deprived, through a series of shocking frauds, of credits to the amount of from 12 to $20,000, and that justly he was largely a creditor, not a debtor, to the government. . . .

Now, what was the motive for all this relentless persecution? Could it be that my wife was indeed the cause? Was it merely to exclude a female from their "good society"? Was one woman so dangerous to public morals, and so formidable in influence and power, as to require all this strong array of cabinet counsellors—combination of members of congress—confederacy of fashionable ladies? Was it for that, attacks were made upon the integrity of her husband; and honor, truth and candor sacrificed? The idea is truly ridiculous! She was lone and powerless. Those who liked her society, sought it; and those who did not, kept away. Neither she nor her husband, entered into cabals and intrigues, to the prejudice and injury of others. Their own multiplied wrongs, they bore with as much patience as could be expected, from mortals endowed with human passions and sensibilities. A common understanding prevailed, express in relation to one family, and which was also understood in relation to others, that each should seek their own associates, according to their own will, uninfluenced and unrestrained. The *motive*, therefore, was not to exclude us from society. It is a matter altogether *too small* to account for the acts and the untiring zeal of so many *great men*.

Was the *motive* merely to exclude me from the cabinet? Was my presence there, dangerous to the interest of the country, or to its institutions? Had I the power or disposition to injure the one, or overthrow the other? Was it pretended that I wanted the ability, intelligence or integrity, necessary to the management of the department of war? Of its management, there has been no complaint, while it was in my hands! I left it at least as prosperous as I found it! Was it suspected that I was not true to the president, and would prove false and faithless to his administration? A confidential intercourse of more than fifteen years, the highest admiration of his character, and the deep personal interest felt in the success of his administration, were surely sufficient to guard me against that. Nothing of this sort entered into the minds of my traducers. They had no desire for my exclusion on account of any suspicions entertained, that I would willingly do injury to the interests of the country, its institutions, or to the president! To what then shall we look for this *motive*? An ardent friend to the vice president, in 1829, in one short sentence disclosed it:

"*Major Eaton is not the friend of Mr. Calhoun,*"

It was this which rendered me unfit for the cabinet, and for the respectable society of Messrs. Ingham, Branch, and Berrien. I could not, perhaps, be used to promote the views of Mr. Calhoun, and might exert an influence to induce general Jackson to stand a second election. It was not thought that in my hands the influence and patronage of the war department, could be used in favor of a successor. In that they did me justice. It was not so used, nor ever would have been. It was a subject about which I spoke not, and felt not. Not even was I solicitous for general Jackson again to be selected, except on the ground that his principles and the course of his administration, when fairly tested, should be found in accord with the general sense of the people and the country. . . .

Their plan was that general Jackson should be president but for four years, and that Mr. Calhoun should succeed him. . . . The moment, however, that Mr. Van Buren was appointed secretary of state, jealousy and fear arose, and then the desire was to place around the president as many of Mr. Calhoun's friends as possible, to counteract the apprehended and dreaded influence; a part of which I most gratuitously was supposed to be. Devoted, as I was said to be, to gen. Jackson, and the success of his administration, my appointment was calculated rather to thwart than to promote their ulterior designs. It was deemed necessary to prevent it; but if that could not be effected, then adequate means were to be resorted to, to get me out of the way. All this Mr. Ingham and Mr. Berrien foresaw. Two of my colleagues, if not the third, were in the secret, and used the influence and importance which office gave them and their families, to promote and further their grand design. . . .

You can perceive the reasons why I and my family have been so relentlessly pursued by the friends of Mr. Calhoun; and you perceive the origin of the progressive and concerted attacks, first upon me, next upon Mr. Van Buren, and lastly, upon the president, that the one might be sent to Russia, the other to Albany, and the third to the solitude of the Hermitage. All has originated in the restless spirit of Mr. Calhoun and his partizans, and in a determination that general Jackson should be president but for four years, and that Mr. Calhoun must and should be his successor.

8. The Seminole Affair

THE ISSUE that finally led to the estrangement of Jackson and Calhoun and provoked the dissolution of the cabinet was the Seminole affair. This dispute went back to the Monroe administration when General Jackson invaded Florida in order to suppress Indian invasions of the United States. Because his actions constituted an act of war there were many who wished to censure him for his unauthorized invasion. But Jackson insisted he had authority from President Monroe. The censure attempt failed, however, largely through the efforts of the Secretary of State, John Quincy Adams, although Jackson somehow got the idea that his principal defender in the cabinet had been the then Secretary of War, John C. Calhoun. Not until early in his first administration was Jackson given documentary evidence by William H. Crawford, the Secretary of the Treasury under Monroe, that Calhoun had actually sought his punishment. The rupture between the two men was now complete, a rupture that began with the Eaton affair and grew worse with the dissemination of the Vice President's nullification ideas. As his political fortunes soured, Calhoun convinced himself that Van Buren instigated a plot against him in order to insure his succession to the presidency. Consequently, he published a pamphlet in the United States Telegraph on February 17, 1831 to defend his actions and explain what he believed were the circumstances by which Jackson learned what had happened in Monroe's cabinet.

The documents presented here constitute a small number of the letters that Calhoun published and they have been rearranged slightly to make his narrative more coherent and understandable.

A. The Introductory Address of the Vice-President: To the People of the United States

I come before you, as my constituents, to give an account of my conduct in an important political transaction, which has been called in question, and so erroneously represented, that neither justice to myself nor respect for you will permit me any longer to remain silent; I allude to my course, in the deliberations of the Cabinet of Mr. Monroe, on the Seminole question. I know not

SOURCE: *United States Telegraph*, February 17, 21, 23, 26, 1831; *Washington Globe*, February 25, 1831; *Niles Weekly Register*, April 2, 1831.

how I can place more fully before you all the facts and circumstances of the case, than by putting you in possession of the correspondence between General Jackson and myself, which will show the difference between the views that we have respectively taken, and by what means, and through whose agency, this long gone-by affair has been revived.

. . . Previous to my arrival here, I had confined the knowledge of the existence of the correspondence to a few confidential friends, who were politically attached both to General Jackson and myself; not that I had anything to apprehend from its disclosure, but because I was unwilling to increase the existing excitement in the present highly critical state of our political affairs. But when I arrived here, late in December, I found my caution had been of no avail, and that the correspondence was a subject of conversation in every circle, and soon became a topic of free comment in most of the public journals. The accounts of the affair, as is usually the case in such occasions, were, for the most part, grossly distorted, and were, in many instances, highly injurious to my character. . . .

In order to give a clear understanding of the affair, it will be necessary to make a few preliminary remarks.

It appears, from Mr. Forsyth's[1] letter, that it was written in reply to a letter, dated at Savannah, the 25th Jan. 1828, from Mr. Hamilton,[2] who was then on his return from New Orleans, where he had been by the appointment of the Tammany society of New York to represent them, as I understand, in the celebration of the 8th January, 1828. Gen. Jackson had been invited by the legislature of Louisiana, to attend the celebration. Mr. Hamilton on his way to New Orleans passed through this city, in December, 1827, when congress was in session, and after remaining here some days he proceeded to Nashville, and accompanied the general and suite to New Orleans. From Savannah he returned to New York through this place, where he again remained some time, congress being still in session. Whether this letter of Mr. Hamilton to Mr. Forsyth was the commencement of the intrigue, or whether it originated at an earlier date, at this place on his way to Nashville, or while there, I am unable to say; but I cannot doubt that the arrangements for its accomplishment were made on his return from Savannah to this

1. John Forsyth, governor of Georgia.
2. James A. Hamilton of New York, son of Alexander Hamilton and friend of Martin Van Buren.

place. At the time I was decidedly, and I may add, zealously engaged in the support of gen. Jackson. . . .

Mr. Hamilton, while here, requested to have some conversation with me, which on my part was carried on with freedom that is usual between those engaged in the same side of a warm political contest. I viewed him in no other light than that of a warm supporter of general Jackson. In connexion with some remark of his, that there was a rumor of an attack on gen. Jackson for his conduct in the Seminole war, he inquired if any motion had been made in the cabinet to arrest him. To which I replied in the negative. It may be proper to remark here, that no such motion or any other was made. The discussion in reference to the course that might be pursued towards him, took place on a suggestion of the propriety of an inquiry into his conduct, and my answer was therefore in strict conformity to the facts. . . .

Upon his return to New York, I received a letter from him dated the 25th of February, the object of which was, apparently, to know if he understood my conversation correctly. He stated that his object in being thus particular in endeavouring to ascertain from me whether his recollection was faithful or not with regard to the conversation, was because he wished to fulfil the object of his inquiry by confirming major Lewis, a confidential friend of gen. Jackson, in the truth, not with a view to make the publication then, but to be prepared against an apprehended attack, founded on events connected with the Seminole campaign. The disclosure, particularly that the information was intended for major Lewis as a confidential friend of gen. Jackson, excited my suspicion. Circumstances, however, gave my eye a wrong direction, not towards myself, but Mr. Monroe. What they were it becomes necessary to state, with the view of understanding the correspondence which followed with Mr. Hamilton. . . .

B. James A. Hamilton to His Excellency John Forsyth, Governor of Georgia

Savannah, January 29, 1828

Dear sir: It was my intention when I left New Orleans to have taken time to visit our illustrious friend Wm. H. Crawford, but the delays of my journey to Milledgeville, consumed so much of my time as to render it impossible for me to do so.

Whenever you meet him do me the favor to inform him of my intention, as I can with difficulty excuse myself for the omission to do so. I wish you would ascertain from him and communicate to me whether the propriety or necessity for arresting and trying general Jackson was ever presented as a question for the deliberation of Mr. Monroe's cabinet. I understand Mr. Southard,[3] in his *suppressed correspondence*, has asserted that to have been the fact.

I would have written directly to Mr. Crawford, but you know how much delicacy and difficulty there is in making such communications in writing. I want the information not to be used, but in order that I may, in the event of a publication which may come from a high quarter, know where to look for information on this subject. Of course nothing would be published without the consent of Mr. Crawford and yourself. . . .

C. JOHN FORSYTH TO WILLIAM H. CRAWFORD

Senate Chamber, April 16, 1830

Dear sir: The president having learned by some means that I had given the information contained in the enclosed copy of a letter to Mr. Hamilton, of New York, to that gentleman, I have been requested by one of his friends to give the same information for his use. Although I had your express permission to write to Mr. H. I had not *express permission* to make any other use of what you communicated to me, and I do not consider myself at liberty to do more than what I have done without referring the subject again to you. I was more particular than I should otherwise have been by learning that Mr. Calhoun had given a different account of the transaction alluded to. I have thought proper therefore to send you the enclosed, and to know first, whether my statement of our conversation is correct, and secondly, if you have any objection to my complying with the request made to me. . . .

D. GENERAL JACKSON TO MR. CALHOUN

May 13, 1830

Sir: That frankness, which, I trust, has always characterized me through life, towards those with whom I have been in the habits of friendship, induces me to lay before you the enclosed copy of a

---

3. Samuel L. Southard, Secretary of the Navy in the Monroe cabinet.

letter from William H. Crawford, Esq. which was placed in my hands on yesterday. The submission, you will perceive, is authorized by the writer. The statements and facts it presents being so different from what I had heretofore understood to be correct, requires that it should be brought to your consideration. . . . My object in making this communication is to announce to you the great surprise which is felt, and to learn of you whether it be possible that the information is correct; whether it can be, under all the circumstances of which you and I are both informed, that any attempt seriously to affect me was moved and sustained by you in the Cabinet Council, when, as is known to you, I was but executing the *wishes* of the Government, and clothed with the authority to "conduct the war in the manner I might judge the best." . . .

E. Copy of Mr. Crawford's Letter to Mr. Forsyth, Enclosed in the Above

Woodlawn, 30th April, 1830

My Dear Sir: Your letter of the 16th was received by Sunday's mail, together with its enclosure. I recollect having conversed with you at the time and place, and upon the subject, in that enclosure stated, but I have not a distinct recollection of what I said to you, but I am certain there is one error in your statement of that conversation to Mr. ————. I recollect distinctly what passed in the Cabinet meeting, referred to in your letter to Mr. ————.

Mr. Calhoun's proposition in the Cabinet was, that General Jackson should be punished in some form, or reprimanded in some form; I am not positively certain which. As Mr. Calhoun did not propose to arrest General Jackson, I feel confident that I could not have made use of that word in my relation of the circumstances which transpired in the Cabinet, as I have no recollection of ever having designedly misstated any transaction in my life, and most sincerely believe I never did. My apology for having disclosed what passed in a Cabinet meeting is this: In the summer after the meeting, an extract of a letter from Washington was published in a Nashville paper in which it was stated that I had proposed to arrest General Jackson, but that he was triumphantly defeated by Mr. Calhoun and Mr. Adams. This letter, I always believed, was written by Mr. Calhoun, or by his directions. It had the desired effect. General Jackson became extremely inimical to me, and friendly to Mr. Calhoun. In stating the argument of Mr. Adams to induce Mr. Monroe to support General Jackson's conduct through-out, adverting to Mr. Monroe's apparent admission, that if a young officer had acted so, he might be safely punished. Mr. Adams said, that if General Jackson had acted so, that if he was a subaltern officer, *shooting was too good for him.* This, however, was said with a view of driving Mr. Monroe to an unlimited support of what General Jackson had done, and not with an unfriendly view to the General. Indeed, my own views on the subject had undergone a material change after the Cabinet had been convened. Mr. Calhoun had made some allusions to a letter the General had written to the President, who had forgotten that he had received such a letter, but said, if he had received such an one, he could find it: and went directly to his cabinet, and brought the letter out. In it General Jackson approved of the determination of the Govern-ment to break up Amelia Island and Galveztown, and gave it also as his opinion that the Floridas ought to be taken by the United States. He added, it might be a delicate matter for the Executive to decide; but if the President approved of it, he had only to give a hint to some confidential member of Congress, say Johnny Ray,[4] and he would do it, and take the responsibility of it on himself. I asked the President if the letter had been answered. He replied, no; for that he had no recollection of having received it. I then said that I had no doubt that General Jackson, in taking Pensacola, believed he was doing what the Executive wished. After that letter was produced, unanswered, I should have opposed the infliction of punishment upon the General, who had considered the silence of the President as a tacit consent; yet it was after this letter was produced and read, that Mr. Calhoun made his proposition to the Cabinet for punishing the General. You may show this letter to Mr. Calhoun, if you please. With the foregoing corrections of what passed in the Cabinet, your account of it to Mr. ————— is cor-rect. Indeed, there is but one inaccurracy in it, and one omission. What I have written beyond them is a mere amplification of what passed in the Cabinet. I do not know that I ever hinted at the letter of the General to the President; yet that letter had a most important bearing upon the deliberations of the Cabinet, at least

4. John Rhea, congressman from Tennessee.

in my mind, and possibly in the minds of Mr. Adams and the President; but neither expressed an opinion upon the subject. It seems it had none upon the mind of Mr. Calhoun, for it made no change in his conduct.

F. MR. CALHOUN TO GENERAL JACKSON

Washington, 25th May, 1830

Sir:—In answering your letter of the 13th instant, I wish to be distinctly understood, that however high my respect is for your personal character, and the exalted station which you occupy, I cannot recognize the right on your part to call in question my conduct on the interesting occasion, in the discharge of a high official duty, and under responsibility to my conscience and my country only. . . .

I had a right, as I supposed, to conclude that you long since knew that the administration, and myself in particular, were of the opinion that the orders under which you acted did not authorize you to occupy the Spanish posts; but I now infer from your letter, to which this is in answer, that such conclusion was erroneous. . . .

Connected with the subject of your orders, there are certain expressions in your letter, which, though I am at a loss to under-stand I cannot pass over in silence. After announcing your surprise at the contents of Mr. Crawford's letter, you ask whether the information is correct . . . that you were "executing the *wishes* of the Government." If by *wishes*, which you have underscored, it be meant that there was any intimation given by myself, directly or indirectly, of the desire of the Government that you should occupy the Spanish posts, so far from being "informed" I had not the slightest knowledge of any such intimation, nor did I ever hear a whisper of any such before. . . .

I was the junior member of the cabinet, and had been but a few months in the administration. As Secretary of War, I was more immediately connected with the questions whether you had tran-scended your orders, and, if so, what course ought to be pursued. I was of the impression that you had exceeded your orders, and had acted on your own responsibility; but I neither questioned your patriotism nor your motives. Believing that there where orders were transcended, investigation, as a matter of course, ought to follow, as due in justice to the Government and the officer, unless there be strong reasons to the contrary. I came to the meeting under the impression that the usual course ought to be pursued in this case, which I supported by presenting fully and freely all the arguments that occurred to me. They were met by other arguments, growing out of a more enlarged view of the subject. . . . After deliberately weighing every question, when the members of the cabinet came to form their final opinion, on a view of the whole ground, it was unanimously determined, as I understood, in favor of the course adopted, and which was fully made known to you by Mr. Monroe's letter of the 19th of July, 1818. I gave it my assent and support, as being that which, under all the circumstances, the public interest required to be adopted. . . .

On a review of this subject, it is impossible not to be struck with the time and mode of bringing on this correspondence. It is now twelve years since the termination of the Seminole War. Few events in our history have caused so much excitement, or been so fully discussed, both in and out of Congress. During a greater part of this long period, Mr. Crawford was a prominent actor on the public stage, seeing and hearing all that occurred, and without restraint, according to his own statement, to disclose freely all he knew; yet not a word is uttered by him in your behalf; but now when you have triumphed over all difficulties, when you no longer require defence, he, for the first time, breaks silence, not to defend you, but to accuse one who gave you every support in your hour of trial in his power when you were fiercely attacked, if not by Mr. Crawford himself, at least by some of his most confidential and influential friends. Nor is the manner less remarkable than the time. Mr. Forsyth, a Senator from Georgia, here in this place, writes to Mr. Crawford, his letter covering certain enclosures, and referring to certain correspondence and conversations in relation to my conduct in the cabinet deliberations on the Seminole question. . . .

Why did not Mr. Forsyth himself show me the letter—the original letter? By what authority did he place a copy in your hands? None is given by the writer. Why is your name interposed? Was it to bring me into conflict with the President of the United States? . . . I have asked the question, Why is this affair brought up at this late period, and in this remarkable manner? . . . I should be blind not to see that this whole affair is a political manoeuvre, in which the design is that you should be the instrument, and myself the victim, but in which the real actors are carefully concealed by an artful movement. . . . Several indications forewarned me, long since, that a blow was mediated against me: I will not say from the quarter from which this comes: but in relation to this subject, more than two years since, I had a correspondence with the District Attorney for the Southern District of New York,[5] on the subject of the proceedings of the cabinet on the Seminole war, which, though it did not then excite particular attention, served to direct my eye to what was going on. . . .

G. GENERAL JACKSON TO MR. CALHOUN

May 30, 1830

Sir:

Your communication of the 29th inst. was handed me this morning just as I was going to church, and of course was not read until I returned. I regret to find that you have entirely mistaken my note of the 13th instant. There is no part of it which calls in question either your conduct or your motives in the case alluded it. Motives are to be inferred from actions, and judged of by our God. It had been intimated to me many years ago, that it was you, and not Mr. Crawford, who had been secretly endeavoring to destroy my reputation. These insinuations I indignantly repelled, upon the ground that you, in all your letters to me, professed to be my personal friend, and approved entirely my conduct in relation to the Seminole campaign. I had too exalted an opinion of your honor and frankness, to believe for one moment that you could be capable of such deception. Under the influence of these friendly feelings (which I always entertained for you) when I was presented with a copy of Mr. Crawford's letter, with that frankness which ever has, and I hope ever will characterize my conduct, I considered it due to you, and the friendly relations which had always existed between us, to lay it forthwith before you, and ask if the statements contained in that letter could be true. I repeat, I had a right to believe that you were my sincere friend and, until now, never expected to have occasion to say to you, in the language of Caesar, Et tu Brute? . . . It is due to myself, however, to state that the knowledge of the Executive documents and orders in my possession will show conclusively that I had authority for all I did, and that your explanation of my powers, as declared to Governor Bibb, shows

5. James A. Hamilton.

your own understanding of them. Your letter to me on the 29th, handed today, and now before me, is the first intimation to me that you ever entertained any other opinion or view of them. Your conduct, words, actions, and letters, I have ever thought, show this. Understanding you now, no further communication with you on this subject is necessary. . . .

H. GENERAL JACKSON TO MR. FORSYTH

. . . I had been informed that Mr. Crawford had made a statement concerning this business, which had come to the knowledge of Col. James A. Hamilton, of New York. On meeting with Col. Hamilton, I inquired of him, and received for answer that he had, but remarked that he did not think it proper to communicate without the consent of the writer. I answered, that, being informed that the Marshall of this District had, to a friend of mine, made a similar statement to that said to have been made by Mr. Crawford, I would be glad to see Mr. Crawford's statement, and desired he would write and obtain his consent. My reasons were, that I had, from the uniform friendly professions of Mr. Calhoun, always believed him my friend in all this Seminole business; and I had a desire to know if in all this I had been mistaken, and whether it was possible for Mr. Calhoun to have acted with such insincerity and duplicity toward me.

I. MR. VAN BUREN TO THE EDITOR OF THE *Telegraph*

Mr. Van Buren transmits the enclosed to the editor of the United States Telegraph, for insertion in his paper of to-morrow February 25, 1831.

Mr. Van Buren desires us, in relation to the correspondence between the vice president and various other persons, which has recently appeared, to make the following statement in his behalf.

He observes that an impression is attempted to be made upon the public mind, that certain applications by James A. Hamilton, esq. of New York, to Mr. Forsyth, . . . for information in regard to certain cabinet transactions during the administration of Mr. Monroe, and which are referred to by the latter gentleman, were so made by Mr. Van Buren's advice or procurement. Leaving the motives and objects of these applications to those who may deem it necessary to notice them, Mr. Van Buren avers that they, and each of them, were not only made without agency of any description on his part, but also without his knowledge; and that he has, at no period, taken any part in the matters connected with them.—He desires us further to say, that every assertion, or insinuation, which has for its object to impute to him any participation in attempts, supposed to have been made in the years 1827 and 1828, to prejudice the vice president in the good opinion of gen. Jackson or at any time, is alike unfounded and unjust. He had no motive or desire to create such an impression, and neither took, advised, nor countenanced, directly, or indirectly, any steps to effect that object. For the correctness of these declarations, he appeals with a confidence which defies contradiction, to all who have been actors in the admitted transactions referred to, or who possess any knowledge on the subject.

Washington, Feb. 25, 1831

9. The Spoils System

JAMES PARTON, one of Jackson's earliest and most successful biographers, concluded reluctantly that the General's administration was a disaster to the country because it inaugurated the spoils system. Actually Jackson neither began the system nor were his removals as ruthless and wholesale as some chose to think. But it cannot be denied that Jackson meant to establish the principle of rotation as his message to Congress clearly states. Unfortunately, there was a great deal of talk about the number of able men who were expelled from office for political reasons, and the remark in the U.S. Senate by William L. Marcy, one of Van Buren's lieutenants, that, "To the Victor belong the spoils of the enemy" tended to give rotation a bad name. The outcries against the executive patronage reached such a pitch, particularly among the Whigs, that the Senate formed a committee to investigate. Headed by John C. Calhoun, the committee not only enumerated the faults of the system but attempted to explain the profound effects "this great, growing and excessive" patronage had on the political life of the country.

SOURCE: Andrew Jackson's First Annual Message, December 8, 1829, James D. Richardson, *Messages and Papers*, II: 1011–12; U.S., Congress, *Senate Documents*, 23d Congress, 2d session, III, document 108.

A. Jackson's First Annual Message

There are, perhaps, few men who can for any great length of time enjoy office and power without being more or less under the influence of feelings unfavorable to the faithful discharge of their public duties. Their integrity may be proof against improper considerations immediately addressed to themselves, but they are apt to acquire a habit of looking with indifference upon the public interests and of tolerating conduct from which an unpracticed man would revolt. Office is considered as a species of property, and government rather as a means of promoting individual interests than as an instrument created solely for the service of the people. Corruption in some and in others a perversion of correct feelings and principles divert government from its legitimate ends and make it an engine for the support of the few at the expense of the many. The duties of all public officers are, or at least admit of being made, so plain and simple that men of intelligence may readily qualify themselves for their performance; and I can not but believe that more is lost by the long continuance of men in office than is generally to be gained by their experience. I submit, therefore, to your consideration whether the efficiency of the Government would not be promoted and official industry and integrity better secured by a general extension of the law which limits appointments to four years.

In a country where offices are created solely for the benefit of the people no one man has any more intrinsic right to official station than another. Offices were not established to give support to particular men at the public expense. No individual wrong is, therefore, done by removal, since neither appointment to nor continuance in office is matter of right. The incumbent became an officer with a view to public benefits, and when these require his removal they are not to be sacrificed to private interests. It is the people, and they alone, who have a right to complain when a bad officer is substituted for a good one. He who is removed has the same means of obtaining a living that are enjoyed by the millions who never held office. The proposed limitation would destroy the idea of property now so generally connected with official station, and although individual distress may be sometimes produced, it would, by promoting that rotation which constitutes a leading principle in the republican creed, give healthful action to the system. . . .

B. "Report of a Senate Committee to Inquire into the Extent of the Executive Patronage, February 9, 1835"

Among the circumstances which have contributed to the great increase of executive patronage of late, the most prominent, doubtless, are the great increase of the expenditure of the Government, which, within the last eight years, (from 1825 to 1833,) has risen from $11,490,460 to $22,713,755, not including payments on account of the public debt; a corresponding increase of officers, agents, contractors and others, dependant on the Government; the vast quantity of land to which the Indian title has, in the same period, been extinguished, and which has been suddenly thrown into the market, accompanied with the patronage incident to holding Indian treaties, and removing the Indians to the west of the Mississippi, and also a great increase of the number and influence of surveyors, receivers, registers, and others employed in the branch of the administration connected with the public lands; all of which have greatly increased the influence of executive patronage over an extensive region, and that the most growing and flourishing portion of the Union. In this connexion, the recent practice of the Government must be taken into estimate, of reserving to individual Indians a large portion of the best land of the country, to which the title of the nation is extinguished, to be disposed of under the sanction of the Executive, on the recommendation of agents appointed solely by him, and which has prevailed to so great an extent of late, especially in the southwestern section of the Union.

It is difficult to imagine a device better calculated to augment the patronage of the Executive, and, with it, to give rise to speculations calculated to deprave and corrupt the community, without benefit to the Indians. But as greatly as these causes have added to the force of patronage of late, there are others of a different nature, which have contributed to give it a far greater and more dangerous influence. At the head of these should be placed the practice so greatly extended, if not for the first time introduced, of removing from office persons well qualified, and who had faithfully performed their duty, in order to fill their places with those who are recommended on the grounds that they belong to the party in power. . . .

In speaking of the practice of removing from office on party ground as of recent date, and, of course, comprehended under the causes which have of late contributed to the increase of executive patronage, your committee are aware that cases of such removals may be found in the early stages of the Government; but they are so few, and exercised so little influence, that they may be said to constitute instances rather than as forming a practice. It is only within the last few years that removals from office have been introduced as a system, and, for the first time, an opportunity has been afforded of testing the tendency of the practice, and witnessing the mighty increase which it has given to the force of executive patronage; and the entire and fearful change, in conjunction with other causes, it is effecting in the character of our political system. Nor will it require much reflection to perceive in what manner it contributes to increase so vastly the extent of executive patronage.

So long as offices were considered as public trusts, to be conferred on the honest, the faithful, and capable, for the common good, and not for the benefit or gain of the incumbent or his party, and so long as it was the practice of the Government to continue in office those who faithfully performed their duties, its patronage, in point of fact, was limited to the mere power of nominating to accidental vacancies or to newly created offices, and could, of course, exercise but a moderate influence, either over the body of the community, or of the office-holders themselves: but when this practice was reversed—when offices, instead of being considered as public trusts, to be conferred on the deserving, were regarded as the spoils of victory, to be bestowed as rewards for partisan services, without respect to merit; when it became to be understood that all who hold office, hold by the tenure of partisan zeal and party service, it is easy to see that the certain, direct, and inevitable tendency of such a state of things, is to convert the entire body of those in office into corrupt and supple instruments of power, and to raise up a host of hungry, greedy, and subservient partisans, ready for every service, however base and corrupt. Were a premium offered for the best means of extending to the utmost the power of patronage; to destroy the love of country, and to substitute a spirit of subserviency and man-worship; to encourage vice and discourage virtue; and, in a word, to prepare for the subversion of liberty, and the establishment of despotism, no scheme more perfect could be devised, and such must be the tendency of the practice, with whatever intention adopted, or to whatever extent pursued. . . .

Your committee will next proceed to inquire what has been the effects of this great, growing and excessive patronage, on our political condition and prospects—a question of the utmost importance in deciding on the expediency of it's reduction. Has it tended to strengthen our political institutions, and to give a stronger assurance of perpetuating them, and, with them, the blessings of liberty to our posterity? Has it purified the public and political morals of our country, and strengthened the ties of patriotism? Or, on the other hand, has it tended to sap the foundation of our institutions; to throw a cloud of uncertainty over the future; to degrade and corrupt the public morals; and to substitute devotion and subserviency to power in the place of that disinterested and noble attachment to principles and country which are essential to the preservation of free institutions? These are the questions to be decided; and it is with profound regret that your committee are constrained, however painful, to say that the decision admits of little doubt. They are compelled to admit the fact, that there never has been a period, from the foundation of the Government, when there were such general apprehensions and doubts as to the permanency and success of our political institutions; when the prospect of perpetuating them, and, with them, our liberty, appeared so uncertain; when public and political morals are more depressed; when attachment to country and principles were more feeble, and devotion to party and power stronger; for the truth of all which they appeal to the observation and reflections of the experienced and enlightened of all parties. If we turn our eyes to the Government, we shall find that, with this increase of patronage, the entire character and structure of the Government itself is undergoing a great and fearful change, which, if not arrested, must, at no distant period, concentrate all its power in a single department.

Your committee are aware that, in a country of such vast extent and diversity of interests as ours, a strong Executive is necessary; and, among other reasons, in order to sustain the Government, by its influence, against the local feelings and interests which it must, in the execution of its duties, necessarily encounter; and it was doubtless with this view mainly that the framers of the Constitution invested the executive powers in a single individual, clothed him with the almost entire patronage of the Government. As long as the influence of the Executive is so moderate as to compel him to identify his administration with the public interest, and to hold his patronage subordinate to the principles and measures necessary to promote the common good, the executive power may be said to act within the sphere assigned to it by the constitution, and may be considered as essential to the ready and equal operation of the Government; but when it becomes so strong as to be capable of sustaining itself by its influence alone, unconnected with any system of measures or policy, it is the certain indication of the near approach of irresponsible and despotic power. When it attains that point it will be difficult to find, anywhere in our system, a power sufficient to restrain its progress to despotism. The very causes which render a strong Executive necessary, the great extent of country and diversity of interests, will form great and almost insuperable impediments to any effectual resistance. Each section, as has been shown, will have its own party and its own favorites, entertaining views of principles and policy so different as to render an united effort against executive power almost impossible, while their separate and disjointed efforts must prove impotent against a power far stronger than either, taken separately; nor can the aid of the States be successfully invoked to arrest the progress to despotism. So far from weakening, they will add strength to executive patronage. A majority of the States, instead of opposing, will be usually found acting in concert with the Federal Government, and, of course, will increase the influence of the Executive; so that, to ascertain his patronage, the sum total of the patronage of all the States, acting in conjunction with the Federal Executive, must be added to his. The two, as things now stand, constitute a joint force, difficult to be resisted.

Against a danger so formidable, which threatens, if not arrested, and that speedily, to subvert the constitution, there can be but one effectual remedy: a prompt and decided reduction of executive patronage; the practicability and means of effecting which, your committee will next proceed to consider.

The first, most simple, and usually the most certain mode of reducing patronage, is to reduce the public income, the prolific source from which it almost exclusively flows. Experience has shown, that it is next to impossible to reduce the public expenditure with an overflowing treasury; and not much less difficult to reduce patronage without a reduction of expenditure; or, in other words, that the most simple and effectual mode of retrenching the superfluous expenditure of the Government; to introduce a spirit of frugality and economy in the administration of public affairs; to correct the corruption and abuses of the Government; and, finally, to arrest the progress of power, is, to leave the money in the pockets of those who made it, where all laws, human and divine, place it, and from which it cannot be removed by Government itself, except for its necessary and indispensible wants, without violation of its highest trust, and the most sacred principles of justice. Yet, as manifest as is this truth, such is our peculiar (it may be said extraordinary) situation, that this simple and obvious remedy to excessive patronage, the reduction of the revenue, can be applied only to a very limited extent. . . .

But the great and alarming strides which patronage has made . . . has demonstrated the necessity of imposing other limitations on the discretionary powers of the Executive: particularly in reference to the General Post Office and the public funds, on which important subject the Executive has an almost unlimited discretion as things now are.

In a government like ours, liable to dangers so imminent from the excess and abuse of patronage, it would seem extraordinary that a department of such vast powers, with an annual income and expenditure so great, and with a host of persons in its service, extending and ramifying itself to the remotest point, and into every neighborhood of the Union, and having a control over the correspondence and intercourse of the whole community, should be permitted to remain so long without efficient checks or responsibility, under the almost unlimited control of the Executive. Such a power, wielded by a single will, is sufficient of itself, when made an instrument of ambition, to contaminate the community, and to control, to a great extent, public opinion. To guard against this danger, and to impose effectual restrictions on Executive patronage, acting through this important department, your committee are of the opinion that an entire re-organization of the department is required; but their labor, in reference to this great subject, has been superseded by the Committee on the Post Office, which has bestowed so much attention on it, and which is so much more minutely acquainted with the diseased state of the department than your committee can be, that it would be presumption on their part to attempt to add to their recommendation.

But, as extensive and dangerous as is the patronage of the Executive through the Post Office Department, it is not much less so in reference to the public funds, over which, as has been stated, it now has *unlimited control*, and through them, over the entire banking system of the country. With a banking system, spread from Maine to Louisiana; from the Atlantic to the utmost west; consisting of not less than five or six hundred banks, struggling among themselves for existence and gain; with an immense public fund, under the control of the Executive, to be deposited in whatever banks he may favor, or to be withdrawn at his pleasure; it is impossible for ingenuity to devise any scheme better calculated to convert the surplus revenue into a most potent engine of power and influence; and, it may be added, of peculation, speculation, corruption, and fraud. The first and most decisive step against this danger is that, already proposed, of distributing the surplus revenue among the States, which will prevent its growing accumulation in the banks, and, with it, the corresponding increase of executive power and influence over the banking system. In addition, your committee has reported a bill to change the deposite banks at the rate of —— per cent per annum for the use of the public funds, to be calculated on the average monthly deposites; to prohibit transfers, except for the purpose of disbursements; and to prevent a removal of the public funds from the banks in which they are now, or may hereafter be deposited, without the consent of Congress, except as is provided in the bill. The object of the bill is to secure to the Government an equivalent for the use of the public funds; to prevent the abuses and influence incident to transfer-warrants; and to place the deposite banks, as far as it may be practicable, beyond the control of the Executive.

In addition to these measures, there are, doubtless, many others connected with the customs, Indian affairs, public lands, army, navy, and other branches of the administration, into which, it is feared, there have crept many abuses, which have unnecessarily increased the expenditures and the number of persons employed, and, with them, the executive patronage; but to reform which would require a more minute investigation into the general state of the administration than your committee can at present bestow. Should the measures which they have recommended receive the sanction of Congress, they feel a strong conviction that they will greatly facilitate the work of carrying accountability, retrenchment, and economy through every branch of the administration, and thereby reduce the patronage of the Executive to those safe and economical limits which are necessary to a complete restoration of the equilibrium of the system, now so dangerously disturbed. Your committee are deeply impressed with the necessity of commencing early, and of carrying through, to its full and final completion, this great work of reform.

The disease is daily becoming more aggravated and dangerous; and, if it be permitted to progress for a few years longer, with the rapidity with which it has of late advanced, it will soon pass beyond the reach of remedy. This is no party question. Every lover of his country and of its institutions, be his party what it may, must see and deplore the rapid growth of patronage, with all its attending evils, and the certain catastrophe which awaits its further progress, if not timely arrested. The question now is not how, or where, or with whom the danger originated, but how it is to be arrested; not the cause, but the remedy; not how our institutions and liberty have been endangered, but how they are to be rescued.

10. The Maysville Veto

THE MAYSVILLE ROAD controversy was another example of party wrangling during the early Jackson administration and demonstrated the conflicting views of the major parties on the question of public works. This Road was a stretch of proposed highway to be constructed from Maysville to Lexington within the state of Kentucky, the home of Jackson's rival, Henry Clay. Friends of the project argued that it was simply an extension of the National Road, which originated at Cumberland, Maryland, and therefore interstate in character. But Van Buren, the chief architect of this veto, denied this contention and labelled the Road intrastate in character and therefore unconstitutional. Since New York had built the Erie Canal at its own expense it is obvious that Van Buren did not relish the idea of the federal government assisting other states to build similar improvements. In any event the bill passed Congress in May, 1830, whereupon Jackson vetoed it. The veto was a blow aimed at Clay and at those who favored the construction of federally sponsored public works.

May 27, 1830

To the House of Representatives.

GENTLEMEN: I have maturely considered the bill proposing to authorize "a subscription of stock in the Maysville, Washington,

SOURCE: James D. Richardson, *Messages and Papers*, II: 1046–1055.

Paris, and Lexington Turnpike Road Company," and now return the same to the House of Representatives, in which it originated, with my objections to its passage. . . .

The constitutional power of the Federal Government to construct or promote works of internal improvement presents itself in two points of view—the first as bearing upon the sovereignty of the States within whose limits their execution is contemplated, if jurisdiction of the territory which they may occupy be claimed as necessary to their preservation and use; the second as asserting the simple right to appropriate money from the National Treasury in aid of such works when undertaken by State authority, surrendering the claim of jurisdiction. In the first view the question of power is an open one, and can be decided without the embarrassments attending the other, arising from the practice of the Government. Although frequently and strenuously attempted, the power to this extent has never been exercised by the Government in a single instance. It does not, in my opinion, possess it; and no bill, therefore, which admits it can receive my official sanction.

But in the other view of the power the question is differently situated. The ground taken at an early period of the Government was "that whenever money has been raised by the general authority and is to be applied to a particular measure, a question arises whether the particular measure be within the numerated authorities vested in Congress. If it be, the money requisite for it may be applied to it; if not, no such application can be made." The document in which this principle was first advanced is of deservedly high authority, and should be held in grateful remembrance for its immediate agency in rescuing the country from much existing abuse and for its conservative effect upon some of the most valuable principles of the Constitution. The symmetry and purity of the Government would doubtless have been better preserved if this restriction of the power of appropriation could have been maintained without weakening its ability to fulfill the general objects of its institution, an effect so likely to attend its admission, notwithstanding its apparent fitness, that every subsequent Administration of the Government, embracing a period of thirty out of the forty-two years of its existence, has adopted a more enlarged construction of the power. It is not my purpose to detain you by a minute recital of the acts which sustain this assertion, but it is proper that I should notice some of the most prominent in order that the reflections which they suggest to my mind may be better understood. . . .

The bill before me does not call for a more definite opinion upon the particular circumstances which will warrant appropriations of money by Congress to aid works of internal improvement, for although the extension of the power to apply money beyond that of carrying into effect the object for which it is appropriated has, as we have seen, been long claimed and exercised by the Federal Government, yet such grants have always been professedly under the control of the general principle that the works which might be thus aided should be "of a general, not local, national, not State," character. A disregard of this distinction would of necessity lead to the subversion of the federal system. That even this is an unsafe one, arbitrary in its nature, and liable, consequently, to great abuses, is too obvious to require the confirmation of experience. It is, however, sufficiently definite and imperative to my mind to forbid my approbation of any bill having the character of the one under consideration. I have given to its provisions all the reflection demanded by a just regard for the interests of those of our fellow-citizens who have desired its passage, and by the respect which is due to a coordinate branch of the Government, but I am not able to view it in any other light than as a measure of purely local character; or, if it can be considered national, that no further distinction between the appropriate duties of the General and State Governments need be attempted, for there can be no local interest that may not with equal propriety be denominated national. It has no connection with any established system of improvements; is exclusively within the limits of a State, starting at a point on the Ohio River and running out 60 miles to an interior town, and even as far as the State is interested conferring partial instead of general advantages.

Considering the magnitude and importance of the power, and the embarrassments to which, from the very nature of the thing, its exercise must necessarily be subjected, the real friends of internal improvement ought not to be willing to confide it to accident and chance. What is properly *national* in its character or otherwise is an inquiry which is often extremely difficult of solution. The appropriations of one year for an object which is considered national may be rendered nugatory by the refusal of a succeeding Congress to continue the work on the ground that it is local. No aid can be derived from the intervention of corporations. The question regards the character of the work, not that of those by whom it is to be accomplished. Notwithstanding the union of the Government with the corporation by whose immediate agency any work of internal improvement is carried on, the inquiry will still remain, Is it national and conducive to the benefit of the whole, or local and operating only to the advantage of a portion of the Union? . . .

Through the favor of an overruling and indulgent Providence our country is blessed with general prosperity and our citizens exempted from the pressure of taxation, which other less favored portions of the human family are obliged to bear; yet it is true that many of the taxes collected from our citizens through the medium of imposts have for a considerable period been onerous. In many particulars these taxes have borne severely upon the laboring and less prosperous classes of the community, being imposed on the necessaries of life, and this, too, in cases where the burthen was not relieved by the consciousness that it would ultimately contribute to make us independent of foreign nations for articles of prime necessity by the encouragement of their growth and manufacture at home. They have been cheerfully borne because they were thought to be necessary to the support of Government and the payment of the debts unavoidably incurred in the acquisition and maintenance of our national rights and liberties. But have we a right to calculate on the same cheerful acquiescence when it is known that the necessity for their continuance would cease were it not for irregular, improvident, and unequal appropriations of the public funds? Will not the people demand, as they have a right to do, such a prudent system of expenditure as will pay the debts of the Union and authorize the reduction of every tax to as low a point as the wise observance of the necessity to protect that portion of our manufactures and labor whose prosperity is essential to our national safety and independence will allow? When the national debt is paid, the duties upon those articles which we do not raise may be repealed with safety, and still leave, I trust, without oppression to any section of the country, an accumulating surplus fund, which may be beneficially applied to some well-digested system of improvement.

Under this view the question as to the manner in which the Federal Government can or ought to embark in the construction of roads and canals, and the extent to which it may impose burthens on the people for these purposes, may be presented on its own merits, free of all disguise and of every embarrassment, except such as may arise from the Constitution itself. Assuming these suggestions to be correct, will not our constituents require the observance of a course by which they can be effected? Ought they not to require it? With the best disposition to aid, as far as I can conscientiously, in furtherance of works of internal improvement, my opinion is that the soundest views of national policy at this time point to such a course. Besides the avoidance of an evil influence upon the local concerns of the country, how solid is the advantage which the Government will reap from it in the elevation of its character! How gratifying the effect of presenting to the world the sublime spectacle of a Republic of more than 12,000,000 happy people, in the fifty-fourth year of her existence, after having passed through two protracted wars—the one for the acquisition and the other for the maintenance of liberty—free from debt and with all her immense resources unfettered! What a salutary influence would not such an exhibition exercise upon the cause of liberal principles and free government throughout the world! Would we not ourselves find in its effect an additional guaranty that our political institutions will be transmitted to the most remote posterity without decay? A course of policy destined to witness events like these can not be benefited by a legislation which tolerates a scramble for appropriations that have no relation to any general system of improvement, and whose good effects must of necessity be very limited. In the best view of these appropriations, the abuses to which they lead far exceed the good which they are capable of promoting. They may be resorted to as artful expedients to shift upon the Government the losses of unsuccessful private speculation, and thus, by ministering to personal ambition and self-aggrandizement, tend to sap the foundations of public virtue and taint the administration of the Government with a demoralizing influence.

In the other view of the subject, and the only remaining one which it is my intention to present at this time, is involved the expediency of embarking in a system of internal improvement without a previous amendment of the Constitution explaining and defining the precise powers of the Federal Government over it. Assuming the right to appropriate money to aid in the construction of national works to be warranted by the contemporaneous and continued exposition of the Constitution, its insufficiency for the successful prosecution of them must be admitted by all candid minds. If we look to usage to define the extent of the right, that will be found so variant and embracing so much that has been overruled as to involve the whole subject in great uncertainty and to render the execution of our respective duties in relation to it replete with difficulty and embarrassment. It is in regard to such works and the acquisition of additional territory that the practice obtained its first footing. In most, if not all, other disputed questions of appropriation the construction of the Constitution may be regarded as unsettled if the right to apply money in the enumerated cases is placed on the ground of usage.

This subject has been one of much, and, I may add, painful, reflection to me. It has bearings that are well calculated to exert a powerful influence upon our hitherto prosperous system of government, and which, on some accounts, may even excite despondency in the breast of an American citizen. I will not detain you with professions of zeal in the cause of internal improvements. If to be their friend is a virtue which deserves commendation, our country is blessed with an abundance of it, for I do not suppose there is an intelligent citizen who does not wish to see them flourish. But though all are their friends, but few, I trust, are unmindful of the means by which they should be promoted; none certainly are so degenerate as to desire their success at the cost of that sacred instrument with the preservation of which is indissolubly bound our country's hopes. If different impressions are entertained in any quarter; if it is expected that the people of this country, reckless of their constitutional obligations, will prefer their local interest to the principles of the Union, such expectations will in the end be disappointed; or if it be not so, then indeed has the world but little to hope from the example of free government. When an honest observance of constitutional compacts can not be obtained from communities like ours, it need not be anticipated elsewhere, and the cause in which there has been so much martyrdom, and from which so much was expected by the friends of liberty, may be abandoned, and the degrading truth that man is unfit for self-government admitted. And this will be the case if *expediency* be made a rule of construction in interpreting the Constitution. Power in no government could desire a better shield for the insidious advances which it is ever ready to make upon the checks that are designed to restrain its action.

But I do not entertain such gloomy apprehensions. If it be the wish of the people that the construction of roads and canals should be conducted by the Federal Government, it is not only highly expedient, but indispensably necessary, that a previous amendment of the Constitution, delegating the necessary power and defining and restricting its exercise with reference to the sovereignty of the States, should be made. Without it nothing extensively useful can be effected. The right to exercise as much jurisdiction as is necessary to preserve the works and to raise funds by the collection of tolls to keep them in repair can not be dispensed with. The Cumberland road should be an instructive admonition of the consequences of acting without this right. Year after year contests are witnessed, growing out of efforts to obtain the necessary appropriations for completing and repairing this useful work. Whilst one Congress may claim and exercise the power, a succeeding one may deny it; and this fluctuation of opinion must be unavoidably fatal to any scheme which from its extent would promote the interests and elevate the character of the country. The experience of the past has shown that the opinion of Congress is subject to such fluctuations.

If it be the desire of the people that the agency of the Federal Government should be confined to the appropriation of money in aid of such undertakings, in virtue of State authorities, then the occasion, the manner, and the extent of the appropriations should be made the subject of constitutional regulation. This is the more necessary in order that they may be equitable among the several States, promote harmony between different sections of the Union and their representatives, preserve other parts of the Constitution from being undermined by the exercise of doubtful powers or the too great extension of those which are not so, and protect the whole subject against the deleterious influence of combinations to carry by concert measures which, considered by themselves, might meet but little countenance.

That a constitutional adjustment of this power upon equitable principles is in the highest degree desirable can scarcely be doubted, nor can it fail to be promoted by every sincere friend to the success of our political institutions. In no government are appeals to the source of power in cases of real doubt more suitable than in ours. No good motive can be assigned for the exercise of power by the constituted authorities, while those for whose benefit it is to be exercised have not conferred it and may not be willing to confer it. It would seem to me that an honest application of the conceded powers of the General Government to the advancement of the common weal present a sufficient scope to satisfy a reasonable ambition. The difficulty and supposed impracticability of obtaining an amendment of the Constitution in this respect is, I firmly believe, in a great degree unfounded. The time has never yet been when the patriotism and intelligence of the American people were not fully equal to the greatest exigency, and it never will when the subject calling forth their interposition is plainly presented to them. To do so with the questions involved in this bill, and to urge them to an early, zealous, and full consideration of their deep importance, is, in my estimation, among the highest of our duties. . . .

11. Henry Clay's American System

HENRY CLAY's "American System" was an ingenious attempt to harmonize the various economic interests of the country. He advocated protective tariffs, internal improvements and a sound banking system in an effort to create a "genuine American policy" free from European domination. Unfortunately, Jackson struck repeated blows at the System: he vetoed the Maysville Road; vetoed the Bank bill; and forced the Congress into a partial retreat from protection. In the following speech delivered in the Senate on February 2, 3 and 6, 1832, Clay offered the standard arguments for the protective tariff in an effort to stimulate the growth of industry. But the South would have none of it, and the tariff question helped trigger the nullification controversy of 1832–33.

. . . I pass, with pleasure, to two general propositions which cover the entire ground of debate. The first is, that under the operation of the American system, the objects which it protects and fosters are brought to the consumer at cheaper prices than they commanded prior to its introduction, or, than they would command if it did not exist. If that be true, ought not the country to be contented and satisfied with the system, unless the second proposi-

SOURCE: Henry Clay, *The Works of Henry Clay*, Calvin Colton, ed., Volume V (New York, 1857), pp. 464–5, 467, 471–3, 475, 477–8.

tion, which I mean presently also to consider, is unfounded? And that is, that the tendency of the system is to sustain, and that it has upheld, the prices of all our agricultural and other produce, including cotton.

And is the fact not indisputable, that all essential objects of consumption affected by the tariff, are cheaper and better since the act of 1824, than they were for several years prior to that law? I appeal for its truth to common observation, and to all practical men. I appeal to the farmer of the country, whether he does not purchase on better terms his iron, salt, brown sugar, cotton goods, and woolens, for his laboring people? And I ask the cotton planter if he has not been better and more cheaply supplied with his cotton-bagging? . . .

Gentlemen are no doubt surprised at these facts. They should not underrate the energies, the enterprise, and the skill of our fellow-citizens. I have no doubt they are every way competent to accomplish whatever can be effected by any other people, if encouraged and protected by the fostering care of our own government. Will gentlemen believe the fact, which I am authorized now to state, that the United States, at this time, manufacture one half the quantity of cotton which Great Britain did in 1816! We possess three great advantages: first, the raw material; second, water-power instead of that of steam, generally used in England; and, third, the cheaper labor of females. In England, males spin with the mule and weave; in this country, women and girls spin with the throstle, and superintend the power-loom. And can there be any employment more appropriate? Who has not been delighted with contemplating the clock-work regularity of a large cotton manufactory? I have often visited them at Cincinnati and other places, and always with increased admiration. The women, separated from the other sex, work in apartments, large, airy, well warmed, and spacious. Neatly dressed, with ruddy complexions, and happy countenances, they watch the work before them, mend the broken threads, and replace the exhausted balls or broaches. At stated hours they are called to their meals, and go and return with light and cheerful step. At night they separate, and repair to their respective houses, under the care of a mother, guardian, or friend. . . .

But it is argued, that if, by the skill, experience, and perfection, which we have acquired in certain branches of manufacture, they can be made as cheap as similar articles abroad, and enter fairly into competition with them, why not repeal the duties as to those articles? And why should we? Assuming the truth of the supposition, the foreign article would not be introduced in the regular course of trade, but would remain excluded by the possession of the home market, which the domestic article had obtained. The repeal, therefore, would have no legitimate effect. But might not the foreign article be imported in vast quantities, to glut our markets, break down our establishments, and ultimately to enable the foreigner to monopolize the supply of our consumption? America is the greatest foreign market for European manufactures. It is that to which European attention is constantly directed. If a great house becomes bankrupt there, its store-houses are emptied, and the goods are shipped to America, where, in consequence of our auctions, and our custom-house credits, the greatest facilities are afforded in the sale of them. Combinations among manufacturers might take place, or even the operations of foreign governments might be directed to the destruction of our establishments. A repeal, therefore, of one protecting duty, from some one or all of these causes, would be followed by flooding the country with the foreign fabric, surcharging the market, reducing the price, and a complete prostration of our manufactories; after which the foreigner would leisurely look about to indemnify himself in the increased prices which he would be enabled to command by his monopoly of the supply of our consumption. What American citizen, after the government had displayed this vacillating policy, would be again tempted to place the smallest confidence in the public faith, and adventure once more in this branch of industry? . . .

I have now to consider the remaining of the two propositions which I have already announced. That is, second, that under the operation of the American system, the products of our agriculture command a higher price than they would do without it, by the creation of a home market; and by the augmentation of wealth produced by manufacturing industry, which enlarges our powers of consumption both of domestic and foreign articles. The importance of the home market is among the established maxims which are universally recognized by all writers and all men. However some may differ as to the relative advantages of the foreign and the home market, none deny to the latter great value and high consideration.

It is nearer to us; beyond the control of foreign legislation; and undisturbed by those vicissitudes to which all international intercourse is more or less exposed. The most stupid are sensible of the benefit of a residence in the vicinity of a large manufactory, or of a market town, of a good road, or of a navigable stream, which connects their farms with some great capital. If the pursuits of all men were perfectly the same, although they would be in possession of the greatest abundance of the particular produce of their industry, they might, at the same time, be in extreme want of other necessary articles of human subsistence. The uniformity of the general occupation would preclude all exchanges, all commerce. It is only in the diversity of the vocations of the members of a community that the means can be found for those salutary exchanges which conduce to the general prosperity. And the greater that diversity, the more extensive and the more animating is the circle of exchange. Even if foreign markets were freely and widely open to the reception of our agricultural produce, from its bulky nature, and the distance of the interior, and the dangers of the ocean, large portions of it could never profitably reach the foreign market. . . .

What would be the condition of the farming country of the United States—of all that portion which lies north, east, and west of James river, including a large part of North Carolina—if a home market did not exist for this immense amount of agricultural produce? Without the market, where could it be sold? In foreign markets? If their restrictive laws did not exist, their capacity would not enable them to purchase and consume this vast addition to their present supplies, which must be thrown in, or thrown away, but for the home market. But their laws exclude us from their markets. . . .

I have hitherto considered the question in reference only to a state of peace; but a season of war ought not to be entirely overlooked. We have enjoyed nearly twenty years of peace; but who can tell when the storm of war shall again break forth? Have we forgotton, so soon, the privations to which not merely our brave soldiers and our gallant tars were subjected, but the whole community, during the last war, for the want of absolute necessaries? To what an enormous price they rose! And how inadequate the supply was at any price! The statesman who justly elevates his views will look behind as well as forward, and at the existing state of things; and he will graduate the policy, which he recommends, to the probable exigences which may arise in the Republic. Taking this comprehensive range, it would be easy to show that the higher prices of peace, if prices were higher in peace, were more than compensated by the lower prices of war, during which, supplies of all essential articles are indispensable to its vigorous, effectual, and glorious prosecution. I conclude this part of the argument with the hope that my humble exertions have not been altogether unsuccessful in showing,

First, that the policy which we have been considering ought to continue to be regarded as the genuine American system.

Secondly, that the free trade system, which is proposed as its substitute, ought really to be considered as the British colonial system.

Thirdly, that the American system is beneficial to all parts of the Union, and absolutely necessary to much the larger portion.

Fourthly, that the price of the great staple of cotton, and of all our chief productions of agriculture, has been sustained and upheld, and a decline averted, by the protective system.

Fifthly, that if the foreign demand for cotton has been at all diminished by the operation of that system, the diminution has been more than compensated in the additional demand created at home.

Sixthly, that the constant tendency of the system, by creating competition among ourselves, and between American and European industry, reciprocally acting upon each other, is to reduce prices of manufactured objects.

Seventhly, that in point of fact, objects within the scope of the policy of protection have greatly fallen in price.

Eighthly, that if, in a season of peace, these benefits are experienced, in a season of war, when the foreign supply might be cut off, they would be much more extensively felt.

Ninthly, and finally, that the substitution of the British colonial system for the American system, without benefiting any section of the Union, by subjecting us to a foreign legislation, regulated by foreign interests, would lead to the prostration of our manufactories, general impoverishment, and ultimate ruin. . . .

12. Indian Removal

THE REMOVAL of the Indian tribes west of the Mississippi River is one of the darkest and saddest pages in American history. Jackson initiated their removal and Congress authorized the action in 1830. There is some evidence that Jackson's actions were motivated by concern for the survival of the Indians, but it is also clear that he shared Western prejudice against the red men and wanted them out of the way. He signed over ninety treaties with various tribes promising them lands in the West in exchange for their lands east of the Mississippi. As it developed, the tribes were virtually expelled from their homes and pressed along a "trail of tears" to find starvation and death on the western plains. Several times savage fighting broke out, such as the Black Hawk and Second Seminole Wars, but eventually the Indians were subdued, their lands sequestered and most of the tribes driven westward.

A. INSTRUCTIONS TO GENERALS WILLIAM CARROLL
AND JOHN COFFEE FROM JOHN H. EATON,
SECRETARY OF WAR, MAY 30, 1829

Department of War

Sir: A crisis in our Indian affairs has arrived. Strong indications are seen of this in the circumstance of the Legislatures of Georgia and Alabama extending their laws over the Indians within their respective limits. These acts, it is reasonable to presume, will be followed by the other States interested in those portions of their soil now in the occupancy of the Indians. In the right to exercise such jurisdiction the Executive of the United States fully concurs; and this has been officially announced to the Cherokee Indians. The President is of opinion that the only mode left for the Indians to escape the effects of such enactments, and consequences more destructive and which are consequent on their contiguity to the whites, is, *for them to emigrate.* He sees the peculiarly delicate and dangerous grounds

SOURCE: *Senate Documents,* 21st Congress, 1st session, document # 1, serial 160; 23d Congress, 2nd session, document # 1, serial 266; *House Documents,* 24th Congress, 1st session, document # 2, serial 286; 27th Congress, 3d session, document # 219 (# 86), serial 425.

they occupy. He is sincerely anxious, by the exercise of the powers vested in him, and the application of any means, applicable to the great object, to save these people, and relieve the States. He is of opinion, if the Indians can be approached in any way that shall elude their prejudices, and enlightened as to their true relation to the States, upon the one hand, and what would be their relation, in the West, and to the General Government, on the other, they would consent to avoid the evil effects of the first, and realize for themselves and posterity the benefits of the last. He proposes to make the effort with the Cherokees and Creeks, and would extend it also to the Choctaws and Chickasaws, were there means at his disposal that could be made applicable to the effort among them. It is the wish of the President, as well from your known acquaintance with the Indian character, as from their knowledge of you, that you would undertake to enlighten the Cherokees and Creeks on the great subject of their best interests. . . .

Nothing is more certain than that, if the chiefs and influential men could be brought into the measure, the rest would implicitly follow. It becomes, therefore, a matter of necessity, if the General Government would benefit these people, that it move upon them in the line of their own prejudices; and by the adoption of any proper means, break the power that is warring with their best interests. The question is, how can this be best done? Not, it is believed, for the reasons suggested, by the means of a general council. There they would be awakened to all the intimations which those who are opposed to their exchange of country might throw out; and the consequence would be—what it has been—a firm refusal to acquiesce. The best resort is believed to be that which is embraced in an appeal to the chiefs and influential men— not together, but apart, at their own houses and by a proper exposition of their real condition, rouse them to think upon that; whilst offers to them, of extensive reservations in fee simple, and other rewards, would, it is hoped, result in obtaining their acquiescence. This had, their people, as a body, it is believed, would gladly go.

The President views the Indians as the children of the Government. He see what is best for them; and that a perseverence in their refusal to fly the dangers that surround them, must result in their misery, and final destruction. He would, if appeals to reason fail, induce them, by rewards, to avoid the threatened calamity.

Your first business, should you consent to engage in this work of mercy to the Indians, would be to ascertain upon whom, as pivots, the will of the Cherokees and Creeks turns. Go to them not as a negotiator, but friend. Open to each a view of his danger, and the danger that threatens his people. This may be made up of references to their present state, as to numbers, when compared with the past; the causes that have produced this thinning of their numbers; and here you might enlarge of their comparative degradation as a people, and the total impossibility of their ever attaining to higher privileges while they retain their present relations to a people who seek to get rid of them; to the inefficiency of their own laws for their advancement; and finally to the fact that these will be superseded and trodden underfoot, by the exercise, over them, of the laws of the States. And here you might amply illustrate the really difficult relation which the Cherokees, particularly, bear to this question, by the passing over them of the various laws of *four States!*

You might then enlarge upon the advantage of their condition in the West. Both those tribes have a fine and fertile and abundant country, west of the Arkansas and Mississippi. There the General Government could, and *would* protect them fully in the possession of the soil, and their right to self government, and improve them by instruction to be afforded to their children, &c. There they might grow up in every succeeding generation to be our equals in privileges, civil and religious; and by acceding to the kind wishes of the President, confer upon their prosperity lasting benefits and honors, whilst, by refusing to comply, they must, necessarily, entail destruction upon their race. . . .

B. Report from the Office of Indian Affairs, Department of War, November 25, 1834, Signed by Elbert Herring and Addressed to Lewis Cass, Secretary of War

. . . The interposition of the Government of the United States, in behalf of the Indian race, is now matter of history. That race seemed to be fast sinking in the overwhelming wave of white population; both physically and morally, it was unable to withstand the competition. It became degraded and wretched, and was rapidly vanishing from the face of the earth. The policy instituted for their protection and perpetuation was not only humane, but was also essential to the object, if, by any means, it might be attained. As such, it has carried the national sympathy along with it, and is now, as it were, incorporated with our national feelings. . . .

In carrying out the general principles of this policy, measures have been adopted for the execution of the several treaties with the Cherokees, Creeks, Seminoles, Appalachicolas, Quapaws, the united bands of Otoes and Missourias, of the river Platte, and the four confederated bands of Pawnees of the Platte, and the Loup Fork, all of which were ratified at the last session of Congress. Preparatory steps have also been taken for the removal of the Creeks and Seminoles, and it is expected that a considerable portion of those tribes will be removed beyond the Mississippi during the ensuing season, and find a happier home in the domains set apart for their residence, under the guarantee of the United States.

In pursuance of instructions from the department, General William Marshall, Indian agent for the Miamies, opened a negotiation recently with the chiefs of that tribe, for the purchase of their land in the State of Indiana. He has succeeded in procuring from them a cession of two hundred thousand acres, on terms advantageous to themselves and to the United States. It may be considered the precursor to a total cession of their remaining land in that State, and their consequent emigration to the western territory, a result desirable in many respects, especially connected with advantages to a portion of our citizens, and doubly gratifying from its being compatible with the best interests of the tribe.

The alteration proposed by a resolution of the Senate, at the last session of Congress, in the boundaries of the land granted by the Chicago treaty of 1833 to the united nation of Chippewa, Ottawa and Pottawatimie Indians, has received their assent, under certain modifications, specified in their agreement of the first of October last.

C. Report of Commissary General of Subsistence, Department of War, November 12, 1835, Signed by Geo. Gibson and Addressed to Lewis Cass, Secretary of War

. . . The efforts to effect Indian emigration have, during the past year, met with no very encouraging success; yet have they been most strenuous. No proper expedient has been left untried to accelerate the departure for their destined homes of the tribes east of the Mississippi; and the exertions though unsuccessful in a great degree, have cost much labor and expense it is hoped not without the promise of ultimate benefits. . . . The business of Indian removal is necessarily expensive. The Indians are uncertain in their movements, slow and vacillating. Easily operated upon by designing men, they readily believe every thing told them in opposition to the benevolent design of the Government. Thus have been caused the great expenses incident to both partial successes and to complete failures in removing them. Without, then, continued vigilance on the part of those engaged in the general superintendence of the operations, the failures must be more disastrous still; whilst every effort, successful or unsuccessful, calls for the most careful instructions and the most exact examination into the mode of their execution. . . .

It remains for me to advert to the embarrassments which have obstructed the emigration of Indians within a year or two past, and to the prospects in view for the removal of all those from the east of the Mississippi to the new country, who have in treaty stipulations agreed to go. All the tribes on this side of the Mississippi have long been surrounded by a white population more or less dense. They have, in many instances, formed connections with the whites; and they are in constant traffic with the white traders, to whom they are, it is believed always in debt. The traders have much power over them, for besides that which the creditor can, in every stage of society, exercise over the debtor, the successful trader, being a man of opulence, and not unfrequently of great sagacity, becomes the counsellor of the Indian, and sways him with all the potency of this double influence. The annuities are the principal source of remuneration to those who trust the Indians with goods. In many cases they are paid, notwithstanding all the precautions of the officers of the United States, acting under the law of Congress and the regulations of the War Department, also directly into the hands of the traders, sometimes without the formality of counting the specie of which they consist. It is very natural to suppose that it is the interest of the traders to keep the Indians from emigration; and in every attempt made by the agents of the Government to raise an emigrating party, this has been reported to be the case. . . . To deprive the Indians, then, of this the strongest of all inducements for remaining on this side of the Mississippi, (for, with every allowance on account of the attachments incidental to locality, they will pursue their pecuniary interests,) let the annuities be paid west of the Mississippi, and there is no reason to doubt that the scheme of emigration would meet with little future opposition. . . . Without some determined effort on the part of the United States, it cannot be disguised, that the Indians will perseveringly linger in their old haunts, and thus in a measure defeat that plan of benevolence which, it is conceded by the country, is, above all other things, the best calculated to promote their permanent welfare. . . .

D. A. J. RAINES TO C. A. HARRIS, COMMISSIONER OF INDIAN AFFAIRS, JUNE 4, 1838

Fort Smith

The 15th of June the contractors made a beef issue of four months at one time; the cattle were issued on foot, and not slaughtered—stock cattle, bulls, and steers. These cattle the Indians received at 738 pounds each. The same cattle were averaged to the contractor from the Missouri speculator at 425 pounds each, which was a big average; cheating the Indians out of 313 pounds on each head—more than one-third of their entire beef ration. The corn came in sacks, and was issued as the agent of the contract saw fit. Not one bushel was measured; no, sir, not a bushel. There was more than one-third of the corn ration saved to the contractor. For instance: at the depot at the North fork, where the largest number of Indians was fed, it required 6,500 bushels of corn per month; and the issue at that point did not exceed 3,500 bushels per month. The same course was pursued by all the commissaries at the different depots. . . . The corn issue was made to the 15th of September. . . . From that time until the contract expired for those Indians that were here, (the Creek warriors having not yet arrived), their corn ration was purchased by the contractors, say about 40,000 bushels, at fifty cents per bushel, in specie, which closed the contract. . . . Now, sir, I know there was not 40,000 bushels of corn made in the whole Creek nation, old and new emigrants all put together. The new emigration did not get to their new homes in time enough to build houses, make fences, clear ground, and make a crop, except in a few cases. What then, sir, is not the situation of these Indians that have been supplied by this contract? Out of the 16,200 persons, not one-half of them have a *mouthful* of provisions, and are entirely destitute. You may anticipate the result. The $20,000 paid by the contractors to the Indians for their corn ration enabled them to buy that amount of whiskey. Sir, I have seen 2,000 Indians drunk at the North fork of the Canadian, or Canadian depot, in one day. This the contractors had nothing to do with; but, sir, to my knowledge, last year there were more than 400 barrels of whiskey sold at this point. Oh! the misery and wretchedness that presents itself to our view in going among these people. The fell destroyer Death last year visited nearly every house, and, sir, I have witnessed entire families prostrated with sickness—not one able to give help to the other; and these poor people were made the instruments of enriching a few unprincipled and wicked contractors. And yet the world will call these men honest. . . .

Justice can be done to these Indians if you would appoint some man (none of your milk-and-cider cits, ruffle-shirt men) to superintend all issues made to these people. He might arrange his issue days, so as to be at all the different issues for one nation of people. Let him be paid well; let him be a man that has no price for his honor, but is above price. . . .

If you adopt this course, perhaps you may avert an evil which is gathering in this horizon, which will burst over a frontier people with ten-fold vengeance—more severe than any thing in the annuals of Indian warfare.

Why should these people remain quiet on your border? Have they done so when they were surrounded by a white population? No; they have shown their teeth, and some of them have *bit* badly. Will they not in a few years be better able to go to war, and present a stronger front than they ever have been? Have they not a country of a thousand miles extent to the Rocky mountains, where they can retreat, if they are hard *pushed?* Can you chastise them in this vast region, if they were driven to extremities? No, sir, never.

Turn your eyes to Florida, sir. What has been the cause of this war? Why brought about? You must answer, injustice. They wished to remain near the bones of their fathers, and you said it should not be. They have cost the Government, I am told, $15,000,000. Your armies have been defeated—many of your best officers found a bloody grave; and yet they are not conquered. Can you picture to your mind's eye the carnage and bloodshed—the murder and rapine—that would follow, should these Indians take up the rife, and sound the tocsin of war? And why should they not? They are the same Indians; and you have placed them in a better position to defend themselves than they have ever been in before. Beware, then, of the result. Let us have *justice* on our side; do what you can to correct the evils. . . . You are a man of too much good mind to let what I have written fall to the ground. . . .

III

The Bank War and Growth
of Presidential Power

13. Jackson on the Second Bank

THE SINGLE most important event during the entire middle period of
American history was the struggle Andrew Jackson waged against the
Second Bank of the United States. The Bank War, as it was called, gave
rise to the Whig party, fashioned the character of the Democratic party
in terms of leadership, principles and organizational discipline for nearly
a generation, and it became the instrument by which the powers of the
executive office were vastly expanded. Its influence on the American
economy is still debated by historians, some arguing that it condemned
the nation to a century of unsound finance and other contending that its
economic repercussions were considerably less significant than its political effects. In the following document Jackson explains his objections to
the Bank in his own words. Its value is that it comes from Jackson directly, while his famous Bank Veto is largely the work of Amos Kendall
and other members of the cabinet.

Bank. Message for 1830—

The importance of this subject requires that I should again call
the attention of Congress to the approaching expiration of the
charter of the United States Bank. Nothing has occured to lesson
in any degree, the dangers which many of our safest statesmen
apprehend from that institution as it present organised, nor is the
opinion of its unconstitutionality les extensive or les deeply im-
presed. In the spirit of improvement and compromise which dis-
tinguishes our country and institution, it becomes us to inquire,
whether it be not possible to secure the advantages afforded by the

SOURCE: Andrew Jackson's Memorandum Book 1829–32, Jackson
    Papers, Library of Congress.

present Bank, through the agency of a Bank of the United States so modified in its principles and structure as to abrogate constitutional and other objections.

It is thought practicable to organize such a Bank with the necessary offices as a Branch of the Treasury Department, based on the public deposits, without power to make loans on purchased property, which shall remit the funds of the Govt without charge, and find a moderate premium upon exchange furnished private citizens, the means of paying its expenses. Not being a corporate body having no stockholders, debtors or property, and but five officers, it would not be obnoxious to the constitutional objections which are urged against the present Bank; and having no means to operate on the hopes, fears or interests of large masses of the community, it would be shorn of the influence which makes that Bank formidable. The states would be strengthened by having in their hands the means of furnishing the local paper currency through their own Banks, while the Bank of the United States, though issuing no paper, would check the issues of the State, while taking their notes in deposit and for exchange only so long as they continue to be redeemed with specie. In times of public emergency, the capacities of such an institution might be enlarged by an act of Congress.

These suggestions are made, not so much as a recommendation, as with a view of calling the attention of Congress to the possible modifications of a system which cannot continue to exist in its present form without occasional collisions with the local authorities and perpetual office pensions and discontents on the part of the States and the people.

Therefore the following—

Outlines of a substitute of the United States Bank is presented for your consideration

The objections to the present Bank are:

1. It is unconstitutional;
2. It is dangerous to Liberty.

Yet this Bank renders important services to the Government and the country.

It cheapens and facilitates all the fiscal operations of the government.

It tends in some degree to equalise domestic exchange and produce a sound and uniform currency.

A substitute for the present Bank is desired, which shall yield all its benefits, and be obnoxious to some of its objections.

Banks do two kinds of business:

1. They discount notes and bills for which they give their own paper.

2. They deal in exchange.

These two kind of business have no necessary connection. There may be Banks of discount exclusively, and Banks of exchange exclusively. Both may be Banks of deposit.

The United States may establish a Bank of Exchange exclusively based on Government and individual deposits. This Bank may have branches whenever the government may think necessary.

They may be cloathed only with the power to sell exchange on each other; and require to transmit government funds without charge.

They need only have such offices as their duty require, checked by frequent and rigid inspection.

The whole may be placed under the direction of the Secretary of the Treasury, through a separate bureau.

The present Bank is unconstitutional:

1. Because it is a corporation which Congress has no constitutional power to establish.

2. Because it withdraws the business of Bank discounts and the property of private citizens from the operation of State laws, and from the taxing power of the States in which it is employed.

3. Because it purchases land and other real estate within the States without their consent, under an authority purporting to be derived from Congress, when the General Government itself possesses no such constitutional power.

The proposed substitute would not be a corporation, but a branch of the Treasury Department; it would hold no property real or personal, and would withdraw none from the operation of the State laws.

The present Bank is dangerous to Liberty:

1. Because in the number, wealth, and standing of its officers and stockholders, in its power to make loans or withold them, to call oppressively upon its debtors or indulge them, build houses, rent lands & houses, and make donations for political or other purposes, it embodies a forceful influence which may be wielded for the

agrandisement of a favorite individual, a particular interest, or a separate party.

2. Because it concentrates in the hands of a few men, a power over the money of the country, which may be perverted to the oppresion of the people, and in times of public calamity, to the embarrasment of the government.

3. Because much of its stock is owned by foreigners, through the management of which an avenue is opened to a foreign influence in the most vital concern of the Republic.

4. Because it always is governed by interest and will even support *him* who supports *it*. An ambitious or dishonest president may thus always unite all of its power and influence in his support, while an honest one who thwarts its views, will never fail to encounter the weight of its opposition.

5. It weakens the States and strengthens the General Government.

The proposed substitute would have few officers and no stockholders, make no loans, have no debtors, build no houses, rent no lands or houses make no donations, and would be entirely destitute of the influence which arises from the hopes, fears and avarice of thousands. It would oppres no man, and being part of the government, would always aid its operations. It would have no stock and could not be reached by foreign influence. It would afford less aid to a dishonest president than the present Bank, and would never be opposed to an honest one. It would strengthen the States, by leaving to their Banks the whole business of discounts and the furnishing the local currency. It would strengthen the General Government les than the part office and less than the present Bank when it acts in concert with the national authorities.

The proposed substitute would cheapen and facilitate all the fiscal operations of the government as completely as the present Bank. . . . In time of war the capacities of this Bank might be increased by an act of Congres. Such a Bank would not be unconstitutional, not dangerous to liberty, and would yield to the government all the facilities afforded by the present Bank. Further than this perhaps the general government ought not to look. But its incidental advantages to the country would severely be inferior to those afforded by the present Bank while it would destroy a favored monopoly.

Again the U.S. Bank is unconstitutional and unpolitic.

Unconstitutional because:

1st Congress has no power to legislate upon any subject unles such power is expresly given in some part of the constitution, or is necesary and proper for the attainment of some object for the attainment of which there is an expres grant.

Before the formation of the Federal constitution each state was sovereign, and independent, within its own limits, and no state is deprived by the constitution of any it once posesed unles in the exercise of its own sovereign powers has made an expres surrender to the Federal Government.

Who can point his finger to the paragraph in the constitution by which this power is confered & I answer—no person. Had it been intended to confer so important a power by the framers of that institution the grant would have been clear and explicit. Now all ought to admit if such power exists it is doubtful from what paragraph it is to be infered some of its advocates deduce it from one passage—some from another, and the very circumstance of their disagreement, is a strong argument that it cannot be, legitimately, deduced from any of the grants of power which have been made—it has been very appropriately termed a "vagrant power crawling over the constitution, feeling for a soft place in the instrument, where it can make a settlement." . . .

Other considerations I think satisfactorily shew—the framers of the constitution never intended to give Congres the power claimed. . . .

But suppose we admit that from the power to coin money the Congress has the power to regulate the currency both metalic and paper, still it has no power to create the Bank; because if that power is inferred for such purpose we must allow Congres power to transfer to a few individuals Directors and Stockholders the powers of a Sovereign upon a subject of vital importance to the well being of the whole society—This cannot have been the intention of the Framers of the constitution—Whatever sovereign powers are confered upon Congres must be exercised by Congres and cannot be transfered to any other body, to be enacted by itself.—But if Congres had a general power to create a corporation for purposes of Banking, it cannot have the power to create a corporation composed partly of individuals and partly of the Government itself.—A portion of the funds constituting the capital of this Bank belongs to the Federal Government—exclusive priviledges are granted for twenty years, the money of the government is intermixed with that

of individuals and a monopoly quaranteed during the existence of
the charter—In principle and in fact a partnership is formed
between the Government and a few of the citizens, by virtue of
which those individuals have priviledges and interests supported,
aided and sanctioned, separate and distinct from the rest of the
community where the intention of the Federal Government was to
keep up equality, and not to enact separate interests— . . . It has
been sometimes urged that this question of power to charter the
Bank has been settled by legislative judicial and executive determi-
nations. I answer no.—It is one of the cases, in which precedent
ought not readily to conclude us—A frequent recurrence to fundamental principles is esential to the preservation of liberty.—This is
one of the cases in which that maxim should have its full influence,
for if this power is once yielded and it is distinctly understood that
it is not again to be questioned, I firmly believe a monopoly is
created, a priviledged order established that will eventually change
the fundamental principles of our government.—

Impolitic—

But if we yield to the Federal Government this power, it is one
which ought not to be exercised—Because if it puts the community,
at large and their property at the mercy of a corporation which will in
the end pursue its own interest—It will have millions of capital—The
deposits of the Government, averaging probably about Six millions
more, as well as the deposits of individuals to a much larger amount.
With these means and backed by the name and influence of the
United States, it is to have the power to establish as many Branches
in its respective States as it choose, and these States are to have no
power to impose a collect of any tax—When it is the interest of the
Bank to give an artificial value to property they will accomodate
freely, increase *beyond* the *interest* of *society* the amount of the
circulating medium and thus give a high nominal value to property,
and whenever it suits their purposes they can curtail their accom-
odations call upon many debtors at the same time reflow the circulating medium to any amount they choose and this repres the
price of property and becomes the purchasers of it for thrifting
considerations—

They will likewise have the power of setting the rates of exchange both foreign and domestic at such rates as may best
promote their own interests—making them low when they wish to
purchase Bills, and high whenever it may best suit them to sell—

These are powers so vast, and the temptations to use them so great, that no man who loves his country and wishes society protected against avarice and injustice, ought willingly to see confered upon any set man whatsoever.—

2nd. The charter prohibits the Bank from loaning to the Government without a law, but there is nothing to compel them to make a loan in case a law should authorise it, no matter how urgent or presing the wants of the Government may be—Thus the Government may be placed at the mercy of the Bank in times of public calamity and distres.—

3rd. The directors of the Bank through donations from its extensive funds and other uses of them may operate upon public opinion injuriously in political or party struggle.—

4th. Foreigners now use, and may here after be to much connexion this former between them the Government and citizen Stockholders an avenue is opened for the corrupting influence of foreign governments in the political concerns of the American people, which it is to be feared will prove ultimately destructive of our best interests.—

5th. It has failed in time past, and will do so in future, if it be its interest accomplish the objects for which it was chartered.—it does not furnish a paper currency signed by the officers of the principal Bank, with the genuinenes of which society can readily inform themselves, and which can be conveniently converted into specie: but on the contrary has substituted for notes of five and ten dollars drafts or orders signed by the Presidents of the respectives Branches addresed to the Cashier's of the Principal Bank in Philadelphia, and payable there—Thus multiplying signatures contrary to the intention of the charter, and to an extent which puts it out of the power of society to distinguish between the genuine and counterfiet, and if they could do so, fixes the place of payment so distant from the places of the issues, as to prelude the probability of a call for specie at the place of payment.—

6th. When such Bank shall have been a short time in operation and its Branches planted in the respective States, it can and probably will control the election, and through them the politics of the country.—It will always be governed by a view of its own interest, and opposing those who may have independence enough to resist, or object to its unjust pretentions.—The time of a application for a renewal of the charter is a practical proof of this position.—The present charter does not expire till the Spring 1836—Yet the application is made and proper at the present sesion for a renewal as the Presidential Election will take place before another sesion of Congres, from a belief that the Chief Magistrate will not dare to provoke their opposition to his *reelection* by freely exercising his constitutional power should a Bill be now pushed for his signature. Should this bold attempt be yielded, the charter will be made perpetual by the same means, no matter how injuriously it may be operating on society at large.—

7th. If we admit that the Federal Government has the power to incorporate individuals to enable them to carry on a Banking busines and that the interests of the Government as well as of society requires an exercise of the power still, I deny that another charter ought to be granted to the Stockholders of the existing Bank.—They have had the exclusive privilege for twenty years, why not make a new charter telling all others of our own citizens have an equal opportunity to become and thus partake of the benefits— Equality and fairnes would require this—Shall it be allowed that the old Stockholders many of them foreigners shall have this privilege to the exclusion of every other citizen? Surely this is unreasonable and unjust, more expecially when others are not only willing but anxious to obtain this privilege upon terms more favorable to the Government and more respectful to the Sovreignty of the States— . . .

14. The Bank Veto

DESPITE JACKSON's *known objections to the Bank, Henry Clay persuaded Nicholas Biddle, president of the Bank, to request a recharter in 1832, four years before the present charter expired. Clay needed an issue to run against Jackson in the election of 1832 and only the Bank question was considered potent enough to unseat the popular Jackson. So the bill for recharter was introduced into the Congress and passed both houses. With the considerable help of Amos Kendall and others, Jackson issued a stinging veto, without question the single most important state paper of his administration. Many of the arguments repeat the complaints outlined in the preceding document and can be faulted on economic grounds. But the message is a powerful and dramatic polemic*

SOURCE: James D. Richardson, *Messages and Papers*, II: 1144–5, 1152–4.

*that vibrates with political thunder. It is political propaganda of the
highest order and as such was calculated to rouse the great masses of
Americans to unite behind Jackson in his contest against "privilege and
aristocracy."*

ANDREW JACKSON'S VETO OF THE BANK BILL, JULY 10, 1832

If we must have a bank with private stockholders, every consideration of sound policy and every impulse of American feeling ad-
monishes that it should be *purely* American. Its stockholders
should be composed exclusively of our own citizens, who at least
ought to be friendly to our Government and willing to support it in
times of difficulty and danger. . . .

It is maintained by the advocates of the bank that its constitutionality in all its features ought to be considered as settled by
precedent and by the decision of the Supreme Court. To this
conclusion I can not assent. Mere precedent is a dangerous source
of authority, and should not be regarded as deciding questions of
constitutional power except where the acquiescence of the people
and the States can be considered as well settled. So far from this
being the case on this subject, an argument against the bank might
be based on precedent. One Congress, in 1791, decided in favor of
a bank; another, in 1811, decided against it. One Congress, in 1815,
decided against a bank; another, in 1816, decided in its favor. Prior
to the present Congress, therefore, the precedents drawn from that
source were equal. If we resort to the States, the expressions of
legislative, judicial, and executive opinions against the bank have
been probably to those in its favor as 4 to 1. There is nothing in
precedent, therefore, which, if its authority were admitted, ought
to weigh in favor of the act before me.

If the opinion of the Supreme Court covered the whole ground
of this act, it ought not to control the coordinate authorities of this
Government. The Congress, the Executive, and the Court must
each for itself be guided by its own opinion of the Constitution.
Each public officer who takes an oath to support the Constitution
swears that he will support it as he understands it, and not as it is
understood by others. It is as much the duty of the House of
Representatives, of the Senate, and of the President to decide upon
the constitutionality of any bill or resolution which may be presented to them for passage or approval as it is of the supreme
judges when it may be brought before them for judicial decision.
The opinion of the judges has no more authority over Congress

than the opinion of Congress has over the judges, and on that point the President is independent of both. The authority of the Supreme Court must not, therefore, be permitted to control the Congress or the Executive when acting in their legislative capacities, but to have only such influence as the force of their reasoning may deserve. . . .

Suspicions are entertained and charges are made of gross abuse and violation of its charter. An investigation unwillingly conceded and so restricted in time as necessarily to make it incomplete and unsatisfactory discloses enough to excite suspicion and alarm. In the practices of the principal bank partially unveiled, in the absence of important witnesses, and in numerous charges confidently made and as yet wholly uninvestigated there was enough to induce a majority of the committee of investigation—a committee which was selected from the most able and honorable members of the House of Representatives—to recommend a suspension of further action upon the bill and a prosecution of the inquiry. As the charter had yet four years to run, and as a renewal now was not necessary to the successful prosecution of its business, it was to have been expected that the bank itself, conscious of its purity and proud of its character, would have withdrawn its application for the present, and demanded the severest scrutiny into all its transactions. In their declining to do so there seems to be an additional reason why the functionaries of the Government should proceed with less haste and more caution in the renewal of their monopoly.

The bank is professedly established as an agent of the executive branch of the Government, and its constitutionality is maintained on that ground. Neither upon the propriety of present action nor upon the provisions of this act was the Executive consulted. It has had no opportunity to say that it neither needs nor wants an agent clothed with such powers and favored by such exemptions. There is nothing in its legitimate functions which makes it necessary or proper. Whatever interest or influence, whether public or private, has given birth to this act, it can not be found either in the wishes or necessities of the executive department, by which present action is deemed premature, and the powers conferred upon its agent not only unnecessary, but dangerous to the Government and country.

It is to be regretted that the rich and powerful too often bend the acts of government to their selfish purposes. Distinctions in society will always exist under every just government. Equality of talents, of education, or of wealth can not be produced by human institutions. In the full enjoyment of the gifts of Heaven and the fruits of superior industry, economy, and virtue, every man is equally entitled to protection by law; but when the laws undertake to add to these natural and just advantages artificial distinctions, to grant titles, gratuities, and exclusive privileges, to make the rich richer and the potent more powerful, the humble members of society—the farmers, mechanics, and laborers—who have neither the time nor the means of securing like favors to themselves, have a right to complain of the injustice of their Government. There are no necessary evils in government. Its evils exist only in its abuses. If it would confine itself to equal protection, and, as Heaven does its rains, shower its favor alike on the high and low, the rich and the poor, it would be an unqualified blessing. In the act before me there seems to be a wider and unnecessary departure from these just principles.

Nor is our Government to be maintained or our Union preserved by invasions of the rights and powers of the several States. In thus attempting to make our General Government strong we make it weak. Its true strength consists in leaving individuals and States as much as possible to themselves—in making itself felt, not in its power, but in its beneficence; not in its control, but in its protection; not in binding the States more closely to the center, but leaving each to move unobstructed in its proper orbit.

Experience should teach us wisdom. Most of the difficulties our Government now encounters and most of the dangers which impend over our Union have sprung from an abandonment of the legitimate objects of Government by our national legislation, and the adoption of such principles as are embodied in this act. Many of our rich men have not been content with equal protection and equal benefits, but have besought us to make them richer by act of Congress. By attempting to gratify their desires we have in the results of our legislation arrayed section against section, interest against interest, and man against man, in a fearful commotion which threatens to shake the foundations of our Union. It is time to pause in our career to review our principles, and if possible revive that devoted patriotism and spirit of compromise which distinguished the sages of the Revolution and the fathers of our Union. If we can not at once, in justice to interests vested under improvident legislation, make our Government what it ought to be, we can at least take a stand against all new grants of monopolies and exclusive privileges, against any prostitution of our Government to the advancement of the few at the expense of the many, and in favor of compromise and gradual reform in our code of laws and system of political economy.

I have now done my duty to my country. If sustained by my fellow-citizens, I shall be grateful and happy; if not, I shall find in the motives which impel me ample grounds for contentment and peace. In the difficulties which surround us and the dangers which threaten our institutions there is cause for neither dismay nor alarm. For relief and deliverance let us firmly rely on that kind Providence which I am sure watches with peculiar care over the destinies of our Republic, and on the intelligence and wisdom of our countrymen. Through *His* abundant goodness and *their* patriotic devotion our liberty and Union will be preserved.

ANDREW JACKSON

15. "The Veto and the Bank"

FOLLOWING *the veto message the Democratic press bawled their agreement with Jackson's principal arguments. The Washington Globe, edited by Francis P. Blair and established late in 1830 to serve as the mouthpiece for the Democratic party, unleashed a blistering series of articles against the Bank, of which the following document is one example. The editorial is valuable as an example of Jacksonian rhetoric which was so important to the Democrats in conducting their various campaigns. The rhetoric against the "privileged," "monopolists" and "aristocrats" was particularly telling and cannot be dismissed as meaningless propaganda. Their authors believed what they wrote. Indeed, many Americans were convinced that without the shield of Jackson and his supporters the country would be sacrificed to corruption and privilege.*

The first objection made by the President to the act rechartering the Bank of the United States, ought of itself to be conclusive in a country of equal rights. He shows conclusively, so much so that no advocate of the Bank in the Senate or out of it, has dared to deny it, that the act would have operated as a PRESENT, from the people to the stockholders, of more than SEVEN MILLIONS OF DOLLARS!

SOURCE: *Washington Globe*, July 23, 1832.

The stock of the Bank is 350,000 shares of 100 dollars each, 70,000 of which were subscribed by the government and 280,000 by private citizens. In the original subscriptions for the private stock, there was a gross fraud, as the President of the Bank has recently acknowledged. In page 5 of the "Report of the proceedings of the triennial meeting of the stockholders" held "on the 1st day of September, 1831," he sets forth the number of stockholders in the Bank each year from 1817, the time it commenced operations, down to 1831, inclusive, and appends the following remarks, viz:

"It will here be preceived, that the original subscriptions were divided among a great number of persons, *in order to secure the amount of stock desired, but became afterwards concentrated in the names of the real owners.* The whole number of stockholders was in 1820, 2720. From that period the number has risen to 4145."

Here is a direct confession, that the original subscriptions were in a great measure, fraudulent. Rich men, in order to monopolize the stock, procured others to subscribe for them, with the secret understanding that after the Bank had commenced operations, they should transfer the stock, under the pretence of sale to "the real owners." The extent of this fraud may be perceived by adverting to the statement. It shows, that in 1817, there were 31,349 stockholders, and in the year 1826, 2,720, showing that there were no less than 28,629 fraudulent subscriptions! Not much could be expected from a Bank which commenced in a fraud on the community so stupendous. By these fictitious subscriptions, the honest *bona fide* subscribers were cheated out of a large portion of the stock which properly belonged to them, and the whole concern was thrown into the hands of a few speculators and stockjobbers.

So valuable were the exclusive privileges granted to the corporation, that these artful gentlemen realized in a few years seven or eight millions of dollars by the increase in the value of their stock above par. For every $100 paid in, they realized 125 to $130, which was equivalent to a present from the Government of *seven or eight millions.* As the President well observes, this could not have been guarded against in the original charters, because it could not be foreseen. No blame ought, therefore, to be attached to the Congress of 1816 on that account.

But what apology was there for the Congress of 1832, to give to the holders of this stock *seven or eight millions* more? Certainly, those who had by fraudulent subscriptions originally monopolized the stock and the bounty of the Government, did not deserve to be rewarded by a new gratuity. Nor is there either policy or justice in giving to the foreigners, who own $8,405,500 of the stock, two or three millions at the expense of the American people. Nor is there any propriety in giving, by act of Congress, 25 or 30 per cent, even to the *honest* purchasers of the stock among our own citizens. It is not the business of Congress to make presents, at the expense of the people. As justly and as properly might they appropriate seven or eight millions out of the Treasury, giving each stockholder his share by name. What would be the language of the American people had they appropriated that sum out of the Treasury to a few of our own rich citizens who have fraudulently monopolized a large portion of the stock, and to the nobility and gentry of the British Empire? Would they not have loudly demanded of their representatives, why it was that they had so trifled with their essential interests?

In a list of stockholders, communicated to Congress by the Secretary of the Treasury on the 23d January last, we have the names of those who were to receive this gratuity, and the number of shares held by each. We select a few of the foreigners for the information of the people.

"The Right Honorable Sir William Alexander, Knight, &c. and others," owning $5,000, would have received at least $1,250, not of the *royal*, but of the *republican* bounty.

"The Right Honorable Sarah, Countess Dowager of Castle Stewart," owning $10,000 in stock, would have received $2,500.

"The Most Honorable Francis C. S. Conway, Marquis of Hatff," owning $100,300, would have received at least $25,000!

"Right Honorable Lord Henry Viscount Gage," owning $12,000, would have received $3,000.

"Rev. George Gordon, D. D., Dean of Lincoln," owning $31,100, would have received $7,772.

"Sir William Keppel, General in his Britannic Majesty's forces, Knight Grand Cross of the Order of the Bath, &c.," owning $72,200, would have received $18,050!

"Sir Marmaduke Warren Peacoke, Lt. General, &c. &c.," owning $50,000, would have received $12,500.

"Baring, Brothers & Co.," one of whom was recently selected to constitute a member of a Tory Anti-reform Cabinet in England, but deterred from accepting by the overwhelming power of public opinion in favor of Reform, owning $791,500 in stock, would have

received at least ONE HUNDRED NINETY-SEVEN THOUSAND EIGHT HUN-
DRED SEVENTY-FIVE DOLLARS of our *republican bounty!!*

Is it right for Congress to legislate money at this rate, not only
into the pockets of our own rich citizens, but *into the coffers of the
enemies of Liberty in Great Britain?*

The PEOPLE of the United States can have no inducement to
sanction acts of this kind; but this may not be the case with some
of their members of Congress. Those on whom such *favors* are
bestowed, have favors to give·in return. Some members of Congress
are interested indirectly, if not directly, in the stock of the Bank.
Others have received extensive *accommodations*. Others are their
feed lawyers—feed too at a most extravagant rate. The two leaders
of the Bank phalanx in the Senate, were *Daniel Webster* and
Henry Clay.

The name of Daniel Webster appears on the list of stockholders;
but he declared, in his speech against the veto, that he held no
stock, having probably transferred it after the Bank applied for a
new charter, lest he should appear to vote for giving money directly
to himself. But Daniel Webster's chief interest was not in the
stock which he held. It was discovered by the Committee of Investigation that he had received from the principal Bank, as lawyer's fees, upwards of EIGHT THOUSAND DOLLARS. What he has
received from the Branches, they did not ascertain. In one case
disclosed by the Committee, the Bank gave him *one hundred
dollars* for writing *eight words*, being at the rate of *twelve dollars
fifty cents per word!*—Had not Mr. Webster an interest in a vote
which was to preserve such a *valuable client?*

Mr. Clay, in 1811, voted and spoke against the old Bank of the
United States on the ground that it was both inexpedient and
unconstitutional. At a subsequent time, having suffered great
losses, he quited public life and re-commenced the practice of law.
He was employed to attend to all the law business of the Branches
in Kentucky and Ohio; but what he received for those services, has
never been disclosed. The Committee, however, ascertaind, that
he had received from the principal Bank "for professional services,"
upwards of SEVENTEEN THOUSAND DOLLARS. This much is *certain;*
and it is probable, he has received enough from the Branches to
make it THIRTY THOUSAND! Had Mr. Clay no *interest* in his vote
for this Bank? Had he not a *motive* to be liberal to the Stockholders
of an institution which had been so liberal to him?

But he had another interest. The Bank has undertaken *to make him President!* He himself avows, that the object of the Bank in coming forward now, was to ascertain whether Gen. Jackson would consent to re-charter it or not, that all those interested might go against him, if he would not, in the coming election. And whom will they go *for,* if they go *against* General Jackson? For the opposing candidate, *Mr. Clay.* The object of the Bank, therefore, as Mr. Clay well understood, was to support him for President in case Gen. Jackson refused to award to them a new charter. That he would refuse, Mr. Clay never had a doubt.

In voting to recharter the Bank, therefore, Mr. Clay had both a pecuniary and political interest. It was to him a most valuable client, and it had resolved to put forth all its money and power *to make him President.*

In these interests of leading men in Congress, the people may find the reason why that body was deluded into giving to the titled Aristocracy in England and the moneyed Aristocracy of America, *seven or eight millions of dollars.* They will know how far the *Bank* Candidate for the Presidency deserves the support of those whose interests he has thus endeavored to sacrifice; and they will duly appreciate the firmness and patriotism of that man who dares to set all these corrupt influences at defiance and rely for support on the virtue and intelligence of his countrymen.

16. Henry Clay on the Veto

HENRY CLAY *was genuinely convinced of the Bank's importance to the growth and economy of the American nation. He was not simply using the issue to win election to the presidency, even if he did argue for the premature renewal of the charter. When he read Jackson's message he was all the more disturbed because of the uses to which the veto power was now employed. Moreover, in this Senate speech, he tried to respond to some of the particular complaints lodged by the President against the Bank as well as exonerate himself from the charge of inconsistency in his previous attitudes toward the Bank.*

SOURCE: Henry Clay, *The Works of Henry Clay,* Calvin Colton, ed., Volume VII (New York and London, 1904), pp. 524–30, 532–4.

. . . The veto is an extraordinary power, which, though tolerated by the Constitution, was not expected, by the convention, to be used in ordinary cases. It was designed for instances of precipitate legislation, in unguarded moments. Thus restricted, and it has been thus restricted by all former presidents, it might not be mischievous. During Mr. Madison's administration of eight years, there occurred but two or three cases of its exercise. During the last administration, I do not now recollect that it was once. In a period little upward of three years, the present chief magistrates has employed the veto four times. We now hear quite frequently, in the progress of measures through Congress, the statement that the president will veto them, urged as an objection to their passage.

The veto is hardly reconcilable with the genius of representative government. It is totally irreconcilable with it, if it is to be frequently employed in respect to the expediency of measures, as well as their constitutionality. It is a feature of our government, borrowed from a prerogative of the British king. And it is remarkable, that in England it has grown obsolete, not having been used for upward of a century. . . .

No question has been more generally discussed, within the last two years, by the people at large, and in State Legislatures, than that of the bank. And this consideration of it has been prompted by the president himself. In the first message to Congress (in December, 1829) he brought the subject to the view of that body and the nation, and expressly declared, that it could not, for the interest of all concerned, be "too soon" settled. In each of his subsequent annual messages, in 1830, and 1831, he again invited the attention of Congress to the subject. Thus, after an interval of two years, and after the intervention of the election of a new Congress, the president deliberately renews the chartering of the bank of the United States. And yet his friends now declare the agitation of the question to be premature! It was not premature, in 1829, to present the question, but it is premature in 1832 to consider and decide it! . . .

The friends of the president, who have been for nearly three years agitating this question, now turn round upon their opponents, who have supposed the president quite serious and in earnest, in presenting it for public consideration, and charge them with prematurely agitating it. And that for electioneering purposes!

The other side understands perfectly, the policy of preferring an unjust charge, in order to avoid a well-founded accusation.

If there be an electioneering motive in the matter, who have been actuated by it? Those who have taken the president at his word, and deliberated on a measure which he has repeatedly recommended to their consideration? or those who have resorted to all sorts of means to elude the question—by alternately coaxing and threatening the bank; by an extraordinary investigation into the administration of the bank; and by every species of postponement and procrastination, during the progress of the bill.

Notwithstanding all these dilatory expedients, a majority of Congress, prompted by the will and the best interests of the nation, passed the bill. And I shall now proceed, with great respect and deference, to examine some of the objections to its becoming a law, contained in the president's message, avoiding, as much as I can, a repetition of what gentlemen have said who preceded me. . . .

I voted, in 1811, against the old bank of the United States, and I delivered, on that occasion, a speech, in which, among other reasons, I assigned that of its being unconstitutional. My speech has been read to the Senate, during the progress of this bill, but the reading of it excited no other regret than that it was read in such a wretched, bungling, mangling manner. During a long public life (I mention the fact not as claiming any merit for it), the only great question on which I have ever changed my opinion, is that of the bank of the United States. If the researches of the senator had carried him a little further, he would, by turning over a few more leaves of the same book from which he read my speech, have found that which I made in 1816, in support of the present bank. By the reasons assigned in it for the change of my opinion, I am ready to abide in the judgment of the present generation and of posterity. In 1816, being Speaker of the House of Representatives, it was perfectly in my power to have said nothing and done nothing, and thus have concealed the change of opinion my mind had undergone. But I did not choose to remain silent and escape responsibility. I chose publicly to avow my actual conversion. The war and the fatal experience of its disastrous events had changed me. Mr. Madison, Governor Pleasants, and almost all the public men around me, my political friends, had changed their opinions from the same causes.

The power to establish a bank is deduced from that clause of the Constitution which confers on Congress all. powers necessary and proper to carry into effect the enumerated powers. In 1811, I believed a bank of the United States not necessary, and that a safe reliance might be placed on the local banks, in the administration of the fiscal affairs of the government. The war taught us many lessons, and among others demonstrated the necessity of the bank of the United States, to the successful operations of the government. . . .

The interest which foreigners hold in the existing bank of the United States, is dwelt upon in the message as a serious objection to the recharter. But this interest is the result of the assignable nature of the stock; and if the objection be well founded, it applies to government stock, to the stock in local banks, in canal and other companies, created for internal improvements, and every species of money or movables in which foreigners may acquire an interest. The assignable character of the stock is a quality conferred not for the benefit of foreigners, but for that of our own citizens. And the fact of its being transferred to them is the effect of the balance of trade being against us—an evil, if it be one, which the American system will correct. All governments wanting capital resort to foreign nations possessing it in superabundance, to obtain it. Sometimes the resort is even made by one to another belligerent nation. During our revolutionary war we obtained foreign capital (Dutch and French) to aid us. During the late war American stock was sent to Europe to sell; and if I am not misinformed, to Liverpool. The question does not depend upon the place whence the capital is obtained, but the advantageous use of it. The confidence of foreigners in our stocks is a proof of the solidity of our credit. Foreigners have no voice in the administration of this bank; and if they buy its stock, they are obliged to submit to citizens of the United States to manage it. The senator from Tennessee (Mr. White), asks what would have been the condition of this country if, during the late war, this bank had existed, with such an interest in it as foreigners now hold? I will tell him. We should have avoided many of the disasters of that war, perhaps those of Detroit and at this place. The government would have possessed ample means for its vigorous prosecution; and the interest of foreigners, British subjects especially, would have operated upon them, not upon us. Will it not be a serious evil to be obliged to remit in specie to foreigners the eight millions which they now have in this bank, instead of retaining that capital within the country to stimulate its industry and enterprise? . . .

The president tells us, that if the executive had been called upon to furnish the project of a bank, the duty would have been cheerfully performed; and he states that a bank, competent to all the duties which may be required by the government, might be so organized as not to infringe on our delegated powers, or the reserved rights of the States. The president is a co-ordinate branch of the legislative department. As such, bills which have passed both Houses of Congress are presented to him for his approval or rejection. The idea of going to the president for the project of a law, is totally new in the practice, and utterly contrary to the theory of the government. What should we think of the Senate calling upon the House, or the House upon the Senate, for the project of law!

In France, the king possessed the initiative of all laws, and none could pass without its having been previously presented to one of the chambers by the crown through the ministers. Does the president wish to introduce the initiative here? Are the powers of recommendation, and that of veto, not sufficient? Must all legislation, in its commencement and in its termination concentrate in the president? When we shall have reached that state of things, the election and annual session of Congress will be a useless charge upon the people, and the whole business of government may be economically conducted by ukases and decrees. . . .

There are some parts of this message that ought to excite deep alarm; and that especially in which the president announces, that each public officer may interpret the Constitution as he pleases. His language is, "Each public officer, who takes an oath to support the Constitution, swears that he will support it as he understands it, and not as it is understood by others." * * * "The opinion of the judges has no more authority over Congress than the opinion of Congress has over the judges; and on that point the president is independent of both." Now, Mr. President, I conceive, with great deference, that the president has mistaken the purport of the oath to support the Constitution of the United States. No one swears to support it as he understands it, but to support it simply as it is in truth. . . .

17. Daniel Webster on the Veto

DANIEL WEBSTER regarded himself as a constitutional authority and so his criticism of the veto naturally pursued a legal and constitutional argument. Clearly he saw that Jackson was deliberately altering the process of government and claiming for the executive the "power of originating laws." In this speech, delivered in the Senate immediately after the veto was returned, Webster tried to warn his colleagues and the country to the danger of expanding presidential power. A "new epoch" had arrived, he said. "We are entering on experiments, with the government and the Constitution of the country, hitherto untried, and of fearful and appalling aspect."

. . . [The Bank] bill was not passed for the purpose of benefiting the present stockholders. Their benefit, if any, is incidental and collateral. Nor was it passed on any idea that they had a *right* to a renewed charter, although the message argues against such right, as if it had been somewhere set up and asserted. No such right has been asserted by any body. Congress passed the bill, not as a bounty or a favor to the present stockholders, nor to comply with any demand of right on their part; but to promote great public interest, for great public objects. . . .

Sir, the object aimed at by such institutions is to connect the public safety and convenience with private interests. It has been found by experience, that banks are safest under private management, and that government banks are among the most dangerous of all inventions. Now, Sir, the whole drift of the message is to reverse the settled judgment of all the civilized world, and to set up government banks, independent of private interest or private control. For this purpose the message labors, even beyond the measure of all its other labors, to create jealousies and prejudices, on the ground of the alleged benefit which individuals will derive from the renewal of this charter. Much less effort is made to show that government, or the public, will be injured by the bill, than that individuals will profit by it. . . .

SOURCE: Daniel Webster, *The Works of Daniel Webster*, Volume III (Boston, 1864): 424, 433–5, 446–7.

The President is as much bound by the law as any private citizen, and can no more contest its validity than any private citizen. He may refuse to obey the law, and so may a private citizen; but both do it at their own peril, and neither of them can settle the question of its validity. The President may say a law is unconstitutional, but he is not the judge. Who is to decide that question? The judiciary alone possesses this unquestionable and hitherto unquestioned right. The judiciary is the constitutional tribunal of appeal for the citizens, against both Congress and the executive, in regard to the constitutionality of laws. It has this jurisdiction expressly conferred upon it, and when it has decided the question, its judgment must, from the very nature of all judgments that are final, and from which there is no appeal, be conclusive. Hitherto, this opinion, and a correspondent practice, have prevailed, in America, with all wise and considerate men. If it were otherwise, there would be no government of laws; but we should all live under the government, the rule, the caprices, of individuals. If we depart from the observance of these salutary principles, the executive power becomes at once purely despotic; for the President, if the principle and the reasoning of the message be sound, may either execute or not execute the laws of the land, according to his sovereign pleasure. He may refuse to put into execution one law, pronounced valid by all branches of the government, and yet execute another, which may have been by constitutional authority pronounced void.

On the argument of the message, the President of the United States holds, under a new pretence and a new name, a *dispensing power* over the laws as absolute as was claimed by James the Second of England, a month before he was compelled to fly the kingdom. That which is now claimed by the President is in truth nothing less, and nothing else, than the old dispensing power asserted by the kings of England in the worst of times; the very climax, indeed, of all the preposterous pretensions of the Tudor and the Stuart races. According to the doctrines put forth by the President, although Congress may have passed a law, and although the Supreme Court may have pronounced it constitutional, yet it is, nevertheless, no law at all, if he, in his good pleasure, sees fit to deny it effect; in other words, to repeal and annul it. Sir, no President and no public man ever before advanced such doctrines in the face of the nation. There never before was a moment in which any

President would have been tolerated in asserting such a claim to despotic power. After Congress has passed the law, and after the Supreme Court has pronounced its judgment on the very point in controversy, the President has set up his own private judgment against its constitutional interpretation. It is to be remembered, Sir, that it is the present law, it is the act of 1816, it is the present charter of the bank, which the President pronounces to be unconstitutional. It is no bank *to be created*, it is no law proposed to be passed, which he denounces; it is the *law now existing*, passed by Congress, approved by President Madison, and sanctioned by a solemn judgment of the Supreme Court, which he now declares unconstitutional, and which, of course, so far as it may depend on him, cannot be executed. If these opinions of the President be maintained, there is an end of all law and all judicial authority. Statutes are but recommendations, judgments no more than opinions. Both are equally destitute of binding force. Such a universal power as is now claimed for him, a power of judging over the laws and over the decisions of the judiciary, is nothing else but pure despotism. It conceded to him, it makes him at once what Louis the Fourteenth proclaimed himself to be when he said, "I am the State.". . .

When the message denies, as it does, the authority of the Supreme Court to decide on constitutional questions, it effects, so far as the opinion of the President and his authority can effect it, a complete change in our government. It does two things; first, it converts constitutional limitations of power into mere matters of opinion, and then it strikes the judicial department, as an efficient department, out of our system. But the message by no means stops even at this point. Having denied to Congress the authority of judging what powers may be constitutionally conferred on a bank, and having erected the judgment of the President himself into a standard by which to try the constitutional character of such powers, and having denounced the authority of the Supreme Court to decide finally on constitutional questions, the message proceeds to claim for the President, not the power of approval, but the primary power, the power of originating laws. The President informs Congress, that *he* would have sent them such a charter, if it had been properly asked for, as they ought to confer. He very plainly intimates, that, in his opinion, the establishment of all laws, of this nature at least, belongs to the functions of the executive government; and that Congress ought to have waited for the manifestation of the executive will,. before it presumed to touch the subject. Such, Mr. President, stripped of their disguises, are the real pretences set up in behalf of the executive power in this most extraordinary paper.

Mr. President, we have arrived at a new epoch. We are entering on experiments, with the government and the Constitution of the country, hitherto untried, and of fearful and appalling aspect. This message calls us to the contemplation of a future which little resembles the past. Its principles are at war with all that public opinion has sustained, and all which the experience of the government has sanctioned. It denies first principles; it contradicts truths, heretofore received as indisputable. It denies to the judiciary the interpretation of law, and claims to divide with Congress the power of originating statutes. It extends the grasp of executive pretension over every power of the government. But this is not all. It presents the chief magistrate of the Union in the attitude of arguing away the powers of that government over which he has been chosen to preside; and adopting for this purpose modes of reasoning which, even under the influence of all proper feeling towards high official station, it is difficult to regard as respectable. It appeals to every prejudice which may betray men into a mistaken view of their own interests, and to every passion which may lead them to disobey the impulses of their understanding. It urges all the specious topics of State rights and national encroachment against that which a great majority of the States have affirmed to be rightful, and in which all of them have acquiesced. It sows, in an unsparing manner, the seeds of jealousy and ill-will against that government of which its author is the official head. It raises a cry, that liberty is in danger, at the very moment when it puts forth claims to powers heretofore unknown and unheard of. It affects alarm for the public freedom, when nothing endangers that freedom so much as its own unparalleled pretences. This, even, is not all. It manifestly seeks to inflame the poor against the rich; it wantonly attacks whole classes of the people, for the purpose of turning against them the prejudices and the resentments of other classes. It is a state paper which finds no topic too exciting for its use, no passion too inflammable for its address and its solicitation.

Such is this message. It remains now for the people of the United States to choose between the principles here avowed and their government. These cannot subsist together. The one or the other must be rejected. If the sentiments of the message shall receive general approbation, the Constitution will have perished even earlier than the moment which its enemies originally allowed for the termination of its existence. It will not have survived to its fiftieth year.

18. "Rich and Poor"

MUCH OF *the intense, Jacksonian outbursts against privilege, monopoly and the paper system can be found in the writings of William Leggett, sometime editor of the New York Evening Post and founder of the Plaindealer. A free trade economic liberal, Leggett became the leading spokesman of the Locofoco or Equal Rights party, a radical offshoot from the main Democratic branch in New York. In the following editorial published in the Post on December 6, 1834, the editor praises the virtues and wisdom of the common man, castigates the aristocracy and identifies the "power of monopoly and the encroachments of corporate privileges of every kind" as the power against which all people must array themselves.*

The rich perceive, acknowledge, and act upon a common interest, and why not the poor? Yet the moment the latter are called upon to combine for the preservation of their rights, forsooth the community is in danger. Property is no longer secure and life in jeopardy. This cant has descended to us from those times when the poor and laboring classes had no stake in the community and no rights except such as they could acquire by force. But the times have changed though the cant remains the same. The scrip nobility of this Republic have adopted towards the free people of this Republic the same language which the feudal barons and the despot who contested with them the power of oppressing the people used towards their serfs and villains, as they were opprobriously called.

These would-be lordlings of the Paper Dynasty cannot or will not perceive that there is some difference in the situation and

SOURCE: Theodore Sedgewick, Jr., ed., A Collection of the Political Writings of William Leggett, Volume I (New York, 1840), pp. 106–110.

feelings of the people of the United States and those of the despotic governments of Europe. They forget that at this moment our people—we mean emphatically the class which labors with its own hands—is in possession of a greater portion of the property and intelligence of this country, ay, ten times over, than all the creatures of the "paper credit system" put together. This property is indeed more widely and equally distributed among the people than among the phantoms of the paper system, and so much the better. And as to their intelligence, let any man talk with them, and if he does not learn something it is his own fault. They are as well acquainted with the rights of person and property and have as just a regard for them as the most illustrious lordling of the scrip nobility. And why should they not? Who and what are the great majority of the wealthy people of this city, we may say of this country? Are they not—we say it not in disparagement, but in high commendation—are they not men who began the world compara- tively poor with ordinary education and ordinary means? And what should make them so much wiser than their neighbors? Is it be- cause they live in better style, ride in carriages, and have more money or at least more credit than their poorer neighbors? Does a man become wiser, stronger, or more virtuous and patriotic because he has a fine house over his head? Does he love his country the better because he has a French cook and a box at the opera? Or does he grow more learned, logical, and profound by intense study of the daybook, ledger, bills of exchange, bank promises, and notes of hand?

Of all the countries on the face of the earth or that ever existed on the face of the earth, this is the one where the claims of wealth and aristocracy are the most unfounded, absurd, and ridiculous. With no claim to hereditary distinctions, with no exclusive rights except what they derive from monopolies, and no power of per- petuating their estates in their posterity, the assumption of aristo- cratic airs and claims is supremely ridiculous. Tomorrow they themselves may be beggars for aught they know, or at all events their children may become so. Their posterity in the second gen- eration will have to begin the world again and work for a living as did their forefathers. And yet the moment a man becomes rich among us, he sets up for wisdom; he despises the poor and igno- rant; he sets up for patriotism; he is your only man who has a stake in the community and therefore the only one who ought to have a voice in the state. What folly is this? And how contemptible his presumption? He is not a whit wiser, better, or more patriotic than when he commenced the world, a wagon driver. Nay, not half so patriotic, for he would see his country disgraced a thousand times rather than see one fall of the stocks, unless perhaps he had been speculating on such a contingency. To him a victory is only of consequence as it raises, and a defeat only to be lamented as it depresses a loan. His soul is wrapped up in a certificate of scrip or a bank note. Witness the conduct of these pure patriots during the late war, when they, at least a large proportion of them, not only withheld all their support from the Government but used all their influence to prevent others from giving their assistance. Yet these are the people who alone have a stake in the community and, of course, exclusively monopolize patriotism.

But let us ask what and where is the danger of a combination of the laboring classes in vindication of their political principles or in defense of their menaced rights? Have they not the right to act in concert when their opponents act in concert? Nay, is it not their bounden duty to combine against the only enemy they have to fear as yet in this free country: monopoly and a great paper system that grinds them to the dust? Truly, this is strange republican doctrine, and this is a strange republican country, where men cannot unite in one common effort, in one common cause, without rousing the cry of danger to the rights of person and property. Is not this a government of the people, founded on the rights of the people, and instituted for the express object of guarding them against the encroachments and usurpations of power? And if they are not permitted the possession of common interest, the exercise of a common feeling, if they cannot combine to resist by constitutional means these encroachments, to what purpose were they declared free to exercise the right of suffrage in the choice of rulers and the making of laws?

And what, we ask, is the power against which the people not only of this country but of almost all Europe are called upon to array themselves, and the encroachment on their rights they are summoned to resist? Is it not emphatically the power of monopoly and the encroachments of corporate privileges of every kind which the cupidity of the rich engenders to the injury of the poor?

It was to guard against the encroachments of power, the insatiate ambition of wealth, that this government was instituted by the people themselves. But the objects which call for the peculiar jealousy and watchfulness of the people are not now what they once were. The cautions of the early writers in favor of the liberties of mankind have in some measure become obsolete and inapplicable. We are menaced by our old enemies, avarice and ambition, under a new name and form. The tyrant is changed from a steel-clad feudal baron or a minor despot, at the head of thousands of ruffian followers, to a mighty civil gentleman who comes mincing and bowing to the people with a quill behind his ear, at the head of countless millions of magnificent *promises*. He promises to make everybody rich; he promises to pave cities with gold; and he promises to pay. In short he is made up of promises. He will do wonders such as never were seen or heard of, provided the people will only allow him to make his promises equal to silver and gold and human labor, and grant him the exclusive benefits of all the great blessings he intends to confer on them. He is the sly, selfish, grasping, and insatiable tyrant the people are now to guard against. A *concentrated money power*; a usurper in the disguise of a benefactor; an agent exercising privileges which his principal never possessed; an imposter who, while he affects to wear chains, is placed above those who are free, a chartered libertine that pretends to be manacled only that he may the more safely pick our pockets and lord it over our rights. This is the enemy we are now to encounter and overcome before we can expect to enjoy the substantial realities of freedom.

19. Removal of the Public Deposits

His SPECTACULAR *victory over Henry Clay in the presidential contest of 1832 encouraged Jackson to finish off the Bank by removing the government's deposits. He was delayed in the immediate execution of his plan by the development of the nullification controversy. However, on September 17, 1833, Jackson convened his cabinet, informed them of his decision and asked for their opinions. Several opposed the move; only Roger B. Taney, the Attorney General, argued strongly in its favor. Jackson adjourned the meeting and asked the secretaries to return the*

SOURCE: James D. Richardson, *Messages and Papers*, II: 5–19.

following day to hear an "exposé" which he and Taney had written during the summer detailing his reasons for removal. When the members reconvened the following day, Jackson in this statement recited the reasons for his contemplated action, claiming, at the same time, increased presidential power by virtue of the recent election. The cabinet listened quietly to the reading, said nothing when it was over and after a moment silently left the room.

. . . . The President's convictions of the dangerous tendencies of the Bank of the United States, since signally illustrated by its own acts, were so overpowering when he entered on the duties of Chief Magistrate that he felt it his duty, notwithstanding the objections of the friends by whom he was surrounded, to avail himself of the first occasion to call the attention of Congress and the people to the question of its recharter. The opinions expressed in his annual message of December, 1829, were reiterated in those of December, 1830 and 1831, and in that of 1830 he threw out for consideration some suggestions in relation to a substitute. At the session of 1831–32 an act was passed by a majority of both Houses of Congress rechartering the present bank, upon which the President felt it his duty to put his constitutional veto. In his message returning that act he repeated and enlarged upon the principles and views briefly asserted in his annual message, declaring the bank to be, in his opinion, both inexpedient and unconstitutional, and announcing to his countrymen very unequivocally his firm determination never to sanction by his approval the continuance of that institution or the establishment of any other upon similar principles.

There are strong reasons for believing that the motive of the bank in asking for a recharter at that session of Congress was to make it a leading question in the election of a President of the United States the ensuing November, and all steps deemed necessary were taken to procure from the people a reversal of the President's decision.

Although the charter was approaching its termination, and the bank was aware that it was the intention of the Government to use the public deposit as fast as it has accrued in the payment of the public debt, yet did it extend its loans from January, 1831, to May, 1832, from $42,402,304.24 to $70,428,070.72, being an increase of $28,025,766.48 in sixteen months. It is confidently believed that the leading object of this immense extension of its loans was to bring as large a portion of the people as possible under its power and influence, and it has been disclosed that some of the largest sums were granted on very unusual terms to the conductors of the public press. In some of these cases the motive was made manifest by the nominal or insufficient security taken for the loans, by the large amounts discounted, by the extraordinary time allowed for payment, and especially by the subsequent conduct of those receiving the accommodations.

Having taken these preliminary steps to obtain control over public opinion, the bank came into Congress and asked a new charter. The object avowed by many of the advocates of the bank was to put the President to the test, that the country might know his final determination relative to the bank prior to the ensuing election. Many documents and articles were printed and circulated at the expense of the bank to bring the people to a favorable decision upon its pretensions. Those whom the bank appears to have made its debtors for the special occasion were warned of the ruin which awaited them should the President be sustained, and attempts were made to alarm the whole people by painting the depression in the price of property and produce and the general loss, inconvenience, and distress which it was represented would immediately follow the reelection of the President in opposition to the bank.

Can it now be said that the question of a recharter of the bank was not decided at the election which ensued? Had the veto been equivocal, or had it not covered the whole ground; if it had merely taken exceptions to the details of the bill or to the time of its passage; if it had not met the whole ground of constitutionality and expediency, then there might have been some plausibility for the allegation that the question was not decided by the people. It was to compel the President to take his stand that the question was brought forward at that particular time. He met the challenge, willingly took the position into which his adversaries sought to force him, and frankly declared his unalterable opposition to the bank as being both unconstitutional and inexpedient. On that ground the case was argued to the people; and now that the people have sustained the President, notwithstanding the array of influence and power which was brought to bear upon him, it is too late, he confidently thinks, to say that the question has not been decided. Whatever may be the opinions of others, the President considers his reelection as a decision of the people against the bank. In the concluding paragraph of his veto message he said:

> I have now done my duty to my country. If sustained by my fellow-citizens, I shall be grateful and happy; if not, I shall find in the motives which impel me ample grounds for contentment and peace.

He was sustained by a just people, and he desires to evince his gratitude by carrying into effect their decision so far as it depends upon him.

The power of the Secretary of the Treasury over the deposits is unqualified. The provision that he shall report his reasons to Congress is no limitation. Had it not been inserted he would have been responsible to Congress had he made a removal for any other than good reasons, and his responsiblity now ceases upon the rendition of sufficient ones to Congress. The only object of the provision is to make his reasons accessible to Congress and enable that body the more readily to judge of their soundness and purity, and thereupon to make such further provision by law as the legislative power may think proper in relation to the deposit of the public money. . . .

The responsibility is thus thrown upon the executive branch of the Government of deciding how long before the expiration of the charter the public interest will require the deposits to be placed elsewhere; and although according to the frame and principle of our Government this decision would seem more properly to belong to the legislative power, yet as the law has imposed it upon the executive department the duty ought to be faithfully and firmly met, and the decision made and executed upon the best lights that can be obtained and the best judgment that can be formed. It would ill become the executive branch of the Government to shrink from any duty which the law imposes on it, to fix upon others the responsibility which justly belongs to itself. And while the President anxiously wishes to abstain from the exercise of doubtful powers and to avoid all interference with the rights and duties of others, he must yet with unshaken constancy discharge his own obligations, and can not allow himself to turn aside in order to avoid any responsibility which the high trust with which he has been honored requires him to encounter; and it being the duty of one of the Executive Departments to decide in the first instance, subject to the future action of the legislative power, whether the public deposits shall remain in the Bank of the United States until the end of its existence or be withdrawn some time before, the President has felt himself bound to examine the question carefully and deliberately in order to make up his judgment on the subject, and in his opinion the near approach of the termination of the charter and the public considerations heretofore mentioned are of themselves amply sufficient to justify the removal of the deposits, without reference to the conduct of the bank or their safety in its keeping.

But in the conduct of the bank may be found other reasons, very imperative in their character, and which require prompt action. Developments have been made from time to time of its faithlessness as a public agent, its misapplication of public funds, its interference in elections, its efforts by the machinery of committees to deprive the Government directors of a full knowledge of its concerns, and, above all, its flagrant misconduct as recently and unexpectedly disclosed in placing all the funds of the bank, including the money of the Government, at the disposition of the president of the bank as means of operating upon public opinion and procuring a new charter, without requiring him to render a voucher for their disbursement. . . .

If the question of a removal of the deposits presented itself to the Executive in the same attitude that it appeared before the House of Representatives at their last session, their resolution[1] in relation to the safety of the deposits would be entitled to more weight, although the decision of the question of removal has been confided by law to another department of the Government. . . .

A new state of things has, however, arisen since the close of the last session of Congress, and evidence has since been laid before the President which he is persuaded would have led the House of Representatives to a different conclusion if it had come to their knowledge. The fact that the bank controls, and in some cases substantially *owns*, and by its money *supports* some of the leading presses of the country is now more clearly established. Editors to whom it loaned extravagant sums in 1831 and 1832, on unusual time and nominal security, have since turned out to be insolvent,

---

1. Resolution passed by the House of Representatives on March 2, 1833 to the effect that the government's deposits were safe in the U.S. Bank and should be left there.

and to others apparently in no better condition accommodations still more extravagant, on terms more unusual, and some without any security, have also been heedlessly granted.

The allegation which has so often circulated through these channels that the Treasury was bankrupt and the bank was sustaining it, when for many years there has not been less, on an average, than six millions of public money in that institution, might be passed over as a harmless misrepresentation; but when it is attempted by substantial acts to impair the credit of the Government and tarnish the honor of the country, such charges require more serious attention. With six millions of public money in its vaults, after having had the use of from five to twelve millions for nine years without interest, it became the purchaser of a bill drawn by our Government on that of France for about $900,000, being the first installment of the French indemnity. The purchase money was left in the use of the bank, being simply added to the Treasury deposit. The bank sold the bill in England, and the holder sent it to France for collection, and arrangements not having been made by the French Government for its payment, it was taken up by the agents of the bank of Paris with the funds of the bank in their hands. Under these circumstances it has through its organs openly assailed the credit of the Government, and has actually made and persists in a demand of 15 per cent, or $158,842.77, as damages, when no damage, or none beyond some trifling expense, has in fact been sustained, and when the bank had in its own possession on deposit several millions of the public money which it was then using for its own profit. Is a fiscal agent of the Government which thus seeks to enrich itself at the expense of the public worthy of further trust? . . .

It has long been known that the president of the bank, by his single will, originates and executes many of the most important measures connected with the management and credit of the bank, and that the committee as well as the board of directors are left in entire ignorance of many acts done and correspondence carried on in their names, and apparently under their authority. The fact has been recently disclosed that an unlimited discretion has been and is now vested in the president of the bank to expend its funds in payment for preparing and circulating articles and purchasing pamphlets and newspapers, calculated by their contents to operate on elections and secure a renewal of its charter. . . .

The bank is thus converted into a vast electioneering engine, with means to embroil the country in deadly feuds, and, under cover of expenditures in themselves improper, extend its corruption through all the ramifications of society.

Some of the items for which accounts have been rendered show the construction which has been given to the resolutions and the way in which the power it confers has been exerted. The money has not been expended merely in the publication and distribution of speeches, reports of committees, or articles written for the purpose of showing the constitutionality or usefulness of the bank, but publications have been prepared and extensively circulated containing the grossest invectives against the officers of the Government, and the money which belongs to the stockholders and to the public has been freely applied in efforts to degrade in public estimation those who were supposed to be instrumental in resisting the wishes of this grasping and dangerous institution. . . .

It has been alleged by some as an objection to the removal of the deposits that the bank has the power, and in that event will have the disposition, to destroy the State banks employed by the Government, and bring distress upon the country. It has been the fortune of the President to encounter dangers which were represented as equally alarming, and he has seen them vanish before resolution and energy. Pictures equally appalling were paraded before him when this bank came to demand a new charter. But what was the result? Has the country been ruined, or even distressed? Was it ever more prosperous than since that act? The President verily believes the bank has not the power to produce the calamities its friends threaten. The funds of the Government will not be annihilated by being transferred. They will immediately be issued for the benefit of trade, and if the Bank of the United States curtails its loans the State banks, strengthened by the public deposits, will extend theirs. What comes in through one bank will go out through others, and the equilibrium will be preserved. Should the bank, for the mere purpose of producing distress, press its debtors more heavily than some of them can bear, the consequences will recoil upon itself, and in the attempts to embarrass the country it will only bring loss and ruin upon the holders of its own stock. . . .

From all these considerations the President thinks that the State banks ought immediately to be employed in the collection and disbursement of the public revenue, and the funds now in the Bank of the United States drawn out with all convenient dispatch. The safety of the public moneys if deposited in the State banks must be secured beyond all reasonable doubts; but the extent and nature of the security, in addition to their capital, if any be deemed necessary, is a subject of detail to which the Treasury Department will undoubtedly give its anxious attention. The banks to be employed must remit the moneys of the Government without charge, as the Bank of the United States now does; must render all the services which that bank now performs; must keep the Government advised of their situation by periodical returns; in fine, in any arrangement with the State banks the Government must not in any respect be placed on a worse footing than it now is. . . .

It should also be enjoined upon any banks which may be employed that it will be expected of them to facilitate domestic exchanges for the benefit of internal commerce; to grant all reasonable facilities to the payers of the revenue; to exercise the utmost liberality toward the other State banks, and do nothing uselessly to embarrass the Bank of the United States. . . .

It is the desire of the President that the control of the banks and the currency shall, as far as possible, be entirely separated from the political power of the country as well as wrested from an institution which has already attempted to subject the Government to its will. In his opinion the action of the General Government on this subject ought not to extend beyond the grant in the Constitution, which only authorizes Congress "to coin money and regulate the value thereof"; all else belongs to the States and the people, and must be regulated by public opinion and the interests of trade.

The President again repeats that he begs his Cabinet to consider the proposed measure as his own, in the support of which he shall require no one of them to make a sacrifice of opinion or principle. Its responsibility has been assumed after the most mature deliberation and reflection as necessary to preserve the morals of the people, the freedom of the press, and the purity of the elective franchise, without which all will unite in saying that the blood and treasure expended by our forefathers in the establishment of our happy system of government will have been vain and fruitless. Under these convictions he feels that a measure so important to the American people can not be commenced too soon, and he therefore names the 1st day of October next as a period proper for the change of the deposits, or sooner, provided the necessary arrangements with the State banks can be made.

20. Dismissal of the Secretary of the Treasury

ONE SIGNIFICANT *but less important aspect of the Bank War centered around a conflict between the President and the Congress over their respective control of the actions of the Secretary of the Treasury. By law the Secretary is responsible to the Congress for the disposition of public funds, but as a member of the cabinet he is the President's appointee. When the charter establishing the Second Bank was approved the Treasury Secretary was the only person authorized to remove the government's deposits, and he was also required to inform Congress of his action. Jackson appointed William J. Duane his Secretary of the Treasury in June, 1833 with the expectation that Duane would remove the deposits when he instructed him to do so. At one point the Secretary actually agreed to resign his office if he could not execute the President's order. When he was finally ordered by Jackson to begin removal he refused to do it, stating that he wished to delay his decision until Congress convened. Jackson promptly dismissed him. In the process he established the position that the President has an absolute right to dictate the actions of his cabinet members so that they conform to the policy of the administration. Jackson replaced Duane with Taney, and on October 1, 1833 the removal policy was put into operation. The following document, written by Duane, narrates his confrontation with the President.*

. . . On the next day, the members of the cabinet accordingly assembled, and the President caused his secretary to read to them the document, subsequently so well known as "the paper read to the cabinet on the 18th of September."

Very little, if any thing, was said after the paper had been read. As those present were retiring, I approached the President, and asked him to allow me to take and read his exposition. He directed his secretary to deliver it to me, and he did so. I then asked the President, whether I was to understand him as directing me to

SOURCE: William J. Duane, *Narrative and Correspondence concerning the Removal of the Deposites* (Philadelphia, 1838), pp. 100–103.

remove the deposites? He replied, that it was his desire, that I should remove them, but upon his responsibility, adding with great emphasis that, "if I would stand by him it would be the happiest day of his life."

When I retired, I had to consider, not merely whether I ought to remove the deposites, but whether I should resign. I was sensible that I had erred in giving any assurance on the latter point, and doubted whether subsequent occurrences had not absolved me from all obligation to respect it. I desired to avoid a surrender of an important post, and yet wished to part from the President without unkind feeling. It had occurred to me, that I might accomplish both these ends by asking for a written expression of the President's wish that I should retire; and, in giving me such a memorandum, I did not perceive that there would be any committal of himself. It seemed to me that, assailed as I had been and menaced with new attacks, the President, if really my friend, would not desire to tie up my hands.

I was reflecting upon these points, when, early on the morning of the 19th of September, the President sent to inquire, whether I had come to a decision. I replied that I would communicate it on the 21st. On the morning of the same day (19th), the President's secretary called on me to state, that the President had determined to announce the decision on the deposite question, in the Globe of the next day. He then proposed to read to me a paper prepared for that purpose; but I refused to listen to it, stating that I had the President's exposition then before me, and was preparing a defensive paper on my own part; that the President ought to wait one day longer to enable me to present that paper, and to say finally whether I would or would not concur with him; and that any such publication in the Globe, as was proposed, would be a gross indignity to me as an officer and a man. The secretary said, he believed the President would proceed; that the New York Evening Post was urging a decision; and that, as to himself, he had no wish to express. I then at once wrote and delivered to him, a remonstrance against the proposed publication. Nevertheless, on the following day (20th) it appeared in the Globe, as follows:

"We are authorized to state that the deposites of the public money will be changed, from the bank of the U.S. to the state banks, as soon as necessary arrangements can be made for that purpose, and that it is believed they can be completed in Baltimore,

Philadelphia, New York, and Boston, in time to make the change by the 1st of October, and perhaps sooner, if circumstances should render an earlier action necessary on the part of the government.

"It is contemplated, we understand, not to remove at once, the whole of the public money now in deposite in the bank of the U.S., but to suffer it to remain there until it shall be gradually withdrawn by the usual operation of the government. And this plan is adopted in order to prevent any necessity, on the part of the bank of the U.S., for pressing upon the commercial community; and to enable it to afford, if it think proper, the usual facilities to the merchants. It is believed, that by this means the change need not produce any inconvenience to the commercial community, and that circumstances will not require a sudden and heavy call on the bank of the U.S., so as to occasion embarrassment to the institution or the public."

As soon as I read the above quoted annunciation in the Globe, I put aside the defensive exposition which I had been preparing; and, on the 21st of September, wrote and personally delivered to the President the annexed letter. The conversation, which took place on the occasion, was long and occasionally animated. The following brief sketch of a part of it will suffice for the purposes of the present narrative:

Secretary. I have, at length, waited upon you, sir, with this letter.

President. What is it?

S. It respectfully and finally makes known my decision, not to remove the deposites, or resign.

P. Then you do not mean, that we shall part as friends.

S. The reverse, sir, is my desire; but I must protect myself.

P. But you said you would retire, if we could not finally agree.

S. I indiscreetly said so, sir; but I am now compelled to take this course.

P. I have been under an impression that you would resign, even as an act of friendship to me.

S. Personal wishes, sir, must give way. The true question is, which must I observe, my promise to execute my duty faithfully, or my agreement to retire, when the latter conflicts with the former?

P. I certainly never expected that any such difficulties could arise between us; and think you ought still to consider the matter.

S. I have painfully considered it; and hope you will not ask me to make a sacrifice. All that you need is a successor, and him you may have at once.

P. But I do not wish to dismiss you. I·have too much regard for yourself, your family and friends, to take that course.

S. Excuse me, sir, you may only do now what you said, in your letter of the 22d of July, it would be your duty to do, if I then said I would not thereafter remove the deposites.

P. It would be at any time disagreeable to do what might be injurious to you.

S. A resignation, I think, would be more injurious. And permit me to say, that the publication in yesterday's Globe removes all delicacy. A worm if trodden upon will turn. I am assailed in all the leading papers of the administration; and if my friend, you will not tie up my hands.

P. Then, I suppose you mean to come out against me.

S. Nothing is further from my thoughts. I barely desire to do what is now my duty; and to defend myself if assailed hereafter.

[Here the President expatiated on the late disclosures in relation to the bank, the corruptibility of congress, &c.; and at length taking a paper from his drawer said]

P. You have been all along mistaken in your views. Here is a paper that will show you your obligations—that the executive must protect you.

S. I will read it, sir, if such is your wish, but I cannot anticipate a change of opinion.

P. A secretary, sir, is merely an executive agent, a subordinate, and you may say so in self-defence.

S. In this particular case, congress confers a discretionary power, and requires reasons if I exercise it. Surely this contemplates responsibility on my part.

P. This paper will show you, that your doubts are wholly groundless.

S. As to the deposites, allow me, sir, to say, my decision is positive. The only question is as to the mode of my retirement.

P. My dear Mr. Duane; we must separate as friends. Far from desiring, that you should sustain any injury, you know I have intended to give you the highest appointment now in my gift. You shall have the mission to Russia. I would have settled this matter before, but for the delay or difficulty [as I understood the President] in relation to Mr. Buchanan.

S. I am sincerely thankful to you, sir, for your kind disposition, but I beg you to serve me in a way that will be truly pleasing. I desire no new station, and barely wish to leave my present one blameless, or free from apprehension as to the future. Favour me with a written declaration of your desire, that I should leave office, as I cannot carry out your views as to the deposites, and I will take back this letter [the one I had just presented].

P. Never have I had any thing, that has given me more mortification than this whole business. I had not the smallest notion that we could differ.

S. My principles and opinions, sir, are unchanged. We differ only about time—you are for acting now, I am for waiting for congress.

P. How often have I told you, that congress cannot act until the deposites are removed.

S. I am unable, sir, to change my opinion at will upon that point.

P. You are altogether wrong in your opinion, and I thought Mr. Taney would have convinced you that you are.

S. Mr. Taney, sir, endeavoured to prevail on me to adopt his views, but failed. As to the deposites, I barely desired a delay of about ten weeks.

P. Not a day—not an hour; recent disclosures banish all doubt, and I do not see how you can hesitate.

S. I have often stated my reasons. Surely, sir, it is enough that were I to act, I could not give reasons satisfactory to myself.

P. My reasons, lately read in the cabinet, will release you from complaint.

S. I am sorry I cannot view the subject in the same light.

Our conversation was further extended, under varying emotions on both sides; but without any change of opinion or decision—at length I retired. . . .

21. Jackson's "Protest"

THE REMOVAL of the deposits produced an explosion of anger and resentment in the Senate where the Whig party had a majority. That majority not only rejected the arguments presented to them by Secretary Taney for the removal but on March 28, 1834, by a vote of 26 to 20, officially

SOURCE: James D. Richardson, Messages and Papers of the Presidents, III: 69–70, 79, 82–3, 85–6, 90, 92–3.

censured Jackson for this action. Immediately, Jackson fired back a "Protest" message written by Taney, Amos Kendall and Benjamin F. Butler, the new Attorney General, defending his action. More important, he enunciated the novel doctrine that the President is the direct (and sole) representative of the American people since he was the only man elected by all the people. Jackson also claimed that he was directly responsible to the people for his actions, not to Congress as so many presumed. The eventual acceptance of Jackson's doctrine in effect altered the essential character of the presidency. No longer was the chief executive the head of a coordinate branch of the government, responsible to Congress; henceforth he was the spokesman and leader of the American people, the formulator of national policy.

April 15, 1834

To the Senate of the United States:

It appears by the published Journal of the Senate that on the 26th of December last a resolution was offered by a member of the Senate, which after a protracted debate was on the 28th day of March last modified by the mover and passed by the votes of twenty-six Senators out of forty-six who were present and voted, in the following words, viz:

Resolved, That the President, in the late Executive proceedings in relation to the public revenue, has assumed upon himself authority and power not conferred by the Constitution and laws, but in derogation of both.

Having had the honor, through the voluntary suffrages of the American people, to fill the office of President of the United States during the period which may be presumed to have been referred to in this resolution, it is sufficiently evident that the censure it inflicts was intended for myself. Without notice, unheard and untried, I thus find myself charged on the records of the Senate, and in a form hitherto unknown in our history, with the high crime of violating the laws and Constitution of my country.

It can seldom be necessary for any department of the Government, when assailed in conversation or debate or by the strictures of the press or of popular assemblies, to step out of its ordinary path for the purpose of vindicating its conduct or of pointing out any irregularity or injustice in the manner of the attack; but when the Chief Executive Magistrate is, by one of the most important branches of the Government in its official capacity, in a public manner, and by its recorded sentence, but without precedent, competent authority, or just cause, declared guilty of a breach of the laws and Constitution, it is due to his station, to public opinion, and to a proper self-respect that the officer thus denounced should promptly expose the wrong which has been done. . . .

If the resolution had been left in its original form it is not to be presumed that it could ever have received the assent of a majority of the Senate, for the acts therein specified as violations of the Constitution and laws were clearly within the limits of the Executive authority. They are the "dismissing the late Secretary of the Treasury because he would not, contrary to his sense of his own duty, remove the money of the United States in deposit with the Bank of the United States and its branches in conformity with the President's opinion, and appointing his successor to effect such removal, which has been done." But as no other specification has been substituted, and as these were the "Executive proceedings in relation to the public revenue" principally referred to in the course of the discussion, they will doubtless be generally regarded as the acts intended to be denounced as "an assumption of authority and power not conferred by the Constitution or laws, but in derogation of both." It is therefore due to the occasion that a condensed summary of the views of the Executive in respect to them should be here exhibited.

By the Constitution "the executive power is vested in a President of the United States." Among the duties imposed upon him, and which he is sworn to perform, is that of "taking care that the laws be faithfully executed." Being thus made responsible for the entire action of the executive department, it was but reasonable that the power of appointing, overseeing, and controlling those who execute the laws—a power in its nature executive—should remain in his hands. It is therefore not only his right, but the Constitution makes it his duty, to "nominate and, by and with the advice and consent of the Senate, appoint" all "officers of the United States whose appointments are not in the Constitution otherwise provided for," with a proviso that the appointment of inferior officers may be vested in the President alone, in the courts of justice, or in the heads of Departments.

The executive power vested in the Senate is neither that of "nominating" nor "appointing." It is merely a check upon the Executive power of appointment. If individuals are proposed for appointment by the President by them deemed incompetent or unworthy, they may withhold their consent and the appointment can not be made. They check the action of the Executive, but can not in relation to those very subjects act themselves nor direct him. Selections are still made by the President, and the negative given to the Senate, without diminishing his responsibility, furnishes an additional guaranty to the country that the subordinate executive as well as the judicial offices shall be filled with worthy and competent men. . . .

The custody of the public property, under such regulations as may be prescribed by legislative authority, has always been considered an appropriate function of the executive department in this and all other Governments. In accordance with this principle, every species of property belonging to the United States (excepting that which is in the use of the several coordinate departments of the Government as means to aid them in performing their appropriate functions) is in charge of officers appointed by the President, whether it be lands, or buildings, or merchandise, or provisions, or clothing, or arms and munitions of war. The superintendents and keepers of the whole are appointed by the President, responsible to him, and removable at his will.

Public money is but a species of public property. It can not be raised by taxation or customs, nor brought into the Treasury in any other way except by law; but whenever or howsoever obtained, its custody always has been and always must be, unless the Constitution be changed, intrusted to the executive department. No officer can be created by Congress for the purpose of taking charge of it whose appointment would not by the Constitution at once devolve on the President and who would not be responsible to him for the faithful performance of his duties. The legislative power may undoubtedly bind him and the President by any laws they may think proper to enact; they may prescribe in what place particular portions of the public property shall be kept and for what reason it shall be removed, as they may direct that supplies for the Army or Navy shall be kept in particular stores, and it will be the duty of the President to see that the law is faithfully executed; yet will the custody remain in the executive department of the Government. Were the Congress to assume, with or without a legislative act, the power of appointing officers, independently of the President, to take the charge and custody of the public property contained in the military and naval arsenals, magazines, and storehouses, it is believed that such an act would be regarded by all as a palpable usurpation of executive power, subversive of the form as well as the fundamental principles of our Government. But where is the difference in principle whether the public property be in the form of arms, munitions of war, and supplies or in gold and silver or bank notes? None can be perceived; none is believed to exist. Congress can not, therefore, take out of the hands of the executive department the custody of the public property or money without an assumption of executive power and a subversion of the first principles of the Constitution. . . .

Thus was it settled by the Constitution, the laws, and the whole practice of the Government that the entire executive power is vested in the President of the United States; that as incident to that power the right of appointing and removing those officers who are to aid him in the execution of the laws, with such restrictions only as the Constitution prescribes, is vested in the President; that the Secretary of the Treasury is one of those officers; that the custody of the public property and money is an Executive function which, in relation to the money, has always been exercised through the Secretary of the Treasury and his subordinates; that in the performance of these duties he is subject to the supervision and control of the President, and in all important measures having relation to them consults the Chief Magistrate and obtains his approval and sanction; that the law establishing the bank did not, as it could not, change the relation between the President and the Secretary—did not release the former from his obligation to see the law faithfully executed nor the latter from the President's supervision and control; that afterwards and before the Secretary did in fact consult and obtain the sanction of the President to transfers and removals of the public deposits, and that all departments of the Government, and the nation itself, approved or acquiesced in these acts and principles as in strict conformity with our Constitution and laws.

During the last year the approaching termination, according to the provisions of its charter and the solemn decision of the American people, of the Bank of the United States made it expedient, and its exposed abuses and corruptions made it, in my opinion, the duty of the Secretary of the Treasury, to place the moneys of the United States in other depositories. The Secretary did not concur in that opinion, and declined giving the necessary order and direction. So glaring were the abuses and corruptions of the bank, so evident its fixed purpose to persevere in them, and so palpable its design by its money and power to control the Government and change its character, that I deemed it the imperative duty of the Executive authority, by the exertion of every power confided to it by the Constitution and laws, to check its career and lessen its ability to do mischief, even in the painful alternative of dismissing the head of one of the Departments. At the time the removal was made other causes sufficient to justify it existed, but if they had not the Secretary would have been dismissed for this cause only.

His place I supplied by one whose opinions were well known to me, and whose frank expression of them in another situation and generous sacrifices of interest and feeling when unexpectedly called to the station he now occupies ought forever to have shielded his motives from suspicion and his character from reproach. In accordance with the views long before expressed by him he proceeded, with my sanction, to make arrangements for depositing the moneys of the United States in other safe institutions.

The resolution of the Senate as originally framed and as passed, if it refers to these acts, presupposes a right in that body to interfere with this exercise of Executive power. If the principle be once admitted, it is not difficult to perceive where it may end. If by a mere denunciation like this resolution the President should ever be induced to act in a matter of official duty contrary to the honest convictions of his own mind in compliance with the wishes of the Senate, the constitutional independence of the executive department would be as effectually destroyed and its power as effectually tranferred to the Senate as if that end had been accomplished by an amendment of the Constitution. . . .

The dangerous tendency of the doctrine which denies to the President the power of supervising, directing, and controlling the Secretary of the Treasury in like manner with the other executive officers would soon be manifest in practice were the doctrine to be established. The President is the direct representative of the American people, but the Secretaries are not. If the Secretary of the Treasury be independent of the President in the execution of the laws, then is there no direct responsibility to the people in that important branch of this Government to which is committed the care of the national finances. And it is in the power of the Bank of the United States, or any other corporation, body of men, or individuals, if a Secretary shall be found to accord with them in opinion or can be induced in practice to promote their views, to control through him the whole action of the Government (so far as it is exercised by his Department) in defiance of the Chief Magistrate elected by the people and responsible to them. . . .

The resolution of the Senate contains an imputation upon my private as well as upon my public character, and as it must stand forever on their journals, I can not close this substitute for that defense which I have not been allowed to present in the ordinary form without remarking that I have lived in vain if it be necessary to enter into a formal vindication of my character and purposes from such an imputation. In vain do I bear upon my person enduring memorials of that contest in which American liberty was purchased; in vain have I since periled property, fame, and life in defense of the rights and privileges so dearly bought; in vain am I now, without a personal aspiration or the hope of individaul advantage, encountering responsibilities and dangers from which by mere inactivity in relation to a single point I might have been exempt, if any serious doubts can be entertained as to the purity of my purposes and motives. If I had been ambitious, I should have sought an alliance with that powerful institution which even now aspires to no divided empire. If I had been venal, I should have sold myself to its designs. Had I preferred personal comfort and official ease to the performance of my arduous duty, I should have ceased to molest it. In the history of conquerors and usurpers, never in the fire of youth nor in the vigor of manhood could I find an attraction to lure me from the path of duty, and now I shall scarcely find an inducement to commence their career of ambition when gray hairs and a decaying frame, instead of inviting to toil and battle, call me to the contemplation of other worlds, where conquerors cease to be honored and usurpers expiate their crimes. The only ambition I can feel is to acquit myself to Him to whom I must soon render an account of my stewardship, to serve my fellow-men, and live respected and honored in the history of my country. No; the ambition which leads me on is an anxious desire and a fixed determination to return to the people unimpaired the sacred trust they have confided to my charge; to heal the wounds of the Constitution and preserve it from further violation; to persuade my countrymen, so far as I may, that it is not in a splendid government supported by powerful monopolies and aristocratical establishments that they will find happiness or their liberties protection, but in a plain system, void of pomp, protecting all and granting favors to none, dispensing its blessings, like the dews of Heaven, unseen and unfelt save in the freshness and beauty they contribute to produce. It is such a government that the genius of our people requires; such an one only under which our States may remain for ages to come united, prosperous, and free. If the Almighty Being who has hitherto sustained and protected me will but vouchsafe to make my feeble powers instrumental to such a result, I shall anticipate with pleasure the place to be assigned me in the history of my country, and die contented with the belief that I have contributed in some small degree to increase the value and prolong the duration of American liberty.

To the end that the resolution of the Senate may not be hereafter drawn into precedent with the authority of silent acquiescence on the part of the executive department, and to the end also that my motives and views in the Executive proceedings denounced in that resolution may be known to my fellow-citizens, to the world, and to all posterity, I respectfully request that this message and protest may be entered at length on the journals of the Senate.

22. Webster's Reply to the "Protest"

JACKSON's "Protest" constituted a very dangerous challenge to the Whig theory of legislative government. As such it had to be refuted. Daniel Webster understood that Jackson's doctrine represented a significant departure from the essential relationship between the three branches of government structured by the Founding Fathers in the Constitution. Jackson sought to bring the presidency closer to the people, a move that Webster feared would destroy the constitutional balance of power and swing the government into the hands of the chief executive. Rising in the Senate, Webster attacked all the major points contained in the Protest. It was a powerful but ineffectual speech, for Webster was arguing against an idea that quickly found popular acceptance.

. . . The Protest, in the first place, seizes on the fact that all officers must be appointed by the President, or on his nomination;

SOURCE: Daniel Webster, *The Writings and Speeches of Daniel Webster*, Volume VII (Boston, 1903), pp. 130, 131, 138–9, 143–5.

it then assumes the next step, that all officers are, and *must be*, removable at his pleasure; and then, insisting that public money, like other public property, must be kept by *some public officer*, it thus arrives at the conclusion that it *must* always be in the hands of those who are appointed by the President, and who are removable at his pleasure. And it is very clear that the Protest means to maintain that the *tenure of office cannot be so regulated by law, as that public officers shall not be removable at the pleasure of the President.*

The President considers the right of removal as a fixed, vested, constitutional right, which Congress cannot limit, control, or qualify, until the Constitution shall be altered. This, Sir, is doctrine which I am not prepared to admit. I shall not now discuss the question, whether the law may not place the tenure of office beyond the reach of executive pleasure; but I wish merely to draw the attention of the Senate to the fact, that any such power in Congress is denied by the principles and by the words of the Protest. According to that paper, we live under a constitution by the provisions of which the public treasures are, necessarily and unavoidably, always under executive control; and as the executive may remove all officers, and appoint others, at least temporarily, without the concurrence of the Senate, he may hold those treasures, in the hands of persons appointed by himself alone, in defiance of any law which Congress has passed or can pass. It is to be seen, Sir, how far such claims of power will receive the approbation of the country. It is to be seen whether a construction will be readily adopted which thus places the public purse out of the guardianship of the immediate representatives of the people.

But, Sir, there is, in this paper, something even yet more strange than these extraordinary claims of power. There is a strong disposition, running through the whole Protest, to represent the executive department of this government as the peculiar protector of the public liberty, the chief security on which the people are to rely against the encroachment of other branches of the government. . . .

Sir, it exceeds human belief that any man should put sentiments such as this paper contains into a public communication from the President to the Senate. They are sentiments which give us all one master. The Protest asserts an absolute right to remove all persons from office at pleasure; and for what reason? Because they are incompetent? Because they are incapable? Because they are remiss, negligent, or inattentive? No, Sir; these are not the reasons. But he may discharge them, one and all, simply because "he is no longer willing to be responsible for their acts"! It insists on an absolute right in the President to *direct* and *control* every act of every officer of the government, except the judges. It asserts this right of direct *control* over and over again. The President may go into the treasury, among the auditors and comptrollers, and *direct* them how to settle every man's account; what abatements to make from one, what additions to another. He may go into the custom-house, among collectors and appraisers, and may *control* estimates, reductions, and appraisements. It is true that these officers are sworn to discharge the duties of their respective offices honestly and fairly, according to their *own* best abilities, it is true, that many of them are liable to indictment for official misconduct, and others responsible, in suits of individuals, for damages and penalties, if such official misconduct be proved; but notwithstanding all this, the Protest avers that all these officers are but the *President's agents*; that they are but aiding *him* in the discharge of *his* duties; that *he* is responsible for their conduct, and that they are removable at his will and pleasure. And it is under this view of his own authority that the President calls the Secretaries *his* Secretaries, not once only, but repeatedly. After half a century's administration of this government, Sir;—after we have endeavored, by statute upon statute, and by provision following provision, to define and limit official authority; to assign particular duties to particular public servants; to define those duties; to create penalties for their violation; to adjust accurately the responsibility of each agent with his own powers and his own duties; to establish the prevalence of equal rule; to make the law, as far as possible, every thing, and individual will, as far as possible, nothing;—after all this, the astounding assertion rings in our ears, that, throughout the whole range of official agency, in its smallest ramifications as well as in its larger masses, there is but ONE RESPONSIBILITY, ONE DISCRETION, ONE WILL! True indeed is it, Sir, if these sentiments be maintained,—true indeed is it that a President of the United States may well repeat from Napoleon what he repeated from Louis the Fourteenth. "I am the state!" . . .

I will never agree that a President of the United States holds the whole undivided power of office in his own hands, upon the theory that he is responsible for the entire action of the whole body of those engaged in carrying on the government and executing the laws. Such a responsibility is purely ideal, delusive, and vain. There is, there can be, no substantial responsibility, any further than every individual is answerable, not merely in his reputation, not merely in the opinion of mankind, but *to the law*, for the faithful discharge of his own appropriate duties. Again and again we hear it said that the President is responsible to the American people! that he is responsible to the bar of public opinion! For whatever he does, he assumes accountability to the American people! For whatever he omits, he expects to be brought to the high bar of public opinion! And this is thought enough for a limited, restrained, republican government! an undefined, undefinable, ideal responsibility to the public judgment!

Sir, if all this mean any thing, if it be not empty sound, it means no less than that the President may do any thing and every thing which he may expect to be tolerated in doing. He may go just so far as he thinks it safe to go; and Cromwell and Bonaparte went no farther. I ask again, Sir, Is this legal responsibility? Is this the true nature of a government with written laws and limited powers? And allow me, Sir, to ask, too, if an executive magistrate, while professing to act under the Constitution, is restrained only by this responsibility to public opinion, what prevents him, on the same responsibility, from proposing a change in that Constitution? Why may he not say, "I am about to introduce new forms, new principles, and a new spirit; I am about to try a political experiment on a great scale; and when I get through with it, I shall be responsible to the American people, I shall be answerable to the bar of public opinion"?

Connected, Sir, with the idea of this airy and unreal responsibility to the public is another sentiment, which of late we hear frequently expressed; and that is, *that the President is the direct representative of the American people.* This is declared in the Protest in so many words. "The President," it says, "is *the direct representative of the American people.*" Now, Sir, this is not the language of the Constitution. The Constitution nowhere calls him the representative of the American people; still less, their direct representative. It could not do so with the least propriety. He is not chosen directly by the people, but by a body of electors, some of whom are chosen by the people, and some of whom are appointed by the State legislatures. Where, then, is the authority for saying that the President is the *direct representative of the people?* The Constitution calls the members of the other house Representatives, and declares that they shall be chosen by the people; and there are no other direct or immediate representatives of the people in this government. The Constitution denominates the President simply the President of the United States; it points out the complex mode of electing him, defines his powers and duties, and imposes limits and restraints on his authority. With these powers and duties, and under these restraints, be becomes, when chosen, President of the United States. That is his character, and the denomination of his office. How is it, then, that, on this official character, thus cautiously created, limited, and defined, he is to engraft another and a very imposing character, namely, the character *of the direct representative of the American people?* I hold this, Sir, to be mere assumption, and dangerous assumption. If he is the representative of *all* the American people, he is the only representative which they all have. Nobody else presumes to represent all the people. And if he may be allowed to consider himself as the SOLE REPRESENTATIVE OF ALL THE AMERICAN PEOPLE, and is to act under no other responsibility than such as I have already described, then I say, Sir, that the government (I will not say the people) has already a master. I deny the sentiment, therefore, and I protest against the language; neither the sentiment nor the language is to be found in the Constitution of the country; and whoever is not satisfied to describe the powers of the President in the language of the Constitution may be justly suspected of being as little satisfied with the powers themselves. The President is President. His office and his name of office are known, and both are fixed and described by law. Being commander of the army and navy, holding the power of nominating to office and removing from office, and being by these powers the fountain of all patronage and all favor, what does he not become if he be allowed to superadd to all this the character of single representative of the American people? Sir, he becomes what America has not been accustomed to see, what this Constitution has never created, and what I cannot contemplate but with profound alarm. He who may call himself the single representative of a nation, may speak in the name of the nation, may undertake to wield the power of the nation; and who shall gainsay him in whatsoever he chooses to pronounce to be the nation's will? . . .

23. Van Buren's Special Session Message

JACKSON KILLED *the national bank but it was his successor, Martin Van Buren, who lived with the consequences. Shortly after assuming office in 1837 a severe depression struck the nation—a depression, declared New York merchants, resulting from the "interference of the General Government with the commercial and business operations of the country, its intermeddling with the currency, its destruction of the national bank, its attempts to substitute a metallic for a credit currency, and finally, to the issuing by the President of the United States of the Treasury Order known as the 'Specie Circular'."*[2] *Almost immediately after the panic struck banks suspended specie payments—that is they refused to exchange hard money for their notes. Since the Deposit Act of 1836 required those banks receiving government funds to redeem all their notes in gold and silver, the suspension of specie payments convinced Van Buren to abandon the deposit system. He summoned Congress into special session and in his message proposed that the government keep its money in its own depositories or sub-treasuries. This divorce, as it was called, ended the problem of the disposition of government money to prevent its use by private corporations.*

Washington, September 4, 1837
Fellow-Citizens of the Senate and House of Representatives:

The act of the 23d of June, 1836, regulating the deposits of the public money and directing the employment of State, District, and Territorial banks for that purpose, made it the duty of the Secretary of the Treasury to discontinue the use of such of them as should at any time refuse to redeem their notes in specie, and to substitute other banks, provided a sufficient number could be obtained to receive the public deposits upon the terms and condition therein prescribed. The general and almost simultaneous suspension of specie payments by the banks in May last rendered the performance of this duty imperative in respect to those which had been selected under the act, and made it at the same time impracticable to employ the requisite number of others upon the prescribed conditions. The specific regulations established by Con-

SOURCE: James D. Richardson, *Messages and Papers*, III: 324–28, 330–1, 335, 337–8, 344, 346.

2. New York *Evening Post*, April 26, 1837.

gress for the deposit and safe-keeping of the public moneys having thus unexpectedly become inoperative, I felt it to be my duty to afford you an early opportunity for the exercise of your supervisory powers over the subject. . . .

The history of trade in the United States for the last three or four years affords the most convincing evidence that our present condition is chiefly to be attributed to overaction in all the departments of business—an overaction deriving, perhaps, its first impulses from antecedent causes, but stimulated to its destructive consequences by excessive issues of bank paper and by other facilities for the acquisition and enlargement of credit. At the commencement of the year 1834 the banking capital of the United States, including that of the national bank, then existing, amounted to about $200,000,000, the bank notes then in circulation to about ninety-five millions, and the loans and discounts of the banks to three hundred and twenty-four millions. Between that time and the 1st of January, 1836, being the latest period to which accurate accounts have been received, our banking capital was increased to more than two hundred and fifty-one millions, our paper circulation to more than one hundred and forty millions, and the loans and discounts to more than four hundred and fifty-seven millions. To this vast increase are to be added the many millions of credit acquired by means of foreign loans, contracted by the States and State institutions, and, above all, by the lavish accommodations extended by foreign dealers to our merchants. . . .

For the deposit, transfer, and disbursement of the revenue national and State banks have always, with temporary and limited exceptions, been heretofore employed; but although advocates of each system are still to be found, it is apparent that the events of the last few months have greatly augmented the desire, long existing among the people of the United States, to separate the fiscal operations of the Government from those of individuals or corporations.

Again to create a national bank as a fiscal agent would be to disregard the popular will, twice solemnly and unequivocally expressed. On no question of domestic policy is there stronger evidence that the sentiments of a large majority are deliberately fixed, and I can not concur with those who think they see in recent events a proof that these sentiments are, or a reason that they should be, changed. . . .

But it was not designed by the Constitution that the Government should assume the management of domestic or foreign exchange. It is indeed authorized to regulate by law the commerce between the States and to provide a general standard of value or medium of exchange in gold and silver, but it is not its province to aid individuals in the transfer of their funds otherwise than through the facilities afforded by the Post-Office Department. As justly might it be called on to provide for the transportation of their merchandise. These are operations of trade. They ought to be conducted by those who are interested in them in the same manner that the incidental difficulties of other pursuits are encountered by other classes of citizens. Such aid has not been deemed necessary in other countries. Throughout Europe the domestic as well as the foreign exchanges are carried on by private houses, often, if not generally, without the assistance of banks; yet they extend throughout distinct sovereignties, and far exceed in amount the real exchanges of the United States. There is no reason why our own may not be conducted in the same manner with equal cheapness and safety. Certainly this might be accomplished if it were favored by those most deeply interested; and few can doubt that their own interest, as well as the general welfare of the country, would be promoted by leaving such a subject in the hands of those to whom it properly belongs. A system founded on private interest, enterprise, and competition, without the aid of legislative grants or regulations by law, would rapidly prosper; it would be free from the influence of political agitation and extend the same exemption to trade itself, and it would put an end to those complaints of neglect, partiality, injustice, and oppression which are the unavoidable results of interference by the Government in the proper concerns of individuals. All former attempts on the part of the Government to carry its legislation in this respect further than was designed by the Constitution have in the end proved injurious, and have served only to convince the great body of the people more and more of the certain dangers of blending private interests with the operations of public business; and there is no reason to suppose that a repetition of them now would be more successful.

It can not be concealed that there exists in our community opinions and feelings on this subject in direct opposition to each other. A large portion of them, combining great intelligence, activity, and influence, are no doubt sincere in their belief that the operations of trade ought to be assisted by such a connection; they regard a national bank as necessary for this purpose, and they are disinclined to every measure that does not tend sooner or later to the establishment of such an institution. On the other hand, a majority of the people are believed to be irreconcilably opposed to that measure; they consider such a concentration of power danger- ous to their liberties, and many of them regard it as a violation of the Constitution. This collision of opinion has doubtless caused much of the embarrassment to which the commercial transactions of the country have lately been exposed. Banking has become a political topic of the highest interest, and trade has suffered in the conflict of parties. A speedy termination of this state of things, however desirable, is scarcely to be expected. We have seen for nearly half a century that those who advocate a national bank, by whatever motive they may be influenced, constitute a portion of our community too numerous to allow us to hope for an early abandonment of their favorite plan. On the other hand, they must indeed form an erroneous estimate of the intelligence and temper of the American people who suppose that they have continued on slight or insufficient grounds their persevering opposition to such an institution, or that they can be induced by pecuniary pressure or by any other combination of circumstances to surrender principles they have so long and so inflexibly maintained. . . .

Surely banks are not more able than the Government to secure the money in their possession against accident, violence, or fraud. The assertion that they are so must assume that a vault in a bank is stronger than a vault in the Treasury, and that directors, cashiers, and clerks not selected by the Government nor under its control are more worthy of confidence than officers selected from the people and responsible to the Government—officers bound by official oaths and bonds for a faithful performance of their duties, and constantly subject to the supervision of Congress. . . .

The power and influence supposed to be connected with the custody and disbursement of the public money are topics on which the public mind is naturally, and with great propriety, peculiarly sensitive. Much has been said on them in reference to the proposed separation of the Government from the banking institutions; and surely no one can object to any appeals or animadversions on the subject which are consistent with facts and evince a proper respect for the intelligence of the people. If a Chief Magistrate may be allowed to speak for himself on such a point, I can truly say that to me nothing would be more acceptable than the withdrawal from the Executive, to the greatest practicable extent, of all concern in the custody and disbursement of the public revenue; not that I would shrink from any responsibility cast upon me by the duties of my office, but because it is my firm belief that its capacity for usefulness is in no degree promoted by the possession of any patronage not actually necessary to the performance of those duties. But under our present form of government the intervention of the executive officers in the custody and disbursement of the public money seems to be unavoidable; and before it can be admitted that the influence and power of the Executive would be increased by dispensing with the agency of banks the nature of that intervention in such an agency must be carefully regarded, and a comparison must be instituted between its extent in the two cases.

The revenue can only be collected by officers appointed by the President with the advice and consent of the Senate. The public moneys in the first instance must therefore in all cases pass through hands selected by the Executive. Other officers appointed in the same way, or, as in some cases, by the President alone, must also be intrusted with them when drawn for the purpose of disbursement. It is thus seen that even when banks are employed the public funds must twice pass through the hands of executive officers. Besides this, the head of the Treasury Department, who also holds office at the pleasure of the President, and some other officers of the same Department, must necessarily be invested with more or less power in the selection, continuance, and supervision of the banks that may be employed. The question is then narrowed to the single point whether in the intermediate stage between the collection and disbursement of the public money the agency of banks is necessary to avoid a dangerous extension of the patronage and influence of the Executive. . . .

Those who look to the action of this Government for specific aid to the citizen to relieve embarrassments arising from losses by revulsions in commerce and credit lose sight of the ends for which it was created and the powers with which it is clothed. It was established to give security to us all in our lawful and honorable pursuits, under the lasting safeguard of republican institutions. It was not intended to confer special favors on individuals or on any classes of them, to create systems of agriculture, manufactures, or trade, or to engage in them either separately or in connection with individual citizens or organized associations. If its operations were to be directed for the benefit of any one class, equivalent favors must in justice be extended to the rest, and the attempt to bestow such favors with an equal hand, or even to select those who should most deserve them, would never be successful.

All communities are apt to look to government for too much. Even in our own country, where its powers and duties are so strictly limited, we are prone to do so, especially at periods of sudden embarrassment and distress. But this ought not to be. The framers of our excellent Constitution and the people who approved it with calm and sagacious deliberation acted at the time on a sounder principle. They wisely judged that the less government interferes with private pursuits the better for the general prosperity. It is not its legitimate object to make men rich or to repair by direct grants of money or legislation in favor of particular pursuits losses not incurred in the public service. This would be substantially to use the property of some for the benefit of others. But its real duty—that duty the performance of which makes a good government the most precious of human blessings—is to enact and enforce a system of general laws commensurate with, but not exceeding, the objects of its establishment, and to leave every citizen and every interest to reap under its benign protection the rewards of virtue, industry, and prudence. . . .

I deeply regret that events have occurred which require me to ask your consideration of such serious topics. I could have wished that in making my first communication to the assembled repre- sentatives of my country I had nothing to dwell upon but the history of her unalloyed prosperity. Since it is otherwise, we can only feel more deeply the responsibility of the respective trusts that have been confided to us, and under the pressure of difficulties unite in invoking the guidance and aid of the Supreme Ruler of Nations and in laboring with zealous resolution to overcome the difficulties by which we are environed. . . .

24. The Sub-Treasury Speech of Thomas Hart Benton

THOMAS HART BENTON, *Senator from Missouri, was the most articulate critic of the national bank in the United States Senate. Like Jackson he was committed to gold and silver as the circulating medium of exchange. He feared that under the paper, or credit, system the country was saddled with boom or bust financial cycles, that when depression struck credit disappeared and the working class had no money with which to pay their debts. With the financial collapse of 1837 Benton sided with Van Buren in arguing for a divorce of government funds from private banks. It was a long struggle to get Congress to accept this scheme rather than charter another national bank. Not until 1840 did the Independent Treasury or Divorce Bill win approval from Congress. In his Thirty Years View, a work that is partly reminiscences and partly extracts from the Congressional record, Benton reprinted one of his principal speeches in favor of the bill.*

The bill is to divorce the government from the banks, or rather is to declare the divorce, for the separation has already taken place by the operation of law and by the delinquency of the banks. The bill is to declare the divorce; the amendment is to exclude their notes from revenue payments, not all at once, but gradually, and to be accomplished by the 1st day of January, 1841. Until then the notes of specie-paying banks may be received, diminishing one-fourth annually; and after that day, all payments to and from the federal government are to be made in hard money. Until that day, payments from the United States will be governed by existing laws. . . .

I am for this restoration. I am for restoring to the federal treasury the currency of the Constitution. I am for carrying back this government to the solidity projected by its founders. This is a great object in itself—a reform of the first magnitude—a reformation with healing on its wings, bringing safety to the government and blessings to the people. The currency is a thing which reaches every individual, 'and every institution. From the government to

SOURCE: Thomas Hart Benton, *Thirty Years View*, Volume II (New York, 1856), pp. 56–57, 61–62.

the washerwoman, all are reached by it, and all concerned in it; and, what seems parodoxical, all are concerned to the same degree; for all are concerned to the whole extent of their property and dealings; and all is all, whether it be much or little. The government with its many ten millions of revenue, suffers no more in proportion then the humble and meritorious laborer who works from sun to sun for the shillings which give food and raiment to his family. The federal government has deteriorated the currency, and carried mischief to the whole community, and lost its own revenues, and subjected itself to be trampled upon by corporations, by departing from the constitution, and converting this government from a hard-money to a paper money government. The object of the amendment and the bill is to reform these abuses, and it is a reform worthy to be called a reformation—worthy to engage the labor of patriots—worthy to unite the exertions of different parties —worthy to fix the attention of the age—worthy to excite the hopes of the people, and to invoke upon its success the blessings of heaven. . . .

Thus, pecuniary, political, and moral considerations require the government to retrace its steps, to return to first principles, and to restore its fiscal action to the safe and solid path of the constitution. Reform is demanded. It is called for by every public and by every private consideration. Now is the time to make it. The connection between Bank and State is actually dissolved. It is dissolved by operation of law, and by the delinquency of these institutions. They have forfeited the right to the deposits, and lost the privilege of paying the revenue in their notes, by ceasing to pay specie. The government is now going on without them, and all that is wanting is the appropriate legislation to perpetuate the divorce which, in point of fact, has already taken place. Now is the time to act; this the moment to restore the constitutional currency to the federal government; to restore the custody of the public moneys to national keepers; and to avoid, in time to come, the calamitous revulsions and perilous catastrophes of 1814, 1819, and 1837.

And what is the obstacle to the adoption of this course, so imperiously demanded by the safety of the republic and the welfare of the people, and so earnestly recommended to us by the chief magistrate? What is the obstacle—what the power that countervails the Executive recommendation, paralyzes the action of Congress, and stays the march of reform? The banks—the banks—the banks, are this obstacle, and this power. They set up the pretension to force their paper into the federal Treasury, and to force themselves to be constituted that Treasury. Though now bankrupt, their paper dishonored, their doors closed against creditors, every public and every private obligation violated, still they arrogate a supremacy over this federal government; they demand the guardianship of the public moneys, and the privilege of furnishing a federal currency; and, though too weak to pay their debts, they are strong enough to throttle this government, and to hold in doubtful suspense the issue of their vast pretensions.

The President, in his message, recommends four things: first, to discontinue the reception of local bank paper in payment of federal dues; secondly, to discontinue the same banks as depositories of the public moneys; thirdly, to make the future collection and disbursement of the public moneys in gold and silver; fourthly, to take the keeping of the public moneys into the hands of our own officers.

What is there in this but a return to the words and meaning of the constitution, and a conformity to the practice of the government in the first years of President Washington's administration? . . .

The right and the obligation of the government to keep its own moneys in its own hands, results from first principles, and from the great law of self-preservation. Every thing else that belongs to her, she keeps herself; and why not keep that also, without which every thing else is nothing? Arms and ships—provisions, munitions, and supplies of every kind—are kept in the hands of government officers; money is the sinew of war, and why leave this sinew exposed to be cut by any careless or faithless hand? Money is the support and existence of the government—the breath of its nostrils, and why leave this support—this breath—to the custody of those over whom we have no control? How absurd to place our ships, our arms, our military and naval supplies in the hands of those who could refuse to deliver them when requested, and put the government to a suit at law to recover their possession! Every body sees the absurdity of this; but to place our money in the same condition, and, moreover, to subject it to the vicissitudes of trade and the perils of banking, is still more absurd; for it is the life blood, without which the government cannot live—the oil, without which no part of its machinery can move. . . .

The bill reported by the chairman of the Committee on Finance

[Mr. WRIGHT of New York] presents the details of the plan for accomplishing this great result. That bill has been printed and read. Its simplicity, economy, and efficiency strike the sense of all who hear it, and annihilate without argument, the most formidable arguments of expense and patronage, which had been conceived against it. The present officers, the present mints, and one or two more mints in the South, in the West, and in the North, complete the plan. There will be no necessity to carry masses of hard money from one quarter of the Union to another. Government drafts will make the transfer without moving a dollar. A government draft upon a national mint, will be the highest order of bills of exchange. Money wanted by the government in one place will be exchanged, through merchants, for money in another place. Thus it has been for thousands of years, and will for ever be. . . .

IV

Nationalism, States Rights and Nullification

25. The Webster-Hayne Debate

DURING the Age of Jackson the nation veered dangerously close to civil war. Throughout the decade of the 1830s there was intensive analysis and debate over the nature of the Union and the rights of the states. Slavery, western lands, the tariff and sectional rivalry were some of the reasons precipitating a series of quarrels between those of conflicting constitutional viewpoints. The first disagreement occurred on December 29, 1829 when Senator Samuel Foote of Connecticut introduced a resolution, which, among other things, called for the limitation of sales of certain public lands. In response, Senator Thomas Hart Benton rose in the Senate on January 18, 1830 and declared that the resolution would, in effect, check emigration to the new states and territories and therefore limit their settlement. In support of Benton, Senator Robert Y. Hayne of South Carolina spoke at some length and was answered by Daniel Webster of Massachusetts on January 20, 1830. It was now a full scale debate and went beyond western lands to encompass questions like slavery, the tariff and the nature of the Union. Hayne responded to Webster on January 21 and 25 and Webster's celebrated second reply came on January 26 and 27.

A. HAYNE'S OPENING SPEECH

What ought to be the future policy of the Government in relation to the Public Lands? we find the most opposite and irreconcileable opinions between the two parties which I have before described. On the one side it is contended that the public land ought to be reserved as a permanent fund for revenue, and future

SOURCE: *Registers of Debates*, 21st Congress, 1st session, pp. 31–35, 35–41, 43–80.

distribution among the States, while, on the other, it is insisted that the whole of these lands of right belong to, and ought to be relinquished to the States in which they lie. . . .

If I could, by a mere act of my will, put at the disposal of the Federal Government any amount of treasure which I might think proper to name, I should limit the amount to the means necessary for the legitimate purposes of the Government. Sir, an immense national treasury would be a fund for corruption. It would enable Congress and the Executive to exercise a control over States, as well as over great interests in the country, nay, even over corporations and individuals—utterly destructive to the purity, and fatal to the duration of our institutions. It would be equally fatal to the sovereignty and independence of the States. . . .

But, sir, there is another purpose to which it has been supposed the public lands can be applied, still more objectionable. I mean that suggested in a report from the Treasury Department, under the late administration, of so regulating the disposition of the public lands as to create and preserve, in certain quarters of the Union, a population suitable for conducting great manufacturing establishments. It is supposed, sir, by the advocates of the American System, that the great obstacle to the progress of manufactures in this country, is the want of that low and degraded population which infest the cities and towns of Europe, who, having no other means of subsistence, will work for the lowest wages, and be satisfied with the smallest possible share of human enjoyment. And this difficulty it is proposed to overcome, by so regulating and limiting the sales of the public lands, as to prevent the drawing off this portion of the population from the manufacturing States. Sir, it is bad enough that Government should presume to regulate the industry of man; it is sufficiently monstrous that they should attempt, by arbitrary legislation, artificially to adjust and balance the various pursuits of society, and to "organize the whole labor and capital of the country." But what shall we say of the resort to such means for these purposes! What! create a manufactory of paupers, in order to enable the rich proprietors of woolen and cotton factories to amass wealth? From the bottom of my soul do I abhor and detest the idea, that the powers of the Federal Government should ever be prostituted for such purpose. Sir, I hope we shall act on a more just and liberal system of policy. The people of America are, and ought to be for a century to come, essentially an agricultural people: and I can conceive of no policy that can possibly be pursued in relation to the public lands, none that would be more "for the common benefit of all the States," than to use them as the means of furnishing a secure asylum to that class of our fellow-citizens, who in any portion of the country may find themselves unable to procure a comfortable subsistence by the means immediately within their reach. . . .

B. WEBSTER'S FIRST REPLY

. . . The Hon. Gentleman spoke of the whole course and policy of the Government. . . . I wish to see no new powers drawn to the General Government; but I confess I rejoice in whatever tends to strengthen the bond that unites us, and encourages the hope that our Union may be perpetual. And, therefore, I cannot but feel regret at the expression of such opinions as the Gentleman has avowed; because I think their obvious tendency is to weaken the bond of our connexion. I know that there are some persons in the part of the country from which the Hon. Member comes, who habitually speak of the Union in terms of indifference, or even of disparagement. The Hon. Member himself is not, I trust, and can never be one of those. They significantly declare that it is time to calculate the value of the Union; and their aim seems to be to enumerate, and magnify all the evils, real and imaginary, which the Government under the Union produces.

The tendency of all these ideas and sentiments is obviously to bring the Union into discussion, as a mere question of present and temporary expediency—nothing more than a mere matter of profit and loss. The Union to be preserved, while it suits local and temporary purposes to preserve it; and to be sundered whenever it should be found to thwart such purposes. . . . Sir, I deprecate and deplore this tone of thinking and acting. I deem far otherwise of the Union of the States; and so did the framers of the Constitution themselves. What they said I believe; fully and sincerely believe, that the Union of the States is essential to the prosperity and safety of the States. . . .

I come now to that part of the gentleman's speech which has been the main occasion of my addressing the Senate. The East! the obnoxious, the rebuked, the always reproached East! We have come in, sir, on this debate, for even more than a common share of accusation and attack. If the honorable member from South Carolina was not our original accuser, he has yet recited the indictment against us, with the air and tone of a public prosecutor. He has summoned us to plead on our arraignment; and he tells us we are charged with the crime of a narrow and selfish policy; of endeavoring to restrain emigration to the West, and, having that object in view, of maintaining a steady opposition to Western measures and Western interests. And the cause of all this narrow and selfish policy the gentleman finds in the tariff. I think he called it the accursed policy of the tariff. This policy, the gentleman tells us, requires multitudes of dependent laborers, a population of paupers, and that it is to secure these at home that the East opposes whatever may induce to Western emigration. Sir, I rise to defend the East. I rise to repel, both the charge itself, and the cause assigned for it. I deny that the East has, at any time, shown an illiberal policy towards the West. I pronounce the whole accusation to be without the least foundation in any facts, existing either now, or at any previous time. I deny it in the general, and I deny each and all its particulars. I deny the sum total, and I deny the detail. I deny that the East has ever manifested hostility to the West, and I deny that she has adopted any policy that would naturally have led her in such a course. . . .

C. Hayne's Reply to Webster

. . . The honorable gentleman from Massachusetts has gone out of his way to pass a high eulogium on the State of Ohio. In the most impassioned tones of eloquence he described her majestic march to greatness. He told us that, having already left all the other States far behind, she was now passing by Virginia and Pennsylvania, and about to take her station by the side of New York. To all this, sir, I was disposed most cordially to respond. When, however, the gentleman proceeded to contrast the State of Ohio with Kentucky, to the disadvantage of the latter, I listened to him with regret; and when he proceeded further to attribute the great and, as he supposed, acknowledged superiority of the former in population, wealth, and general prosperity to the policy of Nathan Dane of Massachusetts, which had secured to the people of Ohio (by the Ordinance of '87) a population of free-men, I will confess that my feelings suffered a revulsion which I am now unable to describe in any language sufficiently respectful toward the gentleman from Massachusetts. In contrasting the State of Ohio with Kentucky, for the purpose of pointing out the superiority of the former, and of attributing that superiority to the existence of slavery in the one State and its absence in the other, I thought I could discern the very spirit of the Missouri question intruded into this debate for objects best known to the gentleman himself. Did that gentleman, sir, when he formed the determination to cross the Southern border in order to invade the State of South Carolina, deem it prudent or necessary to enlist under his banners the prejudices of the world, which, like Swiss troops, may be engaged in any cause, and are prepared to serve under any leader? Did he desire to avail himself of those remorseless allies, the passions of mankind, of which it may be more truly said than of the savage tribes of the wilderness that their "known rule of warfare is an indiscriminate slaughter of all ages, sexes, and conditions"? Or was it supposed, sir, that, in a premeditated and unprovoked attack upon the South, it was advisable to begin by a gentle admonition of our supposed weakness, in order to prevent us from making that firm and manly resistance due to our own character and our dearest interests? Was the significant hint of the weakness of slaveholding States, when contrasted with the superior strength of free States,—like the glare of the weapon half drawn from its scabbard,—intended to enforce the lessons of prudence and of patriotism which the gentleman had resolved, out of his abundant generosity, gratuitously to bestow upon us? Mr. President, the impression which has gone abroad of the weakness of the South, as connected with the slave question, exposes us to such constant attacks, has done us so much injury, and is calculated to produce such infinite mischiefs, that I embrace the occasion presented by the remarks of the gentleman from Massachusetts to declare that we are ready to meet the question promptly and fearlessly. It is one from which we are not disposed to shrink, in whatever form or under whatever circumstances it may be pressed upon us.

We are ready to make up the issue with the gentleman as to the influence of slavery on individual and national character,—on the prosperity and greatness either of the United States or of particular States. Sir, when arraigned before the bar of public opinion on this charge of slavery, we can stand up with conscious rectitude, plead not guilty, and put ourselves upon God and our country. Sir, we will not consent to look at slavery in the abstract. We will not stop to inquire whether the black man, as some philosophers have contended, is of an inferior race, nor whether his color and condition are the effects of a curse inflicted for the offenses of his ancestors. We deal in no abstractions. We will not look back to inquire whether our fathers were guiltless in introducing slaves into this country. If an inquiry should ever be instituted into these matters, however, it will be found that the profits of the slave trade were not confined to the South. Southern ships and Southern sailors were not the instruments of bringing slaves to the shores of America, nor did our merchants reap the profits of that "accursed traffic." But, sir, we will pass over all this. If slavery, as it now exists in this country, be an evil, we of the present day found it ready made to our hands. Finding our lot cast among a people whom God had manifestly committed to our care, we did not sit down to speculate on abstract questions of theoretical liberty. We met it as a practical question of obligation and duty. . . . What a commentary on the wisdom, justice, and humanity of the Southern slave-owner is presented by the example of certain benevolent associations and charitable individuals elsewhere! Shedding weak tears over sufferings which had existence only in their own sickly imaginations, these "friends of humanity" set themselves systematically to work to seduce the slaves of the South from their masters. By means of missionaries and political tracts, the scheme was in a great measure successful. Thousands of these deluded victims of fanaticism were seduced into the enjoyment of freedom in our Northern cities. And what has been the consequence? Go to these cities now and ask the question. Visit the dark and narrow lanes, and obscure recesses, which have been assigned by common consent as the abodes of those outcasts of the world, the free people of color. Sir, there does not exist, on the face of the whole earth, a population so poor, so wretched, so vile, so loathsome, so utterly destitute of all the comforts, conveniences, and decencies of life, as the unfortunate blacks of Philadelphia, and New York, and Boston. Liberty has been to them the greatest of calamities, the heaviest of curses. Sir, I have had some opportunities of making comparison between the condition of the free negroes of the North and the slaves of the South, and the comparison has left not only an indelible impression of the superior advantages of the latter, but has gone far to reconcile me to slavery itself. . . .

In the course of my former remarks, Mr. President, I took occasion to deprecate, as one of the greatest evils, *the consolidation of this government*. The gentleman takes alarm at the sound. "Consolidation," like the tariff, grates upon his ear. He tells us "we have heard much of late about consolidation; that it is the rallying word for all who are endeavoring to weaken the Union by adding to the power of the States." But consolidation (says the gentleman) was the very object for which the Union was formed; and, in support of that opinion, he read a passage from the address of the President of the Convention to Congress, which he assumed to be an authority on his side of the question. But, sir, the gentleman is mistaken. The object of the framers of the Constitution, as disclosed in that address, was not the consolidation of the government, but "the consolidation of the Union." It was not to draw power from the States in order to transfer it to a great national government, but, in the language of the Constitution itself, "to form a more perfect Union,"—and by what means? By "establishing justice, promoting domestic tranquillity, and securing the blessings of liberty to ourselves and our posterity." This is the true reading of the Constitution. But, according to the gentleman's reading, the object of the Constitution was to consolidate the government, and the means would seem to be, the promotion of injustice, causing domestic discord, and depriving the States and the people of "the blessings of liberty" forever. . . .

But, Mr. President, . . . what are we of the South to think of what we have heard this day? The Senator from Massachusetts tells us that the tariff is not an Eastern measure, and treats it as if the East had no interest in it. The Senator from Missouri insists it is not a Western measure, and that it has done no good to the West. The South comes in, and, in the most earnest manner, represents to you that this measure, which we are told "is of no value to the East or the West," is "utterly destructive of our interests." We represent to you that it has spread ruin and devastation through the land, and prostrated our hopes in the dust. We solemnly declare that we believe the system to be wholly unconstitutional, and a violation of the compact between the States and the Union; and our brethren turn a deaf ear to our complaints, and refuse to relieve us from a system "which not enriches them, but makes us poor indeed." Good God! Mr. President, has it come to this? Do gentlemen hold the feelings and wishes of their brethren at so cheap a rate that they refuse to gratify them at so small a price? Do gentlemen value so lightly the peace and harmony of the country that they will not yield a measure of this description to the affectionate entreaties and earnest remonstrances of their friends? Do gentlemen estimate the value of the Union at so low a price that they will not even make one effort to bind the States together with the cords of affection? And has it come to this? Is this the spirit in which this government is to be administered? If so, let me tell gentlemen, the seeds of dissolution are already sown, and our children will reap the bitter fruit. . . .

Who then, Mr. President, are the true friends of the Union? Those who would confine the federal government strictly within the limits prescribed by the Constitution; who would preserve to the States and the people all powers not expressly delegated, who would make this a federal and not a national Union, and who, administering the government in a spirit of equal justice, would make it a blessing and not a curse. And who are its enemies? Those who are in favor of consolidation; who are constantly stealing power from the States, and adding strength to the federal government; who, assuming an unwarrantable jurisdiction over the States and the people, undertake to regulate the whole industry and capital of the country. . . .

The Senator from Massachusetts, in denouncing what he is pleased to call the Carolina doctrine, has attempted to throw ridicule upon the idea that a State has any constitutional remedy, by the exercise of its sovereign authority, against "a gross, palpable, and deliberate violation of the Constitution." He called it "an idle" or "a ridiculous notion," or something to that effect, and added that it would make the Union a "mere rope of sand." Now, sir, as the gentleman has not condescended to enter into any examination of the question, and has been satisfied with throwing the weight of his authority into the scale, I do not deem it necessary to do more than to throw into the opposite scale the authority on which South Carolina relies; and there, for the present, I am perfectly willing to leave the controversy. The South Carolina doctrine, that is to say, the doctrine contained in an exposition reported by a committee of the Legislature in December, 1828, and published by their authority, is the good old Republican doctrine of '98,—the doctrine of the celebrated "Virginia Resolutions" of that year, and of "Madison's Report" of '99. . . .

Sir, as to the doctrine that the federal government is the exclusive judge of the extent as well as the limitations of its powers, it seems to me to be utterly subversive of the sovereignty and independence of the States. It makes but little difference, in my estimation, whether Congress or the Supreme Court are invested with this power. If the federal government, in all or any of its departments, is to prescribe the limits of its own authority, and the States are bound to submit to the decision, and are not to be allowed to examine and decide for themselves when the barriers of the Constitution shall be overleaped, this is practically "a government without limitation of powers." The States are at once reduced to mere petty corporations, and the people are entirely at your mercy. I have but one word more to add. In all the efforts that have been made by South Carolina to resist the unconstitutional laws which Congress has extended over them, she has kept steadily in view the preservation of the Union by the only means by which she believes it can be long preserved,—a firm, manly, and steady resistance against usurpation. The measures of the federal government have, it is true, prostrated her interests, and will soon involve the whole South in irretrievable ruin. But even this evil, great as it is, is not the chief ground of our complaints. It is the principle involved in the contest, a principle which, substituting the discretion of Congress for the limitations of the Constitution, brings the States and the people to the feet of the federal government, and leaves them nothing they can call their own.

D. Webster's Second Reply

I spoke, sir, of the Ordinance of 1787, which prohibits slavery, in all future times, northwest of the Ohio, as a measure of great wisdom and foresight, and one which had been attended with highly beneficial and permanent consequences. I supposed that, on this point, no two gentlemen in the Senate could entertain different opinions. But the simple expression of this sentiment has led the gentleman not only into a labored defense of slavery, in the abstract and on principle, but also into a warm accusation against me, as having attacked the system of domestic slavery now existing in the Southern States. For all this there was not the slightest foundation in anything said or intimated by me. I did not utter a single word which any ingenuity could torture into an attack on the slavery of the South. I said only that it was highly wise and useful, in legislating for the Northwestern country while it was yet a wilderness, to prohibit the introduction of slaves; and added that I presumed there was no reflecting and intelligent person in the neighboring State of Kentucky who would doubt that, if the same prohibition had been extended at the same early period over that commonwealth, her strength and population would at this day have been far greater than they are. If these opinions be thought doubtful, they are nevertheless, I trust, neither extraordinary nor disrespectful. They attack nobody and menace nobody. And yet, sir, the gentleman's optics have discovered, even in the mere expression of this sentiment, what he calls the very spirit of the Missouri question! He represents me as making an onset on the whole South, and manifesting a spirit which would interfere with and disturb their domestic condition!

Sir, this injustice no otherwise surprises me than as it is committed here, and committed without the slightest pretense of ground for it. I say it only surprises me as being done here; for I know full well that it is and has been the settled policy of some persons in the South, for years, to represent the people of the North as disposed to interfere with them in their own exclusive and peculiar concerns. This is a delicate and sensitive point in Southern feeling; and of late years it has always been touched, and generally with effect, whenever the object has been to unite the whole South against Northern men or Northern measures. This feeling, always carefully kept alive, and maintained at too intense a heat to admit discrimination or reflection, is a lever of great power in our political machine. It moves vast bodies, and gives to them one and the same direction. But it is without adequate cause, and the suspicion which exists is wholly groundless. There is not, and never has been, a disposition in the North to interfere with these interests of the South. Such interference has never been supposed to be within the power of government; nor has it been in any way attempted. The slavery of the South has always been regarded as a matter of domestic policy left with the States themselves, and with which the federal government had nothing to do. Certainly, sir, I am, and ever have been, of that opinion. The gentleman, indeed, argues that slavery in the abstract is no evil. Most assuredly I need not say I differ with him altogether and most widely on that point. I regard domestic slavery as one of the greatest evils, both moral and political. But whether it be a malady, and whether it be curable, and, if so, by what means; or, on the other hand, whether it be the *vulnus immedicabile* of the social system, I leave it to those whose right and duty it is to inquire and to decide. And this I believe, sir, is, and uniformly has been, the sentiment of the North. . . .

On yet another point I was still more unaccountably misunderstood. The gentleman had harangued against "consolidation." I told him, in reply, that there was one kind of consolidation to which I was attached, and that was the consolidation of our Union; that this was precisely that consolidation to which I feared others were not attached, and that such consolidation was the very end of the Constitution, the leading object, as they had informed us themselves, which its framers had kept in view. . . .

I repeat, sir, that, in adopting the sentiment of the framers of the Constitution, I read their language audibly and word for word; and I pointed out the distinction, just as fully as I have now done, between the consolidation of the Union and that other obnoxious consolidation which I disclaimed. And yet the honorable member misunderstood me. The gentleman had said that he wished for no fixed revenue,—not a shilling. If by a word he could convert the Capitol into gold, he would not do it. Why all this fear of revenue? Why, sir, because, as the gentleman told us, it tends to consolidation. Now this can mean neither more nor less than that a common revenue is a common interest, and that all common interests tend to preserve the union of the States. I confess I like that tendency; if the gentleman dislikes it, he is right in deprecating a shilling of fixed revenue. So much, sir, for consolidation. . . .

Sir, let me recur to pleasing recollections; let me indulge in refreshing remembrance of the past; let me remind you that, in early times, no States cherished greater harmony, both of principle and feeling, than Massachusetts and South Carolina. Would to God that harmony might again return! Shoulder to shoulder they went through the Revolution; hand in hand they stood round the administration of Washington, and felt his own great arm lean on them for support. Unkind feeling, if it exist, alienation and distrust, are the growth, unnatural to such soils, of false principles since sown. They are weeds, the seeds of which that same great arm never scattered.

Mr. President, I shall enter on no encomium upon Massachusetts; she needs none. There she is. Behold her, and judge for yourselves. There is her history; the world knows it by heart. The past, at least, is secure. . . .

There yet remains to be performed, Mr. President, by far the most grave and important duty which I feel to be devolved on me by this occasion. It is to state and to defend what I conceive to be the true principles of the Constitution under which we are here assembled. . . .

I understand the honorable gentlemen from South Carolina to maintain that it is a right of the State legislatures to interfere whenever, in their judgment, this government transcends its constitutional limits, and to arrest the operation of its laws.

I understand him to maintain this right as a right existing under the Constitution, not as a right to overthrow it on the ground of extreme necessity, such as would justify violent revolution.

I understand him to maintain an authority, on the part of the States, thus to interfere for the purpose of correcting the exercise of power by the general government, of checking it, and of compelling it to conform to their opinion of the extent of its powers.

I understand him to maintain that the ultimate power of judging of the constitutional extent of its own authority is not lodged exclusively in the general government or any branch of it; but that, on the contrary, the States may lawfully decide for themselves, and each State for itself, whether, in a given case, the act of the general government transcends its power.

I understand him to insist that, if the exigency of the case, in the opinion of any State government, require it, such State government may, by its own sovereign authority, annul an act of the general government which it deems plainly and palpably unconstitutional.

This is the sum of what I understand from him to be the South Carolina doctrine, and the doctrine which he maintains. . . .

We, sir, who oppose the Carolina doctrine do not deny that the people may, if they choose, throw off any government when it becomes oppressive and intolerable, and erect a better in its stead. We all know that civil institutions are established for the public benefit, and that, when they cease to answer the ends of their existence, they may be changed. But I do not understand the doctrine now contended for to be that which, for the sake of distinctness, we may call the right of revolution. I understand the gentleman to maintain that without revolution, without civil commotion, without rebellion, a remedy for supposed abuse and transgression of the powers of the general government lies in a direct appeal to the interference of the State governments.

[Mr. HAYNE here rose and said: He did not contend for the mere right of revolution, but for the right of constitutional resistance. What he maintained was that, in case of a plain, palpable violation of the Constitution by the general government, a State may interpose, and that this interposition is constitutional.]

Mr. WEBSTER resumed:—

So, sir, I understood the gentleman, and am happy to find that I did not misunderstand him. What he contends for is, that it is constitutional to interrupt the administration of the Constitution itself, in the hands of those who are chosen and sworn to administer it, by the direct interference, in form of law, of the States, in virtue of their sovereign capacity.

The inherent right in the people to reform their government I do not deny; and they have another right, and that is, to resist unconstitutional laws without overturning the government. It is no doctrine of mine that unconstitutional laws bind the people. The great question is, Whose prerogative is it to decide on the constitutionality or unconstitutionality of the laws? On that, the main debate hinges.

The proposition that, in case of a supposed violation of the Constitution by Congress, the States have a constitutional right to interfere and annul the law of Congress, is the proposition of the gentleman. I do not admit it. If the gentleman had intended no more than to assert the right of revolution for justifiable cause, he would have said only what all agree to. But I cannot conceive that there can be a middle course between submission to the laws, when regularly pronounced constitutional, on the one hand, and open resistance, which is revolution or rebellion, on the other. I say the right of a State to annul a law of Congress cannot be maintained but on the ground of the inalienable right of man to resist oppression; that is to say, upon the ground of revolution. I admit that there is an ultimate violent remedy, above the Constitution and in defiance of the Constitution, which may be resorted to when a revolution is to be justified. But I do not admit that, under the Constitution and in conformity with it, there is any mode in which a State government, as a member of the Union, can interfere and stop the progress of the general government by force of her own laws, under any circumstances whatever.

This leads us to inquire into the origin of this government and the source of its power. Whose agent is it? Is it the creature of the State legislatures, or the creature of the people? If the government of the United States be the agent of the State governments, then they may control it, provided they can agree in the manner of controlling it; if it be the agent of the people, then the people alone can control it, restrain it, modify or reform it. It is observable enough that the doctrine for which the honorable gentleman contends leads him to the necessity of maintaining not only that this general government is the creature of the States, but that it is the creature of each of the States severally, so that each may assert the power for itself of determining whether it acts within the limits of its authority. It is the servant of four-and-twenty masters, of different wills and different purposes, and yet bound to obey all. This absurdity (for it seems no less) arises from a misconception as to the origin of this government and its true character. It is, sir, the people's Constitution, the people's government, made for the people, made by the people, and answerable to the people. The people of the United States have declared that this Constitution shall be the supreme law. We must either admit the proposition or dispute their authority. The States are unquestionably sovereign, so far as their sovereignty is not affected by this supreme law. But the State legislatures, as political bodies, however sovereign, are yet not sovereign over the people. So far as the people have given power to the general government, so far the grant is unquestionably good, and the government holds of the people, and not of the State governments. We are all agents of the same supreme power, the people. The general government and the State governments derive their authority from the same source. Neither can, in relation to the other, be called primary, though one is definite and restricted, and the other general and residuary. . . .

I must now beg to ask, sir, Whence is this supposed right of the States derived? Where do they find the power to interfere with the laws of the Union? Sir, the opinion which the honorable gentleman maintains is a notion founded in a total misapprehension, in my judgment, of the origin of this government, and of the foundation on which it stands. I hold it to be a popular government, erected by the people; those who administer it responsible to the people; and itself capable of being amended and modified, just as the people may choose it should be. It is as popular, just as truly emanating from the people, as the State governments. It is created for one purpose; the State governments for another. It has its own powers; they have theirs. There is no more authority with them to arrest the operation of a law of Congress than with Congress to arrest the operation of their laws. We are here to administer a Constitution emanating immediately from the people, and trusted by them to our administration. It is not the creature of the State governments. . . . No State law is to be valid which comes in conflict with the Constitution, or any law of the United States passed in pursuance of it. But who shall decide this question of interference? To whom lies the last appeal? This, sir, the Constitution itself decides also, by declaring *"that the judicial power shall extend to all cases arising under the Constitution and laws of the United States."* These two provisions cover the whole ground. They are, in truth, the keystone of the arch! With these it is a government; without them it is a confederation. In pursuance of these clear and express provisions, Congress established, at its very first session, in the judicial act, a mode for carrying them into full effect, and for bringing all questions of constitutional power to the final decision of the Supreme Court. It then, sir, became a government. It then had the means of self-protection; and but for this, it would, in all probability, have been now among things which are past. Having constituted the government and declared its powers, the people have further said that, since somebody must decide on the extent of these powers, the government shall itself decide; subject always, like other popular governments, to its responsibility to the people. . . .

For myself, sir, I do not admit the competency of South Carolina, or any other State, to prescribe my constitutional duty, or to settle, between me and the people, the validity of laws of Congress for which I have voted. I decline her umpirage. I have not sworn to support the Constitution according to her construction of its clauses. I have not stipulated, by my oath of office or otherwise, to come under any responsibility, except to the people, and those whom they have appointed to pass upon the question whether laws supported by my votes conform to the Constitution of the country. And, sir, if we look to the general nature of the case, could anything have been more preposterous than to make a government for the whole Union, and yet leave its powers subject, not to one interpretation, but to thirteen or twenty-four interpretations? Instead of one tribunal, established by all, responsible to all, with power to decide for all, shall constitutional questions be left to four-and-twenty popular bodies, each at liberty to decide for itself, and none bound to respect the decisions of others; and each at liberty, too, to give a new construction on every new election of its own members? Would anything with such a principle in it, or rather with such a destitution of all principle, be fit to be called a government? No, sir. It should not be denominated a Constitution. It should be called, rather, a collection of topics for everlasting controversy; heads of debate for a disputatious people. It would not be a government. It would not be adequate to any practical good, or fit for any country to live under. . . .

Mr. President, I have thus stated the reasons of my dissent to the doctrines which have been advanced and maintained. . . . I profess, sir, in my career hitherto, to have kept steadily in view the prosperity and honor of the whole country, and the preservation of our Federal Union. It is to that Union we owe our safety at home and our consideration and dignity abroad. It is to that Union that we are chiefly indebted for whatever makes us most proud of our country. That Union we reached only by the discipline of our virtues in the severe school of adversity. It had its origin in the necessities of disordered finance, prostrate commerce, and ruined credit. Under its benign influences these great interests immediately awoke as from the dead, and sprang forth with newness of life. Every year of its duration has teemed with fresh proofs of its utility and its blessings; and although our territory has stretched out wider and wider, and our population spread farther and farther, they have not outrun its protection or its benefits. It has been to us all a copious fountain of national, social, and personal happiness.

I have not allowed myself, sir, to look beyond the Union, to see what might lie hidden in the dark recess behind. I have not coolly weighed the chances of preserving liberty when the bonds that unite us together shall be broken asunder. I have not accustomed myself to hang over the precipice of disunion, to see whether, with my short sight, I can fathom the depth of the abyss below; nor could I regard him as a safe counselor in the affairs of this government whose thoughts should be mainly bent on considering, not how the Union may be best preserved, but how tolerable might be the condition of the people when it shall be broken up and destroyed. While the Union lasts, we have high, exciting, gratifying prospects spread out before us for us and our children. Beyond that

I seek not to penetrate the veil. God grant that in my day, at least, that curtain may not rise! God grant that on my vision never may be opened what lies behind! When my eyes shall be turned to behold for the last time the sun in heaven, may I not see him shining on the broken and dishonored fragments of a once glorious Union; on States dissevered, discordant, belligerent; on a land rent with civil feuds, or drenched, it may be, in fraternal blood! Let their last feeble and lingering glance rather behold the gorgeous ensign of the republic, now known and honored throughout the earth, still full high advanced, its arms and trophies streaming in their original lustre, not a stripe erased or polluted nor a single star obscured, bearing for its motto no such miserable interrogatory as "What is all this worth?" nor those other words of delusion and folly, "Liberty first and Union afterwards"; but everywhere, spread all over in characters of living light, blazing on all its ample folds, as they float over the sea and over the land, and in every wind under the whole heavens, that other sentiment, dear to every true American heart,—Liberty *and* Union, now and forever, one and inseparable!

26. The Jefferson Birthday Dinner

THE TARIFF of 1828—sometimes referred to as the Tariff of Abomina-
tions—sparked a sectional controversy between the North and the South
over the question of protection, the South contending that protection
was unconstitutional because it aided one section at the expense of
another. Immediately after the passage of the Tariff of 1828, John C.
Calhoun secretly wrote an Exposition and Protest for a South Carolina
legislative committee in which he argued the constitutional right of the
state to nullify the tariff laws of the country unless they were repealed.
This doctrine of nullification was reiterated in the Webster-Hayne debate. Jackson abhorred the doctrine, and although he subscribed to the
philosophy of states rights he rejected the notion that the states acting
on their own could block the execution of federal law. He was given the
opportunity of expressing his views on April 13, 1830 when the Democrats held a commemorative celebration to honor the birthday of
Thomas Jefferson. Since Jackson believed the nullifiers planned to use
the celebration to win support for their doctrine he made a point of at-

SOURCE: *United States Telegraph, April 15, 17, 20, 23, 1830.*

tending the dinner so he could inform the entire nation precisely where he stood. To Jackson, nullification meant disunion, and disunion meant treason.

A. "Our Federal Union: It Must Be Preserved"

The commemoration of the birth-day of the illustrious victory of freedom and benefactor of the United States, was every way worthy of the man and the cause. A greater collection of talent, worth, dignity and virtue, rarely if ever adorned a festive board. Free from all spirit of faction, (although differing in some minor measures) an immense concourse from every part of the Union, joined with the utmost cordiality and enthusiasm in celebrating the birth-day of him whom they loved while living, and honor when dead, whose political principles they adopt as their standard, and will follow as their surest guide for preserving human liberty, extending human happiness, sustaining the Constitution, and perpetuating the Union of these United States. . . .

The celebration was attended by the President of the United States, the Vice President, the Secretaries of State, Treasury, War, Navy, the Postmaster General, and more than a hundred republican members of the two Houses of Congress, together with most of the distinguished officers of the Army and Navy, civil officers of the Government, visitors in the city, and citizens of the District and neighboring cities—The President arrived at 5 o'clock, staid till 10, gave a patriotic toast, and retired.

There were twenty-four regular toasts, and many volunteers given, and in the intervening pauses there were several short, animated, and eloquent speeches delivered. . . .

The dinner was furnished by Mr. Jesse Brown, at the Indian Queen, and in a style unsurpassed for richness, variety, elegance and abundance. The hall was tastefully ornamented with beautiful evergreens; and amidst the freshness of the festoons was discovered a full length portrait of Washington, and two busts of Mr. Jefferson. The size and form of the room are admirably adapted to the accommodation of a large company, being wide enough for two parallel tables, and a cross table at the head, which promoted festivity and sociality, and prevented the dispersion which a single long table creates. . . .

The venerable patriot, the Hon. JOHN ROANE, of Virginia, officiated as President of the Day, assisted by the Hon. GEO. M. BIBB of

Ky.; Hon. LEVI WOODBURY, of New Hampshire; Hon. FELIX GRUNDY, of Tennessee; Hon. C. C. CAMBRELENG, of New York; Hon. WM. F. BORDON, of Va., and the Hon. Mr. OVERTON, of Louisiana, as Vice Presidents. The toasts and speeches are worthy of the distinguished individuals who were present, and the occasion which they are designed to commemorate. . . .

By the President of the United States. Our *Federal* Union: *It must be preserved.*

By the Vice President of the United States. The Union: Next to our liberty, the most dear; may we all remember that it can only be preserved by respecting the rights of the States and distributing equally the benefit and burden of the Union.

By Mr. Van Buren, Secretary of State. Mutual forbearance and reciprocal concession: Through their agency the Union was established. The patriotic spirit from which they emanated will forever sustain it.

By J. H. Eaton, Secretary at War. Public Men: The people will regard with warmest affection those who shall be found to act from principle. . . .

By Mr. Haynes, Chairman of the Committee of Arrangements. The *Union* of the States, and the *Sovereignty* of the States. . . .

The Intelligencer of yesterday, charges that the dinner of the 13th was a political dinner! Unable to condemn the political principles which it was intended to promote, or to censure any thing which appears in the proceedings themselves, we are gravely told that the Editors are not quite sure that the quotations from Mr. Jefferson's writings present his opinions!! Of the President's toast, the Intelligencer says: "We copy the toast just as we find it. The sentiment, which it conveys, is one which it would be very unnatural for a President of the United States not to entertain; but there is something *emphatic* in it, under the circumstances which preceded and attended it. It was as much as to say, in reply to the authors of some of the preceding sentiments. 'You may complain of the Tariff, and perhaps with reason; but so long as it is the law, it had as certainly be maintained, as that my name is ANDREW JACKSON. . . .' "

The President's toast was intended to speak to all parties. It calls as loudly upon the advocates of the tariff to relax unnecessary and oppressive restrictions, as it does on the South to submit with patience to the wholesome operations of public sentiment. . . . Is

THE JEFFERSON BIRTHDAY DINNER

not the Union to be preserved by a careful, a candid, and liberal compromise of interest—an equalization of the benefits and burdens of the Government? If then the present tariff does oppress one section of the country unfairly—if, by its operations, the burdens of Government are unequally distributed, every dictate of patriotism calls upon every citizen to preserve the Union by removing the inequalities, the existing causes of discontent. We are aware that a political party in the country are now endeavoring to revolutionize the Government under the auspices of the tariff. The word is, by some, supposed to have a talismanic effect. In the language of the President, we say that the Union is dearer to us than the tariff. If the South is unjustly oppressed, we would modify the tariff to relieve them from that oppression. Yet it is the duty of the South—it is the duty of all, to maintain that high regard for the Union which would sacrifice every thing short of liberty itself, to preserve it. Let our public men act out the principles of the President's toast. Let them approach the question with a determination to preserve the Union, and it will be preserved. . . .

B. "OLD HICKORY means what he says"

Georgetown, April 25, 1830

Calhoun's friends, by their impatience and intrigues, have done him much injury. Attempts have been made to commit members of Congress and officers of the government in his favor individually. The President believes, that they have been at the bottom of the persecution of Eaton with the view of placing one of themselves in his place. . . . The Jefferson dinner was turned into a piece of political management. The President told me himself that he should not have gone if he had understood it. He further told me that he meant his toast as a rebuke upon the seditious sentiments which were uttered in his presence, and complained bitterly of Green[1] for wilfully perverting it. He said he was a Jeffersonian Democrat, but that many sentiments uttered at the dinner were such as Jefferson abhorred. He could not hear the dissolution of the Union spoken of lightly, and he meant by his toast, that the

SOURCE: Amos Kendall to Francis P. Blair, April 25, 1830, Blair-Lee Papers, Princeton University Library.

1. Duff Green, editor of the United States Telegraph.

Federal Union must be preserved, *Tariff or no Tariff.* Indeed, he was so understood by all present, and I am told it operated as a powerful damper upon some of the Hotspurs, all of whom know that Old Hickory *means what he says.*

In the meantime, Van Buren glides along as smoothly as oil and as silently as a cat. If he is managing at all, it is so adroitly that nobody perceives it. He is evidently gaining from the indiscretions of Calhoun's friends. He has the entire confidence of the President and all his personal friends, while Calhoun is fast losing it. . . .

In fine, I think I perceive the elements of a new division of parties. On one side will be the democracy of the northern, middle, western and part of the southern states, who will go for reform in all the branches of the government, a gradual reduction of duties, so as to bring down the revenue to the proper wants of the government, the lopping off all *splendid appendages* to the government and amplifying its whole machinery, the abandonment of all pretensions to powers which necessarily create collisions with the states, and an honest and efficient administration of the powers which it is deemed constitutional and prudent to exercise.

On the other side, as surprising as it may now seem, I think you will find the previous anti-tariff men of the South and furious tariff men of the North with the corrupt portion of the late coalition party. Indeed, I should not be surprized to see some of the Southern leaders as hotly opposed to Gen. Jackson in a twelve month as the great northern leader is now.

27. Calhoun's Fort Hill Address

WITH HIS estrangement from Jackson virtually complete, Calhoun no longer tried to hide his views about nullification. His Exposition and Protest had been published anonymously in order to protect his position as Vice President and heir-apparent to the presidency. Now that his political fortunes had changed with the ascendency of Van Buren, Calhoun felt no compunction against admitting his political alignment with the nullifiers. Acting on the request of James Hamilton, Jr., the governor of South Carolina, he further elucidated the theoretical basis of

SOURCE: Richard K. Crallé, ed., *The Works of John C. Calhoun,* Volume VI (New York, 1851–56), pp. 59–76.

his doctrine in a statement dated July 26, 1831, and generally known as the "Fort Hill Address." This is the clearest and most cogent explanation of nullification.

The question of the relation which the States and General Government bear to each other is not one of recent origin. From the commencement of our system, it has divided public sentiment. Even in the Convention, while the Constitution was struggling into existence, there were two parties as to what this relation should be, whose different sentiments constituted no small impediment in forming that instrument. . . .

The great and leading principle is, that the General Government emanated from the people of the several States, forming distinct political communities, and acting in their separate and sovereign capacity, and not from all of the people forming one aggregate political community; that the Constitution of the United States is, in fact, a compact, to which each State is a party, in the character already described; and that the several States, or parties, have a right to judge of its infractions; and in case of a deliberate, palpable, and dangerous exercise of power not delegated, they have the right, in the last resort, to use the language of the Virginia Resolutions, "to interpose for arresting the progress of the evil, and for maintaining, within their respective limits, the authorities, rights, and liberties appertaining to them." . . .

It has been well said by one of the most sagacious men of antiquity, that the object of a constitution is, to *restrain the government, as that of laws* is to restain *individuals.* The remark is correct; nor is it less true where the government is vested in a majority, than where it is in a single or a few individuals—in a republic, than a monarchy or aristocracy. No one can have a higher respect for the maxim that the majority ought to govern than I have, taken in its proper sense, subject to the restrictions imposed by the Constitution, and confined to objects in which every portion of the community have similar interests; but it is a great error to suppose, as many do, that the right of a majority to govern is a natural and not a conventional right, and therefore absolute and unlimited. By nature, every individual has the right to govern himself; and governments, whether founded on majorities or minorities, must derive their right from the assent, expressed or implied, of the governed, and be subject to such limitations as they may impose. Where the interests are the same, that is, where the laws that may benefit one will benefit all, or the reverse, it is just and proper to place them under the control of the majority; but where they are dissimilar, so that the law that may benefit one portion may be ruinous to another, it would be, on the contrary, unjust and absurd to subject them to its will; and such I conceive to be the theory on which our Constitution rests.

That such dissimilarity of interests may exist, it is impossible to doubt. They are to be found in every community, in a greater or less degree, however small or homogeneous; and they constitute every where the great difficulty of forming and preserving free institutions. To guard against the unequal action of the laws, when applied to dissimilar and opposing interests, is, in fact, what mainly renders a constitution indispensable; to overlook which, in reasoning on our Constitution, would be to omit the principal element by which to determine its character. Were there no contrariety of interests, nothing would be more simple and easy than to form and preserve free institutions. The right of suffrage alone would be a sufficient guarantee. It is the conflict of opposing interests which renders it the most difficult work of man. . . .

Happily for us, we have no artificial and separate classes of society. We have wisely exploded all such distinctions; but we are not, on that account, exempt from all contrariety of interests, as the present distracted and dangerous condition of our country, unfortunately, but too clearly proves. With us they are almost exclusively geographical, resulting mainly from difference of climate, soil, situation, industry, and production; but are not, therefore, less necessary to be protected by an adequate constitutional provision, than where the distinct interests exist in separate classes. The necessity is, in truth, greater, as such separate and dissimilar geographical interests are more liable to come into conflict, and more dangerous, when in that state, than those of any other description: so much so, that *ours is the first instance on record where they have not formed, in an extensive territory, separate and independent communities, or subjected the whole to despotic sway.* That such may not be our unhappy fate also, must be the sincere prayer of every lover of his country. . . .

The question is new, when applied to our peculiar political organization, where the separate and conflicting interests of society are represented by distinct but connected governments; but it is, in reality, an old question under a new form, long since perfectly solved. Whenever separate and dissimilar interests have been separately represented in any government; whenever the sovereign power has been divided in its exercise, the experience and wisdom of ages have devised but one mode by which such political organization can be preserved,—the mode adopted in England, and by all governments, ancient and modern, blessed with constitutions deserving to be called free,—to give to each co-estate the right to judge of its powers, with a negative or veto on the acts of the others, in order to protect against encroachments the interests it particularly represents: a principle which all of our constitutions recognize in the distribution of power among their respective departments, as essential to maintain the independence of each; but which, to all who will duly reflect on the subject, must appear far more essential, for the same object, in that great and fundamental distribution of powers between the General and State Governments. . . .

Should the General Government and a State come into conflict, we have a higher remedy: the power which called the General Government into existence, which gave it all its authority, and can enlarge, contract, or abolish its powers at its pleasure, may be invoked. The States themselves may be appealed to,—three fourths of which, in fact, form a power, whose decrees are the Constitution itself, and whose voice can silence all discontent. The utmost extent, then, of the power is, that a State, acting in its sovereign capacity as one of the parties to the constitutional compact, may compel the Government, created by that compact, to submit a question touching its infraction, to the parties who created it; to avoid the supposed dangers of which, it is proposed to resort to the novel, the hazardous, and, I must add, fatal project of giving to the General Government the sole and final right of interpreting the Constitution;—thereby reversing the whole system, making that instrument the creature of its will, instead of a rule of action impressed on it at its creation, and annihilating, in fact, the authority which imposed it, and from which the Government itself derives its existence.

That such would be the result, were the right in question vested in the Legislative or Executive branch of the Government, is conceded by all. No one has been so hardy as to assert that Congress or the President ought to have the right, or deny that, if vested finally and exclusively in either, the consequences which I have stated would necessarily follow; but its advocates have been reconciled to the doctrine, on the supposition that there is one department of the General Government which, from it peculiar organization, affords an independent tribunal, through which the Government may exercise the high authority which is the subject of consideration, with perfect safety to all.

I yield, I trust, to few in my attachment to the Judiciary Department. I am fully sensible of its importance, and would maintain it, to the fullest extent, in its constitutional powers and independence; but it is impossible for me to believe it was ever intended by the Constitution that it should exercise the power in question, or that it is competent to do so; and, if it were, that it would be a safe depository of the power.

Its powers are judicial, and not political; and are expressly confined by the Constitution "to all cases in law and equity arising under this Constitution, the laws of the United States, and the treaties made, or which shall be made, under its authority"; and which I have high authority in asserting excludes political questions, and comprehends those only where there are parties amenable to the process of the court. Nor is its incompetency less clear than its want of constitutional authority. There may be many, and the most dangerous infractions on the part of Congress, of which, it is conceded by all, the court, as a judicial tribunal, cannot, from its nature, take cognizance. The Tariff itself is a strong case in point; and the reason applies equally *to all others where Congress pervert a power from an object intended, to one not intended, the most insidious and dangerous of all infractions; and which may be extended to all of its powers, more especially to the taxing and appropriating.* But, supposing it competent to take cognizance of all infractions of every description, the insuperable objection still remains, that it would not be a safe tribunal to exercise the power in question.

It is a universal and fundamental political principle, that the power to protect can safely be confided only to those interested in protecting, or their responsible agents,—a maxim not less true in private than in public affairs. The danger in our system is, that the General Government, which represents the interests of the whole, may encroach on the States, which represent the peculiar and local interests, or that the latter may encroach on the former.

In examining this point, we ought not to forget that the Government, through all its departments, judicial as well as others, is administered by delegated and responsible agents; and that the *power which really controls, ultimately, all the movements, is not in the agents, but those who elect or appoint them.* To understand, then, its real character, and what would be the action of the system in any supposable case, we must raise our view from the mere agents to this high controlling power, which finally impels every movement of the machine. By doing so, we shall find all under the control of the will of a majority, compounded of the majority of the States, taken as political bodies, and the majority of the people of the States, estimated in federal numbers. These, united, constitute the real and final power which impels and directs the movements of the General Government. The majority of the States elect the majority of the Senate; of the people of the States, that of the House of Representatives; the two united, the President; and the President and a majority of the Senate appoint the judges: a majority of whom, and a majority of the Senate and House, with the President, really exercise all the powers of the Government, with the exception of the cases where the Constitution requires a greater number than a majority. The judges are, in fact, as truly the judicial representatives of this united majority, as the majority of Congress itself, or the President, is its legislative or executive representative; and to confide the power to the Judiciary to determine finally and conclusively what powers are delegated and what reserved, would be, in reality, to confide it to the majority, whose agents they are, and by whom they can be controlled in various ways; and, of course, to subject (against the fundamental principle of our system and all sound political reasoning) the reserved powers of the States, with all the local and peculiar interests they were intended to protect, to the will of the very majority against which the protection was intended. Nor will the tenure by which the judges hold their office, however valuable the provision in many other respects, materially vary the case. Its highest possible effect would be to *retard*, and not *finally* to *resist*, the will of a dominant majority. . . .

Against these conclusive arguments, as they seem to me, it is objected that, if one of the parties has the right to judge of infractions of the Constitution, so has the other; and that, consequently, in cases of contested powers between a State and the General

Government, each would have a right to maintain its opinion, as is the case when sovereign powers differ in the construction of treaties or compacts; and that, of course, it would come to be a mere question of force. The error is in the assumption that the General Government is a party to the constitutional compact. The States, as has been shown, formed the compact, acting as sovereign and independent communities. The General Government is but its creature; and though, in reality, a government, with all the rights and authority which belong to any other government, within the orbit of its powers, it is, nevertheless, a government emanating from a compact between sovereigns, and partaking, in its nature and object, of the character of a joint commission, appointed to superintend and administer the interests in which all are jointly concerned; but having, beyond its proper sphere, no more power than if it did not exist. To deny this would be to deny the most incontestable facts and the clearest conclusions; while to acknowledge its truth is, to destroy utterly the objection that the appeal would be to force, in the case supposed. For, if each party has a right to judge, then, under our system of government, the final cognizance of a question of contested power would be in the States, and not in the General Government. It would be the duty of the latter, as in all similar cases of a contest between one or more of the principals and a joint commission or agency, to refer the contest to the principals themselves. Such are the plain dictates of both reason and analogy. On no sound principle can the agents have a right to final cognizance, as against the principals, much less to use force against them to maintain their construction of their powers. Such a right would be monstrous, and has never, heretofore, been claimed in similar cases. . . .

It is thus that our Constitution, by authorizing amendments, and by prescribing the authority and mode of making them, has, by a simple contrivance, with its characteristic wisdom, provided a power which, in the last resort, supersedes effectually the necessity, and even the pretext for force: a power to which none can fairly object; with which the interests of all are safe; which can definitively close all controversies in the only effectual mode, by freeing the compact of every defect and uncertainty, by an amendment of the instrument itself. It is impossible for human wisdom, in a system like ours, to devise another mode which shall be safe and effectual, and, at the same time, consistent with what are the relations and acknowledged powers of the two great departments of our Government. It gives a beauty and security peculiar to our system, which, if duly appreciated, will transmit its blessings to the remotest generations; but, if not, our splendid anticipations of the future will prove but an empty dream. Stripped of all its covering, the naked question is, whether ours is a federal or a consolidated government; a constitutional or absolute one; a government resting ultimately on the solid basis of the sovereignty of the States or on the unrestrained will of a majority; a form of government, as in all other unlimited ones, in which injustice, and violence, and force must finally prevail. *Let it never be forgotten that, where the majority rules without restriction, the minority is the subject;* and that, if we should absurdly attribute to the former the exclusive right of construing the Constitution, there would be, in fact, between the sovereign and subject, under such a government, no Constitution, or, at least, nothing deserving the name, or serving the legitimate object of so sacred an instrument.

How the States are to exercise this high power of interposition, which constitutes so essential a portion of their reserved rights that it *cannot be delegated without an entire surrender of their sovereignty,* and converting our system from a *federal* into a *consolidated* Government, is a question that the States only are competent to determine. The arguments which prove that they possess the power, equally prove that they are, in the language of Jefferson, "*the rightful judges of the mode and measure of redress.*" But the spirit of forbearance, as well as the nature of the right itself, forbids a recourse to it, except in cases of dangerous infractions of the Constitution; and then only in the last resort, when all reasonable hope of relief from the ordinary action of the Government has failed; when, if the right to interpose did not exist, the alternative would be submission and oppression on one side, or resistance by force on the other. That our system should afford, in such extreme cases, an intermediate point between these dire alternatives, by which the Government may be brought to a pause, and thereby an interval obtained to compromise differences, or, if impracticable, be compelled to submit the question to a constitutional adjustment, through an appeal to the States themselves, is an evidence of its high wisdom: an element not, as is supposed by some, of weakness, but of strength; not of anarchy or revolution, but of peace and safety. *Its general recognition would of itself, in a great measure, if not altogether, supersede the necessity of its exercise, by impressing on the movements of the Government that* moderation and justice so essential to harmony and peace, in a country of such vast extent and diversity of interests as ours; and would, if controversy should come, turn the resentment of the aggrieved from the system to those who had abused its powers (a point all-important), and cause them to seek redress, *not in revolution or overthrow, but in reformation.* It is, in fact, properly understood, a substitute,—where the alternative would be force,—tending to prevent, and, if that fails, to correct peaceably the aberrations to which all systems are liable, and which, if permitted to accumulate without correction, must finally end in a general catastrophe. . . .

28. South Carolina's Ordinance of Nullification

THE PASSAGE of a new tariff of 1832 convinced South Carolina nullifiers of the necessity of radical action, although there were other causes for their decision such as their growing concern over the future of slavery in view of abolitionist attacks and repeated Negro uprisings. During the presidential election of 1832 the nullifiers won a two-thirds legislative majority in South Carolina whereupon Governor James Hamilton summoned a special session of the legislature which in turn called for a convention to meet at Columbia on November 19, 1832. By a vote of 136 to 26 the convention adopted an Ordinance of Nullification which brought the state in direct confrontation with the federal government.

To Nullify certain Acts of the Congress of the United States, purporting to be Laws laying Duties and Imposts on the Importation of Foreign Commodities.

Whereas, the Congress of the United States, by various acts, purporting to be acts laying duties and imposts on foreign imports, but in reality intended for the protection of domestic manufactures, and the giving of bounties to classes and individuals engaged in particular employments, at the expense and to the injury and oppression of other classes and individuals, and by wholly exempting from taxation, certain foreign commodities, such as are not produced or manufactured in the United States, to afford a pretext for imposing higher and excessive duties on articles similar to those

SOURCE: *State Papers on Nullification* (Boston, 1834), pp. 29–31.

intended to be protected, hath exceeded its just powers under the Constitution, which confers on it no authority to afford such protection, and hath violated the true meaning and intent of the Constitution, which provides for equality in imposing the burdens of taxation upon the several States and portions of the Confederacy;—And, whereas, the said Congress, exceeding its just power to impose taxes and collect revenue for the purpose of effecting and accomplishing the specific objects and purposes which the Constitution of the United States authorizes it to effect and accomplish, hath raised and collected unnecessary revenue, for objects unauthorized by the Constitution;

We, therefore, the people of the State of South Carolina, in Convention assembled, do declare and ordain, and it is hereby declared and ordained, that the several acts and parts of acts of the Congress of the United States, purporting to be laws for the imposing of duties and imposts on the importation of foreign commodities, and now having actual operation and effect within the United States, and more especially an act entitled "an act in alteration of the several acts imposing duties on imports," approved on the nineteenth day of May, one thousand eight hundred and twenty-eight, and also an act entitled "an act to alter and amend the several acts imposing duties on imports," approved on the fourteenth day of July, one thousand eight hundred and thirty-two, are unauthorized by the Constitution of the United States, and violate the true meaning and intent thereof, and are null, void, and no law, nor binding upon this State, its officers or citizens; and all promises, contracts, and obligations made or entered into, or to be made or entered into with purpose to secure the duties imposed by the said acts, and all judicial proceedings which shall be hereafter had in affirmance thereof, are and shall be held utterly null and void.

And it is further ordained, That it shall not be lawful for any of the constituted authorities, whether of this State, or of the United States, to enforce the payment of duties imposed by the said acts within the limits of this State; but it shall be the duty of the Legislature to adopt such measures, and pass such acts as may be necessary to give full effect to this ordinance, and to prevent the enforcement and arrest of the operation of the said acts and parts of acts of the Congress of the United States, within the limits of this State, from and after the first day of February next, and the duty of all other constituted authorities, and all persons residing or being within the limits of this State, and they are hereby required and enjoined to obey and give effect to this Ordinance, and such acts and measures of the Legislature as may be passed or adopted in obedience thereto.

And it is further ordained, That in no case of law or equity, decided in the Courts of this State, wherein shall be drawn in question the authority of this Ordinance, or the validity of such act or acts of the Legislature as may be passed for the purpose of giving effect thereto, or the validity of the aforesaid acts of Congress, imposing duties, shall any appeal be taken or allowed to the Supreme Court of the United States, nor shall any copy of the record be permitted or allowed for that purpose; and if any such appeal shall be attempted to be taken, the Courts of this State, shall proceed to execute and enforce their judgments, according to the laws and usages of the State, without reference to such attempted appeal, and the person or persons attempting to take such appeal may be dealt with as for a contempt of the Court.

And it is further ordained, That all persons now holding any office of honor, profit or trust, civil or military, under this State (members of the Legislature excepted) shall, within such time and in such manner as the Legislature shall prescribe, take an oath, well and truly to obey, execute and enforce this Ordinance and such act or acts of the Legislature as may be passed in pursuance thereof, according to the true intent and meaning of the same; and, on the neglect or omission of any such person or persons so to do, his or their office or offices shall be forthwith vacated, and shall be filled up, as if such person or persons were dead, or had resigned; and no person hereafter elected to any office of honor, profit or trust, civil or military (members of the Legislature excepted) shall, until the Legislature shall otherwise provide and direct, enter on the execution of his office, or be in any respect competent to discharge the duties thereof, until he shall, in like manner, have taken a similar oath; and no juror shall be impannelled in any of the Courts of this State, in any cause in which shall be in question this Ordinance, or any act of the Legislature passed in pursuance thercof, unless he shall first, in addition to the usual oath, have taken an oath that he will well and truly obey, execute, and enforce this Ordinance, and such act or acts of the Legislature, as may be passed to carry the same into operation and effect, according to the true intent and meaning thereof.

And we, the people of South Carolina, to the end that it may be fully understood by the Government of the United States, and the people of the co-States, that we are determined to maintain this, our Ordinance and declaration, at every hazard, do further declare that we will not submit to the application of force, on the part of the Federal Government, to reduce this State to obedience; but that we will consider the passage by Congress, of any act authorizing the employment of a military or naval force against the State of South Carolina, her constituted authorities or citizens,—or any act, abolishing or closing the ports of this State, or any of them, or otherwise obstructing the free ingress and egress of vessels to and from the said ports,—or any other act on the part of the Federal Government, to coerce the State, shut up her ports, destroy or harass her commerce, or to enforce the acts hereby declared to be null and void, otherwise than through the civil tribunals of the country, as inconsistent with the longer continuance of South Carolina in the Union; and that the people of this State will thenceforth hold themselves absolved from all further obligation to maintain or preserve their political connexion with the people of the other States, and will forthwith proceed to organize a separate Government, and do all other acts and things which sovereign and independent States may of right do.

Done in Convention, at Columbia, the twenty-fourth day of November, in the year of our Lord, one thousand eight hundred and thirty-two, and in the fifty-seventh year of the Declaration of the Independence of the United States of America.

JAMES HAMILTON, JUN., *President of the Convention,*
and Delegate from St. Peters

29. Jackson's Nullification Proclamation

JACKSON *moved decisively against the nullifiers. He transported troops to the federal forts in Charleston harbor, moved arms and ammunition a short distance away in North Carolina, ordered General Winfield Scott to take command in South Carolina and encouraged Unionists within the rebellious state. Withal he proceeded cautiously, trying to be conciliatory; at the same time he clearly indicated that he would not permit*

SOURCE: James D. Richardson, *Message and Papers,* II: 1204–8, 1210–13, 1215, 1217–19.

the humiliation of the country or the violation of its laws. On Decem-
ber 10, 1832, he spoke directly to the people of South Carolina through
his Nullification Proclamation. Although he blended words of warning
with entreaty, he categorically rejected nullification and secession. Much
of the message was the work of Secretary of State Edward Livingston,
particularly in its exposition of the constitutional argument, but the
tone and determination in it was pure Jackson.

To preserve this bond of our political existence from destruction, to maintain inviolate this state of national honor and prosperity, and to justify the confidence my fellow-citizens have reposed in me, I, Andrew Jackson, President of the United States, have thought proper to issue this my proclamation, stating my views of the Constitution and laws applicable to the measures adopted by the convention of South Carolina and to the reasons they have put forth to sustain them, declaring the course which duty will require me to pursue, and, appealing to the understanding and patriotism of the people, warn them of the consequences that must inevitably result from an observance of the dictates of the convention. . . .

The ordinance is founded, not on the indefeasible right of resisting acts which are plainly unconstitutional and too oppressive to be endured, but on the strange position that any one State may not only declare an act of Congress void, but prohibit its execution; that they may do this consistently with the Constitution; that the true construction of that instrument permits a State to retain its place in the Union and yet be bound by no other of its laws than those it may choose to consider as constitutional. It is true, they add, that to justify this abrogation of a law it must be palpably contrary to the Constitution; but it is evident that to give the right of resisting laws of that description, coupled with the uncontrolled right to decide what laws deserve that character, is to give the power of resisting all laws; for as by the theory there is no appeal, the reasons alleged by the State, good or bad, must prevail. . . . But reasoning on this subject is superfluous when our social compact, in express terms, declares that the laws of the United States, its Constitution, and treaties made under it are the supreme law of the land, and, for greater caution, adds "that the judges in every State shall be bound thereby, anything in the constitution or laws of any State to the contrary notwithstanding." And it may be asserted without fear of refutation that no federative government could exist without a similar provision. Look for a moment to the

consequence. If South Carolina considers the revenue laws unconstitutional and has a right to prevent their execution in the port of
Charleston, there would be a clear constitutional objection to their
collection in every other port; and no revenue could be collected
anywhere, for all imposts must be equal. It is no answer to repeat
that an unconstitutional law is no law so long as the question of its
legality is to be decided by the State itself, for every law operating
injuriously upon any local interest will be perhaps thought, and
certainly represented, as unconstitutional, and, as has been shown,
there is no appeal. . . .

I consider, then, the power to annul a law of the United States,
assumed by one State, *incompatible with the existence of the
Union, contradicted expressly by the letter of the Constitution,
unauthorized by its spirit, inconsistent with every principle on
which it was founded, and destructive of the great object for which
it was formed.*

After this general view of the leading principle, we must examine
the particular application of it which is made in the ordinance.

The preamble rests its justification on these grounds: It assumes
as a fact that the obnoxious laws, although they purport to be laws
for raising revenue, were in reality intended for the protection of
manufactures, which purpose it asserts to be unconstitutional; that
the operation of these laws is unequal; that the amount raised by
them is greater than is required by the wants of the Government;
and, finally, that the proceeds are to be applied to objects unauthorized by the Constitution. These are the only causes alleged
to justify an open opposition to the laws of the country and a
threat of seceding from the Union if any attempt should be made
to enforce them. The first virtually acknowledges that the law in
question was passed under a power expressly given by the Constitution to lay and collect imposts; but its constitutionality is drawn in
question from the *motives* of those who passed it. However apparent this purpose may be in the present case, nothing can be
more dangerous than to admit the position that an unconstitutional purpose entertained by the members who assent to a law
enacted under a constitutional power shall make that law void. For
how is that purpose to be ascertained? Who is to make the
scrutiny? How often may bad purposes be falsely imputed, in how
many cases are they concealed by false professions, in how many is
no declaration of motive made? Admit this doctrine, and you give

to the States an uncontrolled right to decide, and every law may be annulled under this pretext. If, therefore, the absurd and dangerous doctrine should be admitted that a State may annul an unconstitutional law, or one that it deems such, it will not apply to the present case.

The next objection is that the laws in question operate unequally. This objection may be made with truth to every law that has been or can be passed. The wisdom of man never yet contrived a system of taxation that would operate with perfect equality. If the unequal operation of a law makes it unconstitutional, and if all laws of that description may be abrogated by any State for that cause, then, indeed, is the Federal Constitution unworthy of the slightest effort for its preservation. We have hitherto relied on it as the perpetual bond of our Union; we have received it as the work of the assembled wisdom of the nation; we have trusted to it as to the sheet anchor of our safety in the stormy times of conflict with a foreign or domestic foe; we have looked to it with sacred awe as the palladium of our liberties, and with all the solemnities of religion have pledged to each other our lives and fortunes here and our hopes of happiness hereafter in its defense and support. Were we mistaken, my countrymen, in attaching this importance to the Constitution of our country? Was our devotion paid to the wretched, inefficient, clumsy contrivance which this new doctrine would make it? Did we pledge ourselves to the support of an airy nothing—a bubble that must be blown away by the first breath of disaffection? Was this self-destroying, visionary theory the work of the profound statesmen, the exalted patriots, to whom the task of constitutional reform was intrusted? Did the name of Washington sanction, did the States deliberately ratify, such an anomaly in the history of fundamental legislation? No; we were not mistaken. The letter of this great instrument is free from this radical fault. Its language directly contradicts the imputation; its spirit, its evident intent, contradicts it. No; we did not err. Our Constitution does not contain the absurdity of giving power to make laws and another to resist them. The sages whose memory will always be reverenced have given us a practical and, as they hoped, a permanent constitutional compact. . . .

The Constitution declares that the judicial powers of the United States extend to cases arising under the laws of the United States, and that such laws, the Constitution, and treaties shall be paramount to the State constitutions and laws. The judiciary act prescribes the mode by which the case may be brought before a court of the United States by appeal when a State tribunal shall decide against this provision of the Constitution. The ordinance declares there shall be no appeal—makes the State law paramount to the Constitution and laws of the United States, forces judges and jurors to swear that they will disregard their provisions, and even makes it penal in a suitor to attempt relief by appeal. It further declares that it shall not be lawful for the authorities of the United States or of that State to enforce the payment of duties imposed by the revenue laws within its limits.

Here is a law of the United States, not even pretended to be unconstitutional, repealed by the authority of a small majority of the voters of a single State. Here is a provision of the Constitution which is solemnly abrogated by the same authority.

On such expositions and reasonings the ordinance grounds not only an assertion of the right to annul the laws of which it complains, but to enforce it by a threat of seceding from the Union if any attempt is made to execute them.

This right to secede is deduced from the nature of the Constitution, which, they say, is a compact between sovereign States who have preserved their whole sovereignty and therefore are subject to no superior; that because they made the compact they can break it when in their opinion it has been departed from by the other States. Fallacious as this course of reasoning is, it enlists State pride and finds advocates in the honest prejudices of those who have not studied the nature of our Government sufficiently to see the radical error on which it rests.

The people of the United States formed the Constitution, acting through the State legislatures in making the compact, to meet and discuss its provisions, and acting in separate conventions when they ratified those provisions; but the terms used in its construction show it to be a Government in which the people of all the States, collectively, are represented. We are one people in the choice of President and Vice-President. Here the States have no other agency than to direct the mode in which the votes shall be given. The candidates having the majority of all the votes are chosen. The electors of a majority of States may have given their votes for one candidate, and yet another may be chosen. The people, then, and not the States, are represented in the executive branch. . . .

The Constitution of the United States, then, forms a *government*, not a league; and whether it be formed by compact between the States or in any other manner, its character is the same. It is a Government in which all the people are represented, which operates directly on the people individually, not upon the States; they retained all the power they did not grant. But each State, having expressly parted with so many powers as to constitute, jointly with the other States, a single nation, can not, from that period, possess any right to secede, because such secession does not break a league, but destroys the unity of a nation; and any injury to that unity is not only a breach which would result from the contravention of a compact, but it is an offense against the whole Union. To say that any State may at pleasure secede from the Union is to say that the United States are not a nation, because it would be a solecism to contend that any part of a nation might dissolve its connection with the other parts, to their injury or ruin, without committing any offense. Secession, like any other revolutionary act, may be morally justified by the extremity of oppression; but to call it a constitutional right is confounding the meaning of terms, and can only be done through gross error or to deceive those who are willing to assert a right, but would pause before they made a revolution or incur the penalties consequent on a failure.

Because the Union was formed by a compact, it is said the parties to that compact may, when they feel themselves aggrieved, depart from it; but it is precisely because it is a compact that they can not. A compact is an agreement or binding obligation. It may by its terms have a sanction or penalty for its breach, or it may not. If it contains no sanction, it may be broken with no other consequence than moral guilt; if it have a sanction, then the breach incurs the designated or implied penalty. A league between independent nations generally has no sanction other than a moral one; or if it should contain a penalty, as there is no common superior it can not be enforced. A government, on the contrary, always has a sanction, express or implied; and in our case it is both necessarily implied and expressly given. An attempt, by force of arms, to destroy a government is an offense, by whatever means the constitutional compact may have been formed; and such government has the right by the law of self-defense to pass acts for punishing the offender, unless that right is modified, restrained, or resumed by the constitutional act. In our system, although it is modified in the case of treason, yet authority is expressly given to pass all laws necessary to carry its powers into effect, and under this grant provision has been made for punishing acts which obstruct the due administration of the laws. . . .

The States severally have not retained their entire sovereignty. It has been shown that in becoming parts of a nation, not members of a league, they surrendered many of their essential parts of sovereignty. The right to make treaties, declare war, levy taxes, exercise exclusive judicial and legislative powers, were all of them functions of sovereign power. The States, then, for all these important purposes were no longer sovereign. The allegiance of their citizens was transferred, in the first instance, to the Government of the United States; they became American citizens and owed obedience to the Constitution of the United States and to laws made in conformity with the powers it vested in Congress. This last position has not been and can not be denied. How, then, can that State be said to be sovereign and independent whose citizens owe obedience to laws not made by it and whose magistrates are sworn to disregard those laws when they come in conflict with those passed by another? What shows conclusively that the States can not be said to have reserved an undivided sovereignty is that they expressly ceded the right to punish treason—not treason against their separate power, but treason against the United States. Treason is an offense against *sovereignty*, and sovereignty must reside with the power to punish it. . . .

This, then, is the position in which we stand: A small majority of the citizens of one State in the Union have elected delegates to a State convention; that convention has ordained that all the revenue laws of the United States must be repealed, or that they are no longer a member of the Union. The governor of that State has recommended to the legislature the raising of an army to carry the secession into effect, and that he may be empowered to give clearances to vessels in the name of the State. No act of violent opposition to the laws has yet been committed, but such a state of things is hourly apprehended. And it is the intent of this instrument to *proclaim*, not only that the duty imposed on me by the Constitution "to take care that the laws be faithfully executed" shall be performed to the extent of the powers already vested in me by law, or of such others as the wisdom of Congress shall devise and intrust to me for that purpose, but to warn the citizens of South Carolina who have been deluded into an opposition to the laws of the danger they will incur by obedience to the illegal and disorganizing ordinance of the convention; to exhort those who have refused to support it to persevere in their determination to uphold the Constitution and laws of their country; and to point out to all the perilous situation into which the good people of that State have been led, and that the course they are urged to pursue is one of ruin and disgrace to the very State whose rights they affect to support.

Fellow-citizens of my native State, let me not only admonish you, as the First Magistrate of our common country, not to incur the penalty of its laws, but use the influence that a father would over his children whom he saw rushing to certain ruin. In that paternal language, with that paternal feeling, let me tell you, my countrymen, that you are deluded by men who are either deceived themselves or wish to deceive you. Mark under what pretenses you have been led on to the brink of insurrection and treason on which you stand. . . .

I have urged you to look back to the means that were used to hurry you on to the position you have now assumed and forward to the consequences it will produce. Something more is necessary. Contemplate the condition of that country of which you still form an important part. Consider its Government, uniting in one bond of common interest and general protection so many different States, giving to all their inhabitants the proud title of *American citizen*, protecting their commerce, securing their literature and their arts, facilitating their intercommunication, defending their frontiers, and making their name respected in the remotest parts of the earth. Consider the extent of its territory, its increasing and happy population, its advance in arts which render life agreeable, and the sciences which elevate the mind! See education spreading the lights of religion, morality, and general information into every cottage in this wide extent of our Territories and States. Behold it as the asylum where the wretched and the oppressed find a refuge and support. Look on this picture of happiness and honor and say, *We too are citizens of America.* Carolina is one of these proud States; her arms have defended, her best blood has cemented, this happy Union. And then add, if you can, without horror and remorse, This happy Union we will dissolve; this picture of peace and prosperity we will deface; this free intercourse we will interrupt; these fertile fields we will deluge with blood; the protection of that glorious flag we renounce; the very name of Americans we discard. . . . The laws of the United States must be executed. I have no discretionary power on the subject; my duty is emphatically pronounced in the Constitution. Those who told you that you might peaceably prevent their execution deceived you; they could not have been deceived themselves. They know that a forcible opposition could alone prevent the execution of the laws, and they know that such opposition must be repelled. Their object is disunion. But be not deceived by names. Disunion by armed force is *treason*. Are you really ready to incur its guilt? If you are, on the heads of the instigators of the act be the dreadful consequences; on their heads be the dishonor, but on yours may fall the punishment. On your unhappy State will inevitably fall all the evils of the conflict you force upon the Government of your country. . . .

Fellow-citizens, the momentous case is before you. On your undivided support of your Government depends the decision of the great question it involves—whether your sacred Union will be preserved and the blessing it secures to us as one people shall be perpetuated. No one can doubt that the unanimity with which that decision will be expressed will be such as to inspire new confidence in republican institutions, and that the prudence, the wisdom, and the courage which it will bring to their defense will transmit them unimpaired and invigorated to our children.

May the Great Ruler of Nations grant that the signal blessings with which He has favored ours may not, by the madness of party or personal ambition, be disregarded and lost; and may His wise providence bring those who have produced this crisis to see the folly before they feel the misery of civil strife, and inspire a returning veneration for that Union which, if we may dare to penetrate His designs, He has chosen as the only means of attaining the high destinies to which we may reasonably aspire. . . .

30. Governor Hayne's Proclamation

To STRENGTHEN *South Carolina's position in Congress, the legislature of the state elected John C. Calhoun to replace Robert Y. Hayne in the Senate. Two days earlier it had elected Hayne as governor, in part because he was considered less radical than his predecessor, James Hamil-*

SOURCE: *Senate Documents,* 22d Congress, 1st session, document # 13, serial 230.

ton, Jr. On December 20, 1832, Hayne issued his Proclamation in response to the legislature's request and in reply to Jackson's Nullification
Proclamation in which he stated South Carolina's constitutional position. He also chided Jackson about obeying the law, as the President
himself had recently refused to execute the order of the Supreme Court
in the case involving Georgia's jurisdiction over the Cherokee Indians.

Whereas the President of the United States hath issued his
proclamation . . .

And whereas the Legislature of South Carolina . . . has
adopted a preamble and resolution to the following effect, viz.

"Whereas, the President of the United States has issued his
proclamation, denouncing the proceedings of this State, calling
upon the citizens thereof to renounce their primary allegiance, and
threatening them with military coercion, unwarranted by the Constitution, and utterly inconsistent with the existence of a free
State: Be it, therefore,

Resolved, That his Excellency the Governor be requested, forthwith, to issue his proclamation, warning the good people of this
State against the attempt of the President of the United States to
seduce them from their allegiance, exhorting them to disregard his
vain menaces, and to be prepared to sustain the dignity, and protect the liberty of the State against the arbitrary measures proposed
by the President."

Now, I, Robert Y. Hayne, Governor of South Carolina, in
obedience to the said resolution, do hereby issue this my proclamation, solemnly warning the good people of this State against the
dangerous and pernicious doctrine promulgated in the said proclamation of the President, as calculated to mislead their judgments
as to the true character of the Government under which they live,
and the paramount obligation which they owe to the State, and
manifestly intended to seduce them from their allegiance, and, by
drawing them to the support of the violent and unlawful measures
contemplated by the President, to involve them in the guilt of
REBELLION. I would earnestly admonish them to beware of the
specious, but false doctrines, by which it is now attempted to be
shown that the several States have not retained their entire sovereignty; that "the allegiance of their citizens was transferred, in the
first instance, to the Government of the United States"; that "a
State cannot be said to be sovereign and independent, whose citizens owe obedience to laws not made by it"; that, "even under the

royal Government, we had no separate character"; that the Constitution has created "a National Government," which is not "a compact between sovereign States"; "that a State has NO RIGHT TO SECEDE": in a word, that ours is a NATIONAL GOVERNMENT, in which the people of all the States are represented, and by which we are constituted "ONE PEOPLE"; and "that our representatives in Congress are all representatives of the United States, and not of the particular States from which they come"—doctrines which uproot the very foundation of our political system; annihilate the rights of the States, and utterly destroy the liberties of the citizen.

It requires no reasoning to show what the bare statement of these propositions demonstrate, that such a Government as is here described has not a single feature of a confederated republic. It is, in truth, an accurate delineation, drawn with a bold hand, of a great consolidated empire—"one and indivisible"; and, under whatever specious form its powers may be masked, it is, in fact, the worst of all despotisms, in which the spirit of an arbitrary Government is suffered to pervade institutions professing to be free. Such was not the Government for which our fathers fought and bled, and offered up their lives and fortunes as a willing sacrifice. Such was not the Government which the great and patriotic men who called the Union into being, in the plenitude of their wisdoms, framed. Such was not the Government which the fathers of the republican faith, led on by the apostle of American liberty, promulgated, and successfully maintained in 1798, and by which they produced the great political revolution effected at that auspicious era. To a Government based on such principles, South Carolina has not been a voluntary party, and to such a Government she never will give her assent. . . .

Here it will be seen that a law of Congress, as such, can have no validity unless made "in pursuance of the Constitution." An unconstitutional act is, therefore, null and void; and the only point that can arise in this case is, whether, to the Federal Government, or any department thereof, has been exclusively reserved the right to decide authoritatively *for the States* this question of constitutionality. If this be so, to which of the departments, it may be asked, is this right of final judgment given? If it be to Congress, then is Congress not only elevated above the other departments of the Federal Government, but it is put above the Constitution itself. This, however, the President himself has publicly and solemnly denied, claiming and exercising—as is known to all the world—the right to refuse to execute acts of Congress and solemn treaties, even after they had received the sanction of every department of the Federal Government.

That the Executive possesses this right of deciding finally and exclusively as to the validity of acts of Congress, will hardly be pretended; and that it belongs to the judiciary, except so far as may be necessary to the decision of questions which may incidentally come before them, in "cases of law and equity," has been denied by none more strongly than the President himself, who, on a memorable occasion, refused to acknowledge the binding authority of the Federal Court, and claimed for himself, and has exercised the right of enforcing the laws, not according to their judgment, but "his own understanding of them." And yet, when it serves the purpose of bringing odium upon South Carolina, "his native State," the President has no hesitation in regarding the attempt of a State to release herself from the control of the federal judiciary, in a matter affecting her sovereign rights, as a violation of the Constitution. . . .

If the President had read the documents which the Convention caused to be forwarded to him for the express purpose of making known her wishes and her views, he would have found that South Carolina asks no more than that the tariff should be reduced to the *revenue standard*; and has distinctly expressed her willingness, that "an amount of duties substantially uniform, should be levied upon protected, as well as unprotected articles, sufficient to raise *the revenue* necessary to meet the demands of the Government for constitutional purposes." He would have found in the exposition put forth by the Convention itself, a distinct appeal to our sister States for the call of a Convention, and the expression of an entire willingness, on the part of South Carolina, to submit the controversy to that tribunal. . . .

The whole argument, so far as it is designed at this time to enter into it, is now disposed of; and it is necessary to advert to some passages in the proclamation which cannot be passed over in silence. The President distinctly intimates that it is his determination to exert the right of putting down the opposition of South Carolina to the tariff, *by force of arms*. He believes himself invested with power to do this under that provision of the Constitution which directs him "to take care that the laws be faithfully executed." Now, if by this it was only meant to be asserted that, under the laws of Congress now of force, the President would feel himself bound to aid the civil tribunals in the manner therein prescribed, supposing such laws to be constitutional, no just exception could be taken to this assertion of Executive duty. But if, as is manifestly intended, the President sets up the claim to judge for himself in what manner the laws are to be enforced, and feels himself at liberty to call forth the militia, and even the military and naval force of the Union against the State of South Carolina, her constituted authorities and citizens, then it is clear that he assumes a power not only not conferred on the Executive by the Constitution, but which belongs to no despot upon earth exercising a less unlimited authority than the Autocrat of all the Russias: an authority which, if submitted to, would at once reduce the free people of these United States to a state of the most abject and degraded slavery. . . .

The President has intimated in his proclamation that a "standing army" is about to be raised to carry secession into effect. South Carolina desires that her true position shall be clearly understood both at home and abroad. Her object is not "disunion"—she has raised no "standing army," and if driven to repel invasion or resist aggression, she will do so by the strong arms and stout hearts of her citizens. South Carolina has solemnly proclaimed her purpose; that purpose is *the vindication of her rights.* . . .

Fellow citizens: In the name and behalf of the State of South Carolina, I do once more solemnly warn you against all attempts to seduce you from your primary allegiance to the State,—I charge you to be faithful to your duty as citizens of South Carolina, and earnestly exhort you to disregard those "vain menaces" of military force, which, if the President, in violation of all his constitutional obligations, and of your most sacred rights, should be tempted to employ, it would become your solemn duty, at all hazards, to resist. I require you to be fully prepared to sustain the dignity and protect the liberties of the State, if need be, with "your lives and fortunes." And may that great and good Being, who, as a "father careth for his children," inspire us with that holy zeal in a good cause, which is the best safeguard of our rights and liberties. . . .

31. "The Union Will Be Preserved"

JACKSON's handling of the nullification controversy was masterful. He did not stumble into acts of violence against the state, as some anticipated. He moved carefully and cautiously, balancing a posture of strength with an attitude of conciliation. He was particularly adroit in encouraging Unionists in South Carolina, such as Joel R. Poinsett, the former minister to Mexico. They were told that military force would be available if necessary and that Jackson would be guided by their advice on the action best calculated to prevent secession. He sent George Breathitt to South Carolina, ostensibly as a postal inspector, but actually as someone to serve as liaison with the Unionists, so that he could have reliable knowledge of what was happening and what the Unionists wished him to do.

Washington, January 24, 1833

My dear Sir, I have recd. yours of the 16th 19th and 20th instant, that of the 16th late last night and hasten to reply by the return express which will leave early tomorrow.

My Message to congress, forwarded to you by the last express was refered to the committee in each house, on the judiciary—that of the Senate has reported a bill which you will receive from the Secretary of the Treasury by the conveyance that will hand you this. you will see from a perusal, that it contains, with the powers now possessed, every authority necessary to enable the executive to execute the revenue laws, and protect our citizens engaged in their support, and to punish all who may attempt to resist their execution by force. This bill has been made the order of the day for Monday next, and altho this delay has been submitted to by the Senate, still I have no doubt but it will pass by a very large majority in both Houses. There will be some intemperate discussion on the bill and on Calhouns, and Grundys resolutions.

It was my duty to make known to Congress, being in session, the

SOURCE: Andrew Jackson to Joel R. Poinsett, January 24, 1833, John S. Bassett, ed., *Correspondence of Andrew Jackson*, V (Washington, D.C., 1926–1935): 11–12.

state of the union, I withheld till the last moment to give Congress time to act before the first of February. having done my duty in this respect, should congress fail to act on the bill, and I shall be informed of the illegal assemblage of an armed force with intention to oppose the execution of the revenue laws, under the late ordinance of So. Carolina, I stand prepared forthwith to issue my proclamation warning them to disperse. should they fail to comply with the proclamation, I will forthwith call into the field, such a force as will overaw resistance, put treason and rebellion down without blood, and arrest and hand over to the judiciary for trial and punishment, the leaders, exciters and promoters of this rebellion and treason.

You need not fear the assemblage of a large force at charleston. give me early information, officially, of the assemblage of a force armed, to carry into effect the ordinance and laws nullifying our revenue laws, and to prevent their execution, and in ten or fifteen days at farthest, I will have in charleston from ten to fifteen thousand well organized troops, well equiped for the field, and twenty thousand, or thirty, more, in their interior. I have a tender of volunteers from every state in the union. I can, if need be, which god forbid, march two hundred thousand men in forty days to quell any and every insurrection, or rebellion that might arise to threaten our glorious confederacy, a union, upon which our liberty, prosperity and happiness rests.

I repeat to the union men again, fear not, *the union will be preserved*, and treason and rebellion promptly put down, when and where it may shew its monster head. you may rest assured that the nullies of Carolina will receive no aid from any quarter. They have been encouraged by a few from Georgia and Virginia, but the united voice of the yeomenry of the country and the tender of volunteers from every state has put this down. They well know I will execute the laws, and that the whole people will support me in it, and preserve the union. even if the Governor of Virginia should have the folly to attempt to prevent the militia from marching thro his state to put the faction in So. Carolina down and place himself at the head of an armed force for such a wicked purpose, I would arrest him at the head of his troops, and hand him over to the civil authority for trial. The volunteers of his own state would enable me to do this. I repeat again my pride and desire is, that the union men may arouse and sustain the majesty of the constitution and

the laws, and save my native state from that disgrace that the nullifiers have brought upon her. give me early intelligence of the assemblage of an armed force any where in the state, under the or-
diance and the laws to nullify and resist the revenue laws of the
united States, and you may rest assured I will act promptly and do
my duty to god and my country, and relieve the good citizens of
that despotism and tyranny, under which the supporters of the
union now labour.

On yesterday the tariff bill would have passed the House of
representatives had it not been for a very insulting and irritating
speech by wilde of Georgia which has threw the whole of Pennsylvania, New York and Ohio into a flame. I am told there is great
excitement, and no hopes now of its passing this session. it is
further believed that the speech was made for this purpose at the
instigation of the nullies who wish no accommodation of the tariff.
This will unite the whole people against the nullifiers, and instead
of carrying the south with the nullies, will have the effect to arouse
them against them when it is discovered their object is nothing
but disunion. The House sat late and I have not heard from it since
7 oclock. I must refer you to Mr. McLane for further information,
as it is very late and my eyes grow dim. Keep me well advised, and
constantly. The armes are placed subject to your requisition, and
under your discretion. I keep no copy, nor have I time to correct
this letter.

In haste very respectfully your friend

32. "Secession Can Never Take Place without Revolution"

To FASHION a compromise that would end the nullification controversy,
Congress hammered out a new tariff bill in 1833, which lowered the
schedule of rates over a ten-year period, and also passed the Force Bill,
authorizing the use of federal troops to insure obedience of the tariff
laws in South Carolina. Jackson signed both bills on March 2, 1833.

SOURCE: Andrew Jackson to Nathaniel Macon, September 2, 1833,
John S. Bassett, ed., Correspondence of Andrew Jackson, V:
176–8.

Nine days later South Carolina, having received no support from other states, reassembled its convention and repealed its nullification of the tariff laws. To save face it also nullified the Force Bill.

Obviously nullification as an instrument of self-protection had failed, but there were many who still believed a state had the legal right to secede. This position was advanced by the most conservative Old Republicans, such as Nathaniel Macon of North Carolina, a venerable congressman and friend of Thomas Jefferson, who had actively opposed the Alien and Sedition Acts and was committed to the doctrines of the Kentucky and Virginia Resolutions. In the summer of 1833 Macon published a letter in the newspapers criticizing Jackson's actions during the nullification controversy. Because he respected the older man, the President wrote to Macon and there followed an exchange of letters. Jackson's response on September 2, 1833, is particularly valuable in explaining his views on secession.

Washington, September 2, 1833.

Dear Sir, I am glad to find, by your letter of August 26th that the position taken by me, against Secession, is the only part of my proclamation, which you condemn. Others have assumed, without specifying in what particulars, that the principles of that paper, are in opposition to those which distinguished the Republican party, during the Era of Mr. Jefferson's administration. You have been frank and specific, but the ground of objection pointed out in your letter to me, so far from making a departure, from the recognized doctrines of the Republicans of that period, is a practical illustration of them. You do not hesitate to admit, that the measures recommended by Mr. Jefferson to enforce the Embargo in the contemplated case of resistance by Massachusetts, and for which you voted, were the same in principle, with those recently adopted to give effect to the revenue laws in South Carolina: but you tell me that "Mr. Jefferson and yourself may have done wrong, in the very hot times in which you acted." Allow me to say, my Dear Sir, that I think you do great injustice to the motives, which actuated yourself and Mr. Jefferson and the Republicans of the times to which you allude. You doubtless considered the union worthless, unless its laws could be enforced, and after great forbearance and due consideration, the deliberate but reluctant resolution was taken, "to provide for calling forth the Militia to execute the laws of the union," if a case of obstruction should arise, within the contemplation of this clause of the constitution. Under circumstances of still greater emergency than those under which Mr Jefferson acted, (when an ordinance had actually passed nullifying the Revenue laws,) I felt it my duty to act with still greater moderation, than his pacific character had dictated on the former occasion. I first warned and appealed to the affections, to the patriotism of my fellow citizens of the South. I exerted my influence to remove the causes employed to excite discontent among them. When troops were enrolled and actually paraded and trained with the avowed design to prevent the collection of revenue after a given day, I still sought to avoid the unhappy collision, by recommending the removal of the custom houses, beyond the jurisdiction and reach of the State threatening to oppose the collection of the revenue; and in the last and worst event, proposed the use of force only to defend the public officers from actual violance, when engaged in the discharge of their duties. The measures of expostulation, and concession in the first instance, of preparation and decision in the last, which the wisdom of Congress sanctioned, I am happy to believe have had the best effects, in securing peace and Stability to the union.

I think you state too broadly your maxim, that "*the Government of the United States and of the states are governments of opinion and not of force*"—or I should rather say, you apply it improperly, as taking all sanction from the laws. I consider all *free* Governments, Governments of opinion, but should hold ours no government at all, if there were no laws to give effect to the public opinion. We live under a government of laws—laws emanating from the public will; but if there were no means of enforcing public opinion, when embodied in a public law, it would be neither a *government of opinion nor force*.

You tell me that a state cannot commit treason. This is very true. But it does not follow, that all the citizens of a state may not commit treason against the united states. "Treason against the united states shall consist only in levying war against them" etc. The State authorities of no one state, have a right to repeal this clause of the constitution, which all the people in each state *severally*, concurred in establishing. If, therefore, South Carolina has authorized by enactments of a convention or of her state Legislature, the citizens of the state, to levy war upon the united states, it would nevertheless have been treason, in all who should have acted under such authority. The authority itself would have been in violation of "*the supreme law of the land*" which the people of

South Carolina, with their own consent, have bound themselves to obey, "any thing in the constitution or laws of any state to the contrary notwithstanding." Your remark that force applied to a state Government, "is not hinted at, in the constitution of the united states, because a state cannot commit treason" and that "it goes on the ground that every state will perform its duty" is, I think met by the passages of the constitution to which I have pointed, as well as its whole tenor. "The constitution of the United States and the laws made in pursuance of it," would never have been declared "the supreme law of the land" with direct and immediate power over individual citizens in every state, "the laws and constitution of any state to the contrary notwithstanding," if the experience under the Articles of Confederation had not shewn that every state, would NOT perform its duty.

If, however, as you imagine "none of the States gave up the right to secede", then, indeed, the establishment of a general Government and "a supreme law of the land" by a solemn compact among the people of the several states respectively, was entirely a nugatory act. There would, then, be no obligation in the constitution or the laws of the United States, but which is still made dependant upon the mere pleasure of the state authorities; and our system would present the absurdity, of establishing a general authority, with the consent of the people in each of the states, having a paramount power, "the constitution and laws of any state to the contrary notwithstanding"—and nevertheless reserving to each and every one of the states, the right to overthrow by a state law, or a clause in a state constitution, the supreme law of the land!!—or in other words, to set it aside, by secession!!

In my opinion, the admission of the right of secession, is a virtual dissolution of the union. If, it were an established principle in any community, that laws are only to have such obligation as each individual might choose in his good pleasure to allow, such society (if society were possible in this state of case) would be without laws or government. So of the states. If the Federal Government and its laws are to be deprived of all authority in a state by its mere declaration, that it secedes, the union and all its attributes, depend upon the breath of every faction, which may obtain a momentary ascendancy in any one state of the confederacy. To insist, that secession is a reserved right, is to insist, that each state reserved the right to put an end to the Government established for the benefit of all and that there are no common obligations among the states. I hold that the states expressly gave up the right to secede, when they entered into the compact binding them in articles of "perpetual union" and more especially, when the present constitution was adopted to establish "a more perfect union" equally unlimited as to duration. That more perfect union consists in "the supreme law of the land" which the Government of the United States is empowered to maintain *within its proper sphere* independently of the state Governments and whether they pass a law or constitutional provision of secession or not—because it is still to be a law of the land, "*any thing in the constitution or law of any state to the contrary notwithstanding.*"

The only right of secession from a Government, and more especially from a government founded upon reciprocal concessions and obligations among the members forming it, is the revolutionary right. Secession can never take place without revolution; and I trust, if it ever should happen, that one section of the union is subjected to intolerable oppression or injustice by another, and no relief can be obtained through the operation of public opinion, upon the constituted authorities, that the right may be as successfully vindicated by the wronged and oppressed against our present Government, as it was against that which we threw off by the revolution, which established it. I send you herewith, the proclamation, the Report from the Department by which it was succeeded, and the law paper consummating them. I hope you will receive them as an earnest of the high respect I bear you: And if on comparing them, you find the principles I have advanced and the measures I have recommended, the same, in effect, with those which were proclaimed and carried out by Mr. Jefferson, yourself, other fathers of the school of 1798, I hope you will do me the justice to beleive, that in following precedents of such high authority, and which have been sanctioned by the almost universal approbation of the country from that time to this, I was altogether unconscious that they were fraught with the dangerous tendencies, imputed in your published letter, to Mr. Carson.

I beg you to beleive that nothing but a wish to vindicate my conduct and consistency to one whose character I so highly esteem, whose probity and pure Patriotism gives weight to his casual opinion, could have induced me to intrude on your retirement and disturb the repose of your age, by a discussion of the topic, which the publication of your letter invited.

With the kindest feelings I am D'r Sir, etc.

V

Economic and Geographic Expansion

33. The Acquisitive Spirit

ALTHOUGH both major parties had their string of newspapers in all the principal cities of the country to explain the party position on the major issues, not until late in the Jacksonian era did magazines appear with the specific purpose of explaining the fundamental principles of the parties. In 1837 the Democrats launched the United States Magazine and Democratic Review, whereupon the Whigs responded with The American Review: A Journal of Politics, Literature, Art and Science, edited by George Hooker Colton. In its first issue the American Review applauded American capitalism as one of the marvels of the age, but it also expressed its concern over the country's restless pursuit of money and profit. This acquisitive spirit, said the Journal, polluted American taste and moral standards and corrupted its sense of humanity. The following selection is one of the best statements on one of the most important themes operating during the Age of Jackson.

. . . All strangers who come among us remark the excessive anxiety written in the American countenance. The widespread comfort, the facilities for livelihood, the spontaneous and cheap lands, the high price of labor, are equally observed, and render it difficult to account for these lines of painful thoughtfulness. It is not poverty, nor tyranny, nor over-competition which produces this anxiety; that is clear. It is the concentration of the faculties upon an object, which in its very nature is unattainable—the perpetual improvement of the outward condition. There are no bounds among us to the restless desire to be better off; and this is the

SOURCE: "Influence of the Trading Spirit upon the Social and Moral Life in America," The American Review: A Whig Journal of Politics, Literature, Art and Science I (January, 1845): 95–98.

ambition of all classes of society. We are not prepared to allow that wealth is more valued in America than elsewhere, but in other countries the successful pursuit of it is necessarily confined to a few, while here it is open to all. No man in America is contented to be poor, or expects to continue so. There are here no established limits within which the hopes of any class of society must be confined, as in other countries. There is consequently no condition of hopes realized, in other words, of contentment. In other lands, if children can maintain the station and enjoy the means, however moderate, of their father, they are happy. Not so with us. This is not the spirit of our institutions. Nor will it long be otherwise in other countries. That equality, that breaking down of artificial barriers which has produced this universal ambition and restless activity in America, is destined to prevail throughout the earth. But because we are in advance of the world in the great political principle, and are now experiencing some of its first effects, let us not mistake these for the desirable fruits of freedom. Commerce is to become the universal pursuit of men. It is to be the first result of freedom, of popular institutions everywhere. Indeed, every land not steeped in tyranny is now feeling this impulse. But while trade is destined to free and employ the masses, it is also destined to destroy for the time much of the beauty and happiness of every land. This has been the result in our own country. We are free. It is a glorious thing that we have no serfs, with the large and unfortunate exception of our slaves—no artificial distinctions—no acknowledged superiority of blood—no station which merit may not fill—no rounds in the social ladder to which the humblest may not aspire. But the excitement, the commercial activity, the restlessness, to which this state of things has given birth, is far from being a desirable or a natural condition. It is natural to the circumstances, but not natural to the human soul. It is good and hopeful to the interests of the race, but destructive to the happiness, and dangerous to the virtue of the generation exposed to it.

Those unaccustomed, by reading or travel, to other states of society, are probably not aware how very peculiar our manner of life here is. The laboriousness of Americans is beyond all comparison, should we except the starving operatives of English factories. And when we consider that here, to the labor of the body is added the great additional labor of mental responsibility and ambition, it is not to be wondered at that as a race, the commercial population is dwindling in size, and emaciated in health, so that *palor* is the national complexion. If this devotion to business were indispensable to living, it would demand our pity. It is unavoidable, we know, in one sense. That is, it is customary—it is universal. . . .

We call our country a *happy* country; happy, indeed, in being the home of noble political institutions, the abode of freedom; but very far from being happy in possessing a cheerful, light-hearted, and joyous people. Our agricultural regions even are infected with the same anxious spirit of gain. If ever the curse of labor was upon the race, it is upon us; nor is it simply now "by the sweat of thy brow thou shalt earn thy bread." Labor for a livelihood is dignified. But we labor for bread, and labor for pride, and *labor* for pleasure. A man's life with us *does* consist of the abundance of the things which he possesseth. To get, and to have the reputation of possessing, is the ruling passion. To it are bent all the energies of nine-tenths of our population. Is it that our people are so much more miserly and earth-born than any other? No, not by any constitutional baseness; but circumstances have necessarily given this direction to the American mind. In the hard soil of our common mother, New England—the poverty of our ancestors—their early thrift and industry—the want of other distinctions than those of property—the frown of the Puritans upon all pleasures; these circumstances combined, directed our energies from the first into the single channel of trade. And in that they have run till they have gained a tremendous head, and threaten to convert our whole people into mere money-changers and producers. Honor belongs to our fathers, who in times of great necessity met the demand for a most painful industry with such manly and unflinching hearts. But what was their hard necessity we are perpetuating as our willing servitude! what they bore as evil we seek as good. We cannot say that the destiny of this country did not demand that the spirit of trade should rule it for centuries. It may be that we are now carrying out only the decree of Providence. But if so, let us consider ourselves as in the wilderness, and not in the promised land. Let us bear the dispensation of God, but not glory in our bondage. If we are doomed to be tradesmen, and nothing but tradesmen—if money, and its influences and authority, are to reign for a season over our whole land, let us not mistake it for the kingdom of heaven, and build triumphal arches over our avenues of trade, as though the Prince of Peace and the Son of God were now and thus to enter in.

It is said that we are not a happy people. And it is true; for we most unwisely neglect all those free fountains of happiness which Providence has opened for all its children. Blessed beyond any people with the means of living, supplied to an unparalleled extent with the comforts and luxuries of life, our American homes are sombre and cheerless abodes. There is even in the air of comfort which their well-furnished apartments wear something uncomfortable. They are the habitations of those who do not live at home. They are wanting in a social and cheerful aspect. They seem fitted more to be admired than to be enjoyed. The best part of the house is for the occasional use of strangers, and not to be occupied by those who might, day by day, enjoy it, which is but one proof among many that we love to appear comfortable rather than to be so. Thus miserable pride hangs like a mill stone about our hospitality. "We sacrifice the hospitality of a year to the prodigality of a night." We are ashamed of any thing but affluence, and when we cannot make an appearance, or furnish entertainments as showy as the richest, we will do nothing. Thus does pride close our doors. Hospitality becomes an event of importance. It is not our daily life, one of our chiefest enjoyments, but a debt, a ceremony, a penance. And not only pride, but anxiety of mind, interferes with sociality. Bent upon one aim, the merchant grudges his thoughts. He cannot expend his energies in social enjoyment. Nay, it is not enjoyment to him; society has nothing of the excitement of business. The excessive pursuit of gain begets a secrecy of thought, a contradiction of ideas, a barrenness of interest, which renders its votary any thing but social or companionable. Conversation incessantly takes an anxious and uninteresting turn; and the fireside becomes only a narrower exchange, and the parlor a more private news-room.

It is rare to see a foreigner without some taste for amusement, some power of relaxing his mind, some interest in the arts, or in literature. This is true even of the less privileged classes. It is rare, on the contrary, to find a *virtuous* American past middle life, who does not regard amusements of all sorts either as childish or immoral; who possesses any acquaintance with or taste for the arts, except it be a natural and rude taste for music; or who reads any thing except newspapers, and only the political or commercial columns of those. It is the want of tastes for other things than business which gives an anxious and unhappy turn to our minds. It cannot be many years before the madness of devoting the whole day to the toils of the counting-house will be acknowledged; before the claim of body and mind to relaxation and cheerful, exhilarating amusement will be seen. We consider the common suspicion which is felt of amusements among thoughtful people to be one of the most serious evils to which our community is exposed. It outlaws a natural taste, and violates and ruins the consciences of the young, by stamping as sinful what they have not the force to refrain from. It makes our places of amusement low, divides the thoughtful and the careless, the grave and the gay, the old and the young, in their pleasures. Children are without the protection of their parents in their enjoyments. And thus, too, is originated one of the greatest curses of our social state—the great want of intimacy and confidence between children and their parents, especially between fathers and sons. . . .

We are more strict in our morals in these Northern States than anywhere in the world, but it is questionable whether our morality is not of a somewhat inferior quality, and in a too narrow view. It is artificial, conventional. There is no quarter of the earth where the Sabbath is more scrupulously observed—where religious institutions are so well supported, or where more abstinence from pleasure is practised. The great virtue of industry prevails. Overt sins are more rare here than elsewhere. As far as morality is restrictive in its nature, it has accomplished a great work in America. The vices or sins which are reducible to statute, or known by name, are generally restrained. We have a large class of persons of extraordinary propriety and faultlessness of life. Our view of morals has a tendency to increase this class. Our pursuits are favorable to it. The love of gain is one of the most sober of all desires. The seriousness of a miser surpasses the gravity of a devotee. Did not every commercial city draw a large body of strangers to it, and attract many reckless and vicious persons, it would wear a very solemn aspect. The pleasure-seeking, the gay, the disorderly, are never the trading population. Large commercial cities tend to great orderliness and decency of manners and morals. But they also tend to very low and barren views of moral excellence. And the American spirit of our own day illustrates this. Our moral sense operates only in one direction. Our virtues are the virtues of merchants, and not of men. We run all to honesty, and mercantile honesty. We do not cultivate the graces of humanity. We have more conscience than heart, and more propriety than either. The fear of evil consequences is more influential than the love of goodness. There is nothing hearty, gushing, eloquent, in the national virtue. You do not see goodness leaking out from the full vessel at every motion it feels. Our goodness is formal, deliberate, premeditated. The upright man is not benevolent, and the just man is not generous. The good man is not cheerful. The religious man is not agreeable. In other words, our morals are partial, and therefore barren. It is not generally understood how great scrupulousness of character may be united with great selfishness, and how, along with a substantial virtue, there may exist the most melancholy deficiencies. This seems to be very common with us, and to be the natural result of our engrossing pursuits. Every one minds his own business, to the extreme peril of his own soul. The apostolic precept, Mind not thine own things, but also the things of another, is in danger of great neglect. Our social condition makes us wary, suspicious, slow to commit ourselves too far in interest for others. The shyness of the tradesman communicates itself to the manners of the visiter; we learn to live within ourselves; we grow unsocial, unfraternal in feeling; and the sensibility, the affection, the cordiality, the forth-putting graces of a warm and virtuous heart, die of disuse. For our part, we are ready to say, let us have more faults and more virtues; more weaknesses and more graces; less punctilio, and more affluence of heart. Let us be less dignified and more cordial; less sanctimonious and more unselfish; less thriving and more cheerful; less toilsome and more social.

We want, as a people, a rounder character. Our humanity is pinched; our tastes are not generous. The domestic and social virtues languish. The dearest relations of life are stripped of beauty; a wretched utility usurps that proper theatre of beautiful sentiment, our very homes. Children grow up unknown to their parents. The mature despise their own youth, and have no sympathy with the romance, the buoyancy, the gayety of their children. Enterprise is our only enthusiasm. We grow to be ashamed of our best affections. We are afraid to acknowledge that we derive enjoyment from trifles, and make apologies for being amused with anything. . . . We fear that the ruling passion of our community, the habits of business which it has established, the anxious and self-concentrated mind which ensues, the morals which it engenders, are very hostile to any thing like perfected humanity. It is very probable that we may have erred in supposing a greatly better state of things to exist in other communities. But we know that we are right as to the positive state of our own, whatever it may be relatively to others. We know, too, very well the almost insuperable difficulties in the way of any individual who shall attempt to withstand the prevailing current of sentiment, or of business habits. But if *none* are to escape, it is well to be aware of the danger; nor must it be assumed that a firm will cannot do much to emancipate a man from the general bondage of trade. Sooner than slave from morning to night at business, we would counsel any man conscious of inward resources, of the desire to cultivate his better nature, his social feelings, his tastes, his generous and cheerful sentiments, to give it up altogether as soon as the most moderate competency is secured; to seek the country—to occupy some of our rich western lands—to do anything which will give him time to enjoy domestic pleasures, to rear his children, to acquaint himself with nature, to read, to meditate. . . .

34. Transportation and Communication

NOTHING galvanized American industry and prepared the country for the industrial revolution as did the coming of the railroads. Not only did it link the nation together, provide distribution of agricultural and manufactured products, and stimulate the growth of urban communities but it also attracted an enormous amount of capital which brought the nation to its "take off" stage of economic development. In the report of the census taken in 1850 the superintendent commented on the fantastic growth of the railroads since their inauguration during the administration of John Quincy Adams. He also described the new communications invention, the telegraph, the first in a series of inventions that ultimately revolutionized communications within the country.

Railroads in the United States.—In no other particular can the prosperity of a country be more strikingly manifested than by the perfection of its roads and other means of internal communication. The system of railroads, canals, turnpikes, post routes, river navigation, and telegraphs, possessed by the United States, presents an indication of its advancement in power and civilization more

SOURCE: Report of the Superintendent of the Census for December 1, 1852, *The Seventh Census* (Washington, D.C., 1853), pp. 98–100, 105–108.

wonderful than any other feature of its progress. In truth, our country in this respect occupies the first place among the nations of the world.

From returns received at this office, in reply to special circulars, and other sources of information, it is ascertained that there were, at the commencement of the year 1852, 10,814 miles of railroads completed and in use; and that 10,898 miles were then in course of construction, with a prospect of being speedily brought into use. While the whole of these 10,898 miles will, beyond reasonable doubt, have been finished within five years, such is the activity with which projects for works of this character are brought forward and carried into effect, that it is not extravagant to assume that there will be completed within the limits of the United States before the year 1860 at least 35,000 miles of railroads.

The Quincy railroad, for the transportation of granite from the quarries at Quincy to Neponset river, and the Mauch Chunk railroad, from the coal mines to the Lehigh river, in Pennsylvania, were the first attempts to introduce that mode of transportation in this country; and their construction and opening, in the years 1826 and 1827, are properly considered the commencement of the American railroad system. From this period until about the year 1848, the progress of the improvements thus begun was interrupted only by the financial revulsion which followed the events of 1836 and 1837. Up to 1848, it is stated that about 6,000 miles had been finished. Since that date an addition of 5,000 miles has been made to the completed roads, and, including the present year, new lines, comprising about 14,000 miles, have been undertaken, surveyed, and mostly placed under contract.

The usefulness and comparative economy of railroads as channels of commerce and travel have become so evident, that they have in some measure superseded canals, and are likely to detract seriously from the importance of navigable rivers for like purposes. In a new country like ours, many items of expense, which go to swell the cost of railroads in England and on the Continent, are avoided. Material is cheap; the right of way usually freely granted; and heavy land damages seldom interpose to retard the progress of an important work. It is difficult to arrive at a clear approximation to the average cost of railroad construction in the United States. Probably the first important work of this class undertaken and carried through in the Union was the cheapest, as it has proved one of the most profitable, ever built. This was the road from Charleston, in South Carolina, to Augusta, on the Savannah river. It was finished and opened for traffic in 1833. The entire expense of building the road and equipping it with engines and cars for passengers and freight was, at the date of its completion, only $6,700 per mile; and all expenditures for repairs and improvements, during the eighteen years that the road has been in operation, have raised the aggregate cost of the whole work to only $1,336,615, or less than $10,000 per mile.

It is estimated that the 2,870 miles of railroads finished in New England have cost $132,000,000, which gives an average of nearly $46,000 per mile. In the middle States, where the natural obstacles are somewhat less, the average expense per mile of the railroads already built is not far from $40,000. Those now in course of completion—as the Baltimore and Ohio railroad, Pennsylvania Central and other lines, the routes of which cross the Alleghany range of mountains—will probably require a larger proportionate outlay, owing to the heavy expense of grading, bridging, and tunnelling. In those States where land has become exceedingly valuable, the cost of extinguishing private titles to the real estate requires, and the damages to property along the routes, form a heavy item in the account of general expenses of building railroads. In the South and West the case is reversed; there the proprietors along the proposed line of a road are often willing and anxious to give as much land as may be needed for its purposes, and accord many other advantages in order to secure its location through or in the vicinity of their possessions. In the States lying in the valleys of the Ohio and Mississippi the cost of grading, also, is much less than at the eastward. Where the country is wooded, the timber can be obtained at the mere cost of removing it from the track; and through prairie districts, Nature seems to have prepared the way for these structures by removing every obstacle from the surface, while fine quarries of stone are to be found in almost every region. These favorable circumstances render the estimate of $20,000 per mile in all the new States safe and reliable.

The primary design of nearly all the great lines of railway in the United States has been to connect the seacoast with the distant interior; to effect which object it was necessary to cross the Alleghanies, which intersect every line of travel diverging to the West from the great commercial cities of the sea board.

The following are some of the vast enterprises which have been undertaken to accomplish this great purpose, which have either been finished or are in such a state of progress as leaves no doubt of their being brought to a successful issue within a few years:

First. The railroads connecting Portland, the commercial capital of Maine, with the British provinces, and through their public works, the St. Lawrence river and the lakes, with the western States of the Union.

Second. The railroads from Boston westward, connecting at Albany with the roads of central New York, and, by the more northern route, traversing New Hampshire and Vermont, continuing towards the West by the Ogdensburg railroad, and bringing Montreal, the chief commercial city of Upper Canada, into communication with the capital of New England.

Third. The New York and Erie railroad, extending from New York city to Lake Erie, and intended to form a part of a continuous line from the Hudson to the Mississippi—a project likely to be effected within the ensuing ten years.

Fourth. The Pennsylvania Central railroad, from Philadelphia to Pittsburgh, with numerous diverging branches, to points north and south of the general direction. This great route will reach St. Louis by a nearly due west course through Ohio, Indiana, and Illinois. The Pennsylvania section will be completed about the end of 1852.

Fifth. The Baltimore and Ohio railroad, one of the most magnificent works of the day, will pass from Baltimore through Maryland and Virginia to Wheeling, on the Ohio. At the latter point, it will form a connexion with the system of roads traversing the West and Northwest. It crosses the Alleghanies by the most favorable passes, and, to avoid a very high grade, a tunnel has been cut, perhaps the longest and most expensive in the world.

Sixth. The roads proposed to be constructed under authority of Virginia, and already commenced, intended to establish communication between tide-water and the interior, and southwestern parts of that State, and to continue the same through Tennessee to the Mississippi. These routes pass through the mountains at the southeast corner of Virginia, and the works are in a state of less forwardness than those upon any other of the great lines referred to in this connexion.

Seventh. The several lines of railroad from Charleston and

Savannah, penetrating South Carolina and Georgia, concentrating in northeastern Alabama, and reaching the level region of the Mississippi by the valley of the Tennessee river. These roads, by their western continuation, will intersect lines running to every important point between the mountains and the Mississippi.

Eighth. The Mobile and Ohio railroad, from the Mexican gulf to Cairo, on the Ohio river, and thence by the Illinois Central railroad to the lakes, a distance in a straight line of about eleven hundred miles. . . .

In the infancy of the American railroad system, a favorite means of providing funds for their construction was the advance of loans from the treasuries of the respective States in which they were situated, but this plan has been superseded by the use of private capital, and, within the last ten years, frequent recourse has been had to the expedient of loans and subscriptions by counties, cities, and towns through which the roads pass. Loans of this character, however, are in all cases made under the grant of authority conferred by the State legislatures. The loans representing these transactions with the stocks of the companies have been estimated to amount to $300,000,000. This sum may be assumed as the amount of the capital invested in those roads now in progress, and those which may have been completed since the opening of the year. If, then, we add this sum to the estimated cost of the roads finished in December, 1851, we shall have $672,770,000 as the total amount of investments in railroads in the United States. . . .

The rates of fare on our railroads are lower than on those of any country of which we have returns, affording the means of comparison. In New England, the average rate per mile is slightly over two cents; from New York to Washington, it is three cents and a half per mile. From New York to Cincinnati, the railroad and steamboat fare together is less than two cents per mile. From New York to Albany, the price of passage is a fraction over one cent per mile, and the average rate upon all the New York railroads has been stated at two cents and one fifth per mile.

Telegraphs.—As telegraphs have formed a subject of inquiry, it is deemed proper to present some account of the information obtained respecting this recent but widely extended and daily enlarging means of communication. At the present time it is a subject engrossing much of the attention of our own citizens, and frequent applications are made to this office, from foreign countries, for information regarding the *minutiæ* of the system as conducted in the United States.

Here, the telegraphic system is carried to greater extent than in any other part of the world, and the numerous lines now in full operation form a net-work over the length and breadth of the land. They are not confined to the populous regions of the Atlantic coast, but extend far into the interior, climb the sides of the highest mountains, and cross the almost boundless prairies; and in a few years a continuous communication will be established between the capital of the nation and the shores of the Pacific, as it now exists between the Atlantic, the great lakes, and the Gulf of Mexico.

It is to American ingenuity that we owe the practical application of the magnetic telegraph for the purpose of communication between distant points, and it has been perfected and improved mainly by American science and skill. While the honor is due to Professor Morse for the practical application and successful prosecution of the telegraph, it is mainly owing to the researches and discoveries of Professor Henry, and other scientific Americans, that he was enabled to perfect so valuable an invention. . . .

During the summer of 1832, Professor S. F. B. Morse, an American, conceived the idea of an electric or electro-magnetic telegraph, and, after numerous experiments, announced his invention to the public in April, 1837.

On the 10th of March, 1837, Hon. Levi Woodbury, then Secretary of the Treasury, issued a circular requesting information in regard to the propriety of establishing a system of telegraphs for the United States, to which Professor Morse replied, giving an account of his invention, its proposed advantages and probable expense. At that time he "presumed five words could be transmitted in a minute." Professor Morse having petitioned Congress for aid to enable him to test the practical operation of his invention, an appropriation of $30,000 was made for this purpose; and in June, 1844, he erected the first telegraphic line in the United States, between Washington and Baltimore, a length of 40 miles.

This line was extended to Philadelphia and New York, a distance of 250 miles. It reached Boston in 1845, and became the great line of the North, from which branched two others, one from Philadelphia to Pittsburg, Cincinnati, and St. Louis, 1,000 miles; the other from New York to Albany, Buffalo, Cleveland, Chicago, and Milwaukie, 1,300 miles. Another line, 1,395 miles in length, connects Buffalo, Niagara, Toronto,˙ Montreal, Quebec, and Halifax.

Two lines run south to New Orleans—one from New York, Washington, and Charleston, 1,966 miles—the other from Cleveland, Ohio, and Cincinnati, via Nashville, 1,200 miles long.

The only line constructed with government aid was that connecting the cities of Washington and Baltimore. The others have been established by private enterprise. This line is at present, perhaps, the best appointed and most reliable in the world. . . .

The amount of business which a well-conducted office can perform is immense. Nearly seven hundred messages, exclusive of those for the press, were sent in one day over the Morse Albany line; and a few days after, the Bain line at Boston sent and received five hundred communications. Another office, with two wires—one five hundred, the other two hundred miles in length—after spending three hours in the transmission of public news, telegraphed, in a single day, four hundred and fifty private messages, averaging twenty-five words each, besides the address, sixty of which were sent in succession, without a word of repetition.

The apparatus cannot be worked successfully without skillful operators, good batteries and machines, and thorough insulation of the conductors. The expense of copper wire, which was at first used, has caused it to be superseded by iron, which is found to answer the purpose as well, though it is requisite to give the iron wire six times the weight of a copper one, to gain the same conducting power with equal lengths. About two hundred and fifty pounds of iron wire are required to a mile. Its insulation is effected by winding it around or passing through caps or knobs of glass, or well-glazed stoneware, or enclosing it with gutta percha. The wires are generally supported on spars or posts, from twenty to thirty feet in height, nine inches in diameter at the base, four and a half at the top, set in the ground five feet deep, and placed from twelve to fifteen rods apart.

Although the wires have been buried in the earth, in some countries, and experiments tried here to effect this object, it would appear, from the latest information received, that this method is unsuccessful, and will be relinquished.

The cost of construction, including wire, posts, labor, &c., is about one hundred and fifty dollars per mile. . . .

The average performance of the Morse instruments is to transmit from eight thousand to nine thousand letters per hour. The usual charge of transmission is twenty-five cents for ten words, or less, sent one hundred miles.

35. Manufactures: Lowell

THE GROWTH of manufacturing in the United States was a steady development over many decades. By the Jacksonian era a number of textile factories were completely operated by machines, and one of the most famous was located in Lowell, Massachusetts. This manufacturing town had the added distinction of employing many young ladies under supervised conditions that attracted widespread interest and praise. Virtually all visitors to the United States had to visit Lowell and see the factories and boarding houses. All commented on their cleanliness and order, contrasting them with the squalor they had seen in European factory towns.

Lowell is one of the newest towns in America, and is strikingly characteristic of the rapidity with which settlements are formed, and cities built and peopled, in this rising country. So recently as 1813, the spot where Lowell stands was without a dwelling; but at the close of that year, when the war with Great Britain had cut off the supplies of manufactured goods from England, and when the prices of all such articles were extravagantly high, two individuals, Captains Whiting and Fletcher, conceived the idea of availing themselves of the water-power here given by the Falls of the Concord and Merrimack rivers, to establish on this spot a cotton manufactory. This was erected on a small scale in a wooden building, costing only 3,000 dollars. In 1818, this was sold to Mr. Hurd, who added to it a brick factory for the manufacture of woollen goods. But in 1826, he becoming insolvent, his works were purchased by a Company; and from that period the works have been so speedily extended, and the population so rapidly increased, by the capital and operations of several other companies entering into the manufacturing enterprise, that there are now 10 companies, or

SOURCE: J. S. Buckingham, *The Eastern and Western States of America*, Volume I (London, 1842), pp. 293–301, 303.

corporations, with a capital of about 10,000,000 dollars, occupying or working 30 mills, giving employment to more than 10,000 operatives, whom 7,000 are females, and paying out 150,000 dollars a month in wages, for the manufacture of more than 8,000,000 dollars' worth of goods in the year. Lowell was incorporated as a city, in 1836; and has now a population of about 20,000 persons, with 12 churches, 25 schools, 4 banks, and 6 newspapers published in the week.

The town is pleasantly and advantageously situated at the con-fluence of the rivers Concord and Merrimack; its water-power is derived through a canal which conveys the water down, by locks, at intervals, from the Falls of Pawtucket above the town, to whatever point may be desired; and the surplus, when used, is drained into one or other of the above-named streams. The canal is a mile and a half long, 60 feet broad, and 8 feet deep, and cost 120,000 dollars. The whole fall of the water is about 30 feet, divided between 3 locks; and the minimum quantity of water supplied is about 2,000 cubic feet per second. This is held to be of sufficient force to carry 286,000 spindles, with all the necessary machinery; but as there are as yet only 150,000 spindles employed in 4,800 looms, there is yet power sufficient for 136,000 spindles more; or enough to turn 10 large mills more than the present number, making 40 in all, before the present water-power shall be exhausted, or it may be necessary to have recourse to steam. There are upwards of 52,000,000 yards of cotton cloth manufactured here in the year, 14,000,000 yards of which are dyed and printed; and about 18,000,000 lbs. of cotton used for this purpose, besides a large quantity of wool. The cotton is wholly from the Southern States of the Union. The wool is chiefly from the Mediterranean.

Besides these larger works, there are in Lowell 10 powder-mills, several flour-mills, large glass-works, flannel-works, bleacheries, machine manufactories, carriage and harness manufactories, iron, brass, tin, and copper works, and founderies, and large establish-ments for making boots and shoes; it is, in short, a perfect hive of industry—there being no mere capitalists or retired tradesmen, few professional persons, and no idlers, in this busy throng—but from sun-rise to sun-set, and for two hours after this during the winter months, every hand is in motion and every eye is on the watch. . . .

The cloth-works and the carpet-manufactory are conducted with all the cleanliness of a parlour; the print-works are also as neat and clean as they are beautiful; but the cotton-works in the Boot Mill (as it is called after Mr. Kirk Boot, one of the early patrons of Lowell) are the perfection of order, beauty, cleanliness, and comfort. I do not remember anything like it in England or Scotland; and though I admire greatly the noble cotton-factory at Providence, and the excellent works at Dover, yet this was greatly superior to either. In general plan, it resembled the best cotton-mills in England, but its superiorities consisted chiefly in these features:—First—more ample space in the area surrounding the building, affording a large and constant supply of fresh air;—Second—more substantial and finished work in the brick, stone, wood, glass, and tile-work of the edifice;—Third—ampler space within, in the breadth of the ascending staircases, the lofty heights of the carding and spinning rooms, and more space between the frames and looms for the persons attending them to move and breathe freely;—Fourth—greater cleanliness in all the floors and walls, more ornament on the machines, and a brighter and more cheerful aspect over all;—Fifth—greater attention to the convenience and comforts of the operatives, in the provisions of accommodations for washing, mirrors for dressing, and neater arrangements for the wardrobes of the females.

All the men that I saw employed in either of these works were better dressed, cleaner, and appeared better fed, healthier, and more contented, than the same class of persons in England; and they have good reason to be so, as they are better paid, earning from 6 to 12 dollars per week, and some of the more skilful 15 dollars—with less cost for living, the enjoyment of all political rights, and the power at any time to emigrate to the West at little charge, whenever their wages should be in danger of being reduced. All the females that we saw—and they exceeded 3,000—were still more superior to the same class of persons in England. They were all remarkably clean, well-dressed, and supplied with requisites for warmth and comfort. . . .

The greater number of the females employed here, are daughters of the farmers in the three States of Massachusetts, New Hampshire, and Vermont. They do not leave their homes from want, but from a love of independence, and a desire to support themselves by their own labour. They therefore rarely come to the factories till they are 15 or 16; and there is a law prohibiting their being employed before they are 14, unless on the condition of their being at school at least three months in the year. When they come, they are in general amply provided with clothes, and every other requisite; and from the first day, they are comfortably accommodated in one of the boarding-houses belonging to the Company in whose factory they may be employed to work. These boarding-houses are neat dwellings, of brick or wood, two and three stories high, built in streets and rows, by the respective Companies, for their own operatives only. They are let at a rent which yields only 5 per cent. interest on their cost (though 10 per cent. is the lowest profit on their working capital), to matrons chosen by the Company, and under their control, as well as responsible to the Directors for the adoption and enforcement of such regulations as they may propose. These matrons are bound to furnish a prescribed number of meals, with regulated quantities and qualities of the articles to the young boarders, at fixed rates; so that there shall be no misunderstanding on either side. The number of boarders that may be taken by each matron, who are mostly widows, is also limited; and no other persons than those actually employed in the factory to which the boarding-house belongs, are permitted to be taken in or entertained at the house, nor are any males admitted among the female boarders there.

Among the regulations by which these establishments are governed, the following deserve mention: 1. Good behaviour in words and actions, and the constant observance of temperance and virtue, and the duties exacted from all, whether in the factory or the boarding-house, as well as diligence and subordination; and any person violating any of the rules and regulations of either branch, are to be punished with instant dismissal. 2. No ardent spirits or intoxicating drinks of any kind are allowed to be used or possessed by any persons, of either sex—agent, overseer, or operative. 3. No games of chance or hazard, such as cards, dice, or backgammon, are at any time allowed. 4. Every person employed must live in one of the boarding-houses, subject to the Company's rules; and all who are not prevented by sickness, must attend divine worship, at such church as they prefer, and rigidly respect the sanctity of the Sabbath. 5. The doors of every boarding-house must be closed at 10 o'clock at night; and no relaxation of this rule to be admitted on any occasion. 6. A report must be made of the misconduct of any individual guilty of a breach of any of these rules, by the matron of the boarding-house, to the Directors of the Company, through the agent of the factory.

The hours of work are from 6 in the morning to 7 in the evening in the summer; and from half-past 6 to half-past 7 in the winter months, with the allowance of one hour to the two meals of break-fast at 8 and dinner at 1 o'clock, supper being taken after their labours are over. On Saturdays the factories are closed at 4 o'clock, so that the labour is 12 hours a day on each day except Saturday, and then only 9. This is no doubt longer than it is desirable that any person should labour continuously, more especially young persons, and still more especially females; but I have no doubt, that from the superior cleanliness, comfort, food, air, and healthful associations by which they are surrounded, their 12 hours' labour here do not produce more fatigue to them, than 10 hours' labour do to the same class of factory-girls in England. . . . What makes this amount of labour more easily borne, however, by the factory operatives here, than it is by their less fortunate sisterhood in Eng-land, is this—that none of them consider it as their permanent condition; all look forward to its termination in a few years at the farthest; and every one must be aware of how much greater a burden can be borne, under the confident hope of its soon ceasing, than could possibly be endured, if the sufferers thought it would last for ever. The men earn here from 12 to 20 dollars a week, and can therefore lay by from 5 to 10 dollars, after providing for every want, so that in two or three years they accumulate enough to go off to the West, and buy an estate at 1¼ dollar an acre, or set up in some small way of business at home. The girls earn from 3 to 5 dollars per week, and the cost of their board being fixed at 1¼ dollar per week, they can lay by, after paying for everything needed, from 1 to 3 dollars per week; and thus in three or four years, they may return home to their father's house with a little capital of from 200 to 300 dollars, and marry advantageously to some young farmer, or other person of their own rank in life. This is sometimes but not often done before they have finished their term of service in the factory; in which case, the female invariably leaves that occupation, and remains at home, nor ever returns to the factory, unless early widowhood and the death of parents should render such a step necessary. The proportion of married women to single employed in these works, is not more than 1 to 100, of those whose husbands are alive; and of widows, about 2 in 100 of the whole number. . . .

All things considered . . . Lowell is certainly one of the most remarkable places under the sun; and it is earnestly to be desired that it should for ever continue to retain all its present features of excellence, for I do not believe there is to be found in any part of the globe a town of 20,000 inhabitants, in which there is so much of unoppressive industry, so much competency of means and contentment of condition, so much purity of morals and gentleness and harmlessness of manners, so little of suffering from excessive labour, intemperance, or ill-health, so small an amount of excitement from any cause, so much of order and happiness, so little of misery or crime, as in this manufacturing town of Lowell, at the present time.

36. Charles River Bridge Case

UNDER THE domination of Chief Justice John Marshall the Supreme Court followed an extremely nationalistic line during the first third of the nineteenth century. The court also defended property rights with a very strict and narrow interpretation of the Constitution. In his two terms in office, Jackson completely changed the court. He was able to appoint five new associate justices—in a court of seven—and then, when Marshall died in 1835, the President appointed Roger B. Taney as chief justice.

The Charles River Bridge case was one of the earliest decisions of the Taney court and in terms of law was the most significant case in the entire Jacksonian era. In the majority decision, Taney placed great emphasis on state and community rights. Where the Marshall court had observed the absolute sanctity of contract, Taney upheld the right of popular majorities acting through their legislatures to regulate property rights and the privileges of corporations. Some historians have seen in this decision a broadening of the free enterprise system because it denied monopolistic claims of older companies whose charters conferred exclusive privileges.

Mr. Chief Justice Taney delivered the opinion of the court.

The questions involved in this case are of the gravest character, and the court have given to them the most anxious and deliberate

SOURCE: Richard Peters, *Reports of Cases Argued . . . in the Supreme Court of the United States . . .* Volume XI (Philadelphia, 1854), pp. 536–37, 544–53.

consideration. The value of the right claimed by the plaintiffs is large in amount; and many persons may no doubt be seriously affected in their pecuniary interests by any decision which the court may pronounce; and the questions which have been raised as to the power of the several states, in relation to the corporations they have chartered, are pregnant with important consequences; not only to the individuals who are concerned in the corporate franchises, but to the communities in which they exist. The court are fully sensible that it is their duty, in exercising the high powers conferred on them by the constitution of the United States, to deal with these great and extensive interests with the utmost caution; guarding, as far as they have the power to do so, the rights of property, and at the same time carefully abstaining from any encroachment on the rights reserved to the states.

It appears, from the record, that in the year 1650, the legislature of Massachusetts granted to the president of Harvard College "the liberty and power," to dispose of the ferry from Charlestown to Boston, by lease or otherwise, in the behalf, and for the behoof of the college: and that, under that grant, the college continued to hold and keep the ferry by its lessees or agents, and to receive the profits of it until 1785. In the last mentioned year, a petition was presented to the legislature, by Thomas Russell and others, stating the inconvenience of the transportation by ferries, over Charles river, and the public advantages that would result from a bridge; and praying to be incorporated for the purpose of erecting a bridge in the place where the ferry between Boston and Charlestown was then kept. Pursuant to this petition, the legislature, on the 9th of March, 1785, passed an act incorporating a company, by the name of "The Proprietors of the Charles River Bridge," for the purposes mentioned in the petition. Under this charter the company were empowered to erect a bridge, in "the place where the ferry was then kept"; certain tolls were granted, and the charter was limited to forty years, from the first opening of the bridge for passengers; and from the time the toll commenced, until the expiration of this term, the company were to pay two hundred pounds, annually, to Harvard College; and, at the expiration of the forty years, the bridge was to be the property of the commonwealth; "saving (as the law expresses it) to the said college or university, a reasonable annual compensation, for the annual income of the ferry, which they might have received had not the said bridge been erected."

The bridge was accordingly built, and was opened for passengers on the 17th of June, 1786. In 1792, the charter was extended to seventy years, from the opening of the bridge; and at the expiration of that time it was to belong to the commonwealth. The corporation have regularly paid to the college the annual sum of two hundred pounds, and have performed all of the duties imposed on them by the terms of their charter.

In 1828, the legislature of Massachusetts incorporated a company by the name of "The Proprietors of the Warren Bridge," for the purpose of erecting another bridge over Charles river. This bridge is only sixteen rods, at its commencement, on the Charlestown side, from the commencement of the bridge of the plaintiffs; and they are about fifty rods apart at their termination on the Boston side. The travellers who pass over either bridge, proceed from Charlestown square, which receives the travel of many great public roads leading from the country; and the passengers and travellers who go to and from Boston, used to pass over the Charles river bridge, from and through this square, before the erection of the Warren bridge.

The Warren bridge, by the terms of its charter, was to be surrendered to the state, as soon as the expenses of the proprietors in building and supporting it should be reimbursed; but this period was not, in any event, to exceed six years from the time the company commenced receiving toll.

When the original bill in this case was filed, the Warren bridge had not been built; and the bill was filed after the passage of the law, in order to obtain an injunction to prevent its erection, and for general relief. The bill, among other things, charged as a ground for relief, that the act for the erection of the Warren bridge impaired the obligation of the contract between the commonwealth and the proprietors of the Charles river bridge; and was therefore repugnant to the constitution of the United States. Afterwards, a supplemental bill was filed, stating that the bridge had then been so far completed, that it had been opened for travel, and that divers persons had passed over, and thus avoided the payment of the toll, which would otherwise have been received by the plaintiffs. . . .

Borrowing, as we have done, our system of jurisprudence from the English law; and having adopted, in every other case, civil and criminal, its rules for the construction of statutes; is there anything in our local situation, or in the nature of our political institutions,

which should lead us to depart from the principle where corporations are concerned? Are we to apply to acts of incorporation, a rule
of construction differing from that of the English law, and, by
implication, make the terms of a charter in one of the states, more
unfavourable to the public, than upon an act of Parliament, framed
in the same words, would be sanctioned in an English court? Can
any good reason be assigned for excepting this particular class of
cases from the operation of the general principle; and for introducing a new and adverse rule of construction in favour of corporations, while we adopt and adhere to the rules of construction
known to the English common law, in every other case, without
exception? We think not; and it would present a singular spectacle
if, while the courts in England are restraining, within the strictest
limits, the spirit of monopoly, and exclusive privileges in nature of
monopolies, and confining corporations to the privileges plainly
given to them in their charter; the courts of this country should be
found enlarging these privileges by implication; and construing a
statute more unfavourably to the public, and to the rights of the
community, than would be done in a like case in an English court
of justice. . . .

But the case most analogous to this, and in which the question
came more directly before the court, is the case of the Providence
Bank v. Billings & Pittmann, 4 Pet. 514; and which was decided in
1830. In that case, it appeared that the legislature of Rhode Island
had chartered the bank, in the usual form of such acts of incorporation. The charter contained no stipulation on the part of the state,
that it would not impose a tax on the bank, nor any reservation of
the right to do so. It was silent on this point. Afterwards, a law was
passed, imposing a tax on all banks in the state; and the right to
impose this tax was resisted by the Providence Bank, upon the
ground, that if the state could impose a tax, it might tax so heavily
as to render the franchise of no value, and destroy the institution;
that the charter was a contract, and that a power which may in
effect destroy the charter is inconsistent with it, and is impliedly
renounced by granting it. But the court said that the taxing power
was of vital importance, and essential to the existence of government; and that the relinquishment of such a power is never to be
assumed. And in delivering the opinion of the court, the late chief
justice states the principle, in the following clear and emphatic
language. Speaking of the taxing power, he says, "as the whole

community is interested in retaining it undiminished, that community has a right to insist that its abandonment ought not to be presumed, in a case in which the deliberate purpose of the state to abandon it does not appear." The case now before the court is, in principle, precisely the same. It is a charter from a state. The act of incorporation is silent in relation to the contested power. The argument in favour of the proprietors of the Charles river bridge, is the same, almost in words, with that used by the Providence Bank; that is, that the power claimed by the state, if it exists, may be so used as to destroy the value of the franchise they have granted to the corporation. The argument must receive the same answer; and the fact that the power has been already exercised so as to destroy the value of the franchise, cannot in any degree affect the principle. The existence of the power does not, and cannot depend upon the circumstance of its having been excised or not.

It may, perhaps, be said, that in the case of the Providence Bank, this court were speaking of the taxing power; which is of vital importance to the very existence of every government. But the object and end of all government is to promote the happiness and prosperity of the community by which it is established; and it can never be assumed, that the government intended to diminish its power of accomplishing the end for which it was created. And in a country like ours, free, active, and enterprising, continually advancing in numbers and wealth; new channels of communication are daily found necessary, both for travel and trade; and are essential to the comfort, convenience, and prosperity of the people. A state ought never to be presumed to surrender this power, because, like the taxing power, the whole community has an interest in preserving it undiminished. And when a corporation alleges, that a state has surrendered for seventy years, its power of improvement and public accommodation, in a great and important line of travel, along which a vast number of its citizens must daily pass; the community have a right to insist, in the language of this court above quoted, "that its abandonment ought not to be presumed, in a case, in which the deliberate purpose of the state to abandon it does not appear." The continued existence of a government would be of no great value, if by implications and presumptions, it was disarmed of the powers necessary to accomplish the ends of its creation; and the functions it was designed to perform, transferred to the hands of privileged corporations. The rule of construction announced by the court, was not confined to the taxing power; nor is it so limited in the opinion delivered. On the contrary, it was distinctly placed on the ground that the interests of the community were concerned in preserving, undiminished, the power then in question; and whenever any power of the state is said to be surrendered or diminished, whether it be the taxing power or any other affecting the public interest, the same principle applies, and the rule of construction must be the same. No one will question that the interests of the great body of the people of the state, would, in this instance, be affected by the surrender of this great line of travel to a single corporation, with the right to exact toll, and exclude competition for seventy years. While the rights of private property are sacredly guarded, we must not forget that the community also have rights, and that the happiness and well being of every citizen depends on their faithful preservation.

Adopting the rule of construction above stated as the settled one, we proceed to apply it to the charter of 1785, to the proprietors of the Charles river bridge. This act of incorporation is in the usual form, and the privileges such as are commonly given to corporations of that kind. It confers on them the ordinary faculties of a corporation, for the purpose of building the bridge; and establishes certain rates of toll, which the company are authorized to take. This is the whole grant. There is no exclusive privilege given to them over the waters of Charles river, above or below their bridge. No right to erect another bridge themselves, nor to prevent other persons from erecting one. No engagement from the state, that another shall not be erected; and no undertaking not to sanction competition, nor to make improvements that may diminish the amount of its income. Upon all these subjects the charter is silent; and nothing is said in it about a line of travel, so much insisted on in the argument, in which they are to have exclusive privileges. No words are used, from which an intention to grant any of these rights can be inferred. If the plaintiff is entitled to them, it must be implied, simply, from the nature of the grant; and cannot be inferred, from the words by which the grant is made. . . .

The inquiry then is, does the charter contain such a contract on the part of the state? Is there any such stipulation to be found in that instrument? It must be admitted on all hands, that there is none—no words that even relate to another bridge, or to the diminution of their tolls, or to the line of travel. If a contract on that subject can be gathered from the charter, it must be by implication; and cannot be found in the words used. Can such an agreement be implied? The rule of construction before stated is an answer to the question. In charters of this description, no rights are taken from the public, or given to the corporation, beyond those which the words of the charter, by their natural and proper construction, purport to convey. There are no words which import such a contract as the plaintiffs in error contend for, and none can be implied; and the same answer must be given to them that was given by this court to the Providence Bank. The whole community are interested in this inquiry, and they have a right to require that the power of promoting their comfort and convenience, and of advancing the public prosperity, by providing safe, convenient, and cheap ways for the transportation of produce, and the purposes of travel, shall not be construed to have been surrendered or diminished by the state; unless it shall appear by plain words, that it was intended to be done. . . .

Indeed, the practice and usage of almost every state in the Union, old enough to have commenced the work of internal improvement, is opposed to the doctrine contended for on the part of the plaintiffs in error. Turnpike roads have been made in succession, on the same line of travel; the later ones interfering materially with the profits of the first. These corporations have, in some instances, been utterly ruined by the introduction of newer and better modes of transportation, and travelling. In some cases, railroads have rendered the turnpike roads on the same line of travel so entirely useless, that the franchise of the turnpike corporation is not worth preserving. Yet in none of these cases have the corporation supposed that their privileges were invaded, or any contract violated on the part of the state. Amid the multitude of cases which have occurred, and have been daily occurring for the last forty or fifty years, this is the first instance in which such an implied contract has been contended for, and this court called upon to infer it from an ordinary act of incorporation, containing nothing more than the usual stipulations and provisions to be found in every such law. The absence of any such controversy, when there must have been so many occasions to give rise to it, proves that neither states, nor individuals, nor corporations, ever imagined that such a contract could be implied from such charters. It shows that the men who voted for these laws, never imagined that they were forming such a contract; and if we maintain that they have made it, we must create it by a legal fiction, in opposition to the truth of the fact, and the obvious intention of the party. We cannot deal thus with the rights reserved to the states; and by legal intendments and mere technical reasoning, take away from them any portion of that power over their own internal police and improvement, which is so necessary to their well being and prosperity. . . .

Let it once be understood that such charters carry with them these implied contracts, and give this unknown and undefined property in a line of travelling; and you will soon find the old turnpike corporations awakening from their sleep, and calling upon this court to put down the improvements which have taken their place. The millions of property which have been invested in railroads and canals, upon lines of travel which had been before occupied by turnpike corporations, will be put in jeopardy. We shall be thrown back to the improvements of the last century, and obliged to stand still, until the claims of the old turnpike corporations shall be satisfied; and they shall consent to permit these states to avail themselves of the lights of modern science, and to partake of the benefit of those improvements which are now adding to the wealth and prosperity, and the convenience and comfort, of every other part of the civilized world. . . .

The judgment of the supreme judicial court of the commonwealth of Massachusetts, dismissing the plaintiffs' bill, must, therefore, be affirmed, with costs. . . .

37. Texas: Clay's "Raleigh Letter"

AFTER TEXAS won its independence from Mexico there was strong feeling in the United States favoring annexation. However, the possibility of war with Mexico and the certain discord to arise over the question of slavery in the area kept the question in abeyance for many years. Henry Clay and Martin Van Buren, the apparent candidates for the presidency in the election of 1844, agreed to eliminate the Texas question from the campaign. Both men published letters in the newspapers explaining their opposition to annexation. In all probability Van Buren lost the

SOURCE: *Niles Weekly Register*, May 4, 1844.

*nomination of the Democratic party to James K. Polk because of his
stand. Clay was nominated by the Whig party, but he lost to Polk in
the election. The expiring administration of John Tyler succeeded in
getting annexation through the Congress just a few days before Polk
took office.*

Raleigh, April 17, 1844

Gentlemen: Subsequent to my departure from Ashland, in December last, I received various communications from popular
assemblages and private individuals, requesting an expression of my
opinion upon the question of the annexation of Texas to the
United States. . . . The rejection of the overture of Texas, some
years ago, to become annexed to the United States, had met with
general acquiescence. Nothing had since occurred materially to
vary the question. I had seen no evidence of a desire being entertained, on the part of any considerable portion of the American
people, that Texas should become an integral part of the United
States. During my sojourn in New Orleans, I had, indeed, been
greatly surprised, by information which I received from Texas, that,
in the course of last fall, a voluntary overture had proceeded from
the executive of the United States to the authorities of Texas to
conclude a treaty of annexation; and that, in order to overcome the
repugnance felt by any of them to a negotiation upon the subject,
strong and, as I believed, erroneous representations had been made
to them of a state of opinion in the Senate of the U. States favorable to the ratification of such a treaty. According to these representations, it had been ascertained that a number of senators,
varying from thirty-five to forty-two, were ready to sanction such a
treaty. I was aware, too, that holders of Texas lands and Texas
scrip, and speculators in them, were actively engaged in promoting
the object of annexation. Still, I did not believe that any executive
of the United States would venture upon so grave and momentous
a proceeding, not only without any general manifestation of public
opinion in favor of it, but in direct opposition to strong and
decided expressions of public disapprobation. But it appears that I
was mistaken. To the astonishment of the whole nation, we are
now informed that a treaty of annexation has been actually concluded, and is to be submitted to the senate for its consideration.
The motives for my silence, therefore, no longer remain, and I feel
it to be my duty to present an exposition of my views and opinions
upon the question, for what they may be worth, to the public

consideration. I adopt this method as being more convenient than several replies to the respective communications which I have received.

I regret that I have not the advantage of a view of the treaty itself, so as to enable me to adapt an expression of my opinion to the actual conditions and stipulations which it contains. Not possessing that opportunity, I am constrained to treat the question according to what I presume to be the terms of the treaty. If, without the loss of national character, without the hazard of foreign war, with the general concurrence of the nation, without any danger to the integrity of the Union, and without giving an unreasonable price for Texas, the question of annexation were presented, it would appear in quite a different light from that in which, I apprehend, it is now to be regarded. . . .

The events which have since transpired in Texas are well known. She revolted against the government of Mexico, flew to arms, and finally fought and won the memorable battle of San Jacinto, annihilating a Mexican army and making a captive of the Mexican president. The signal success of that revolution was greatly aided, if not wholly achieved, by citizens of the United States who had migrated to Texas. These succors, if they could not always be prevented by the government of the United States, were furnished in a manner and to an extent which brought upon us some national reproach in the eyes of an impartial world. And, in my opinion, they impose on us the obligation of scrupulously avoiding the imputation of having instigated and aided the revolution with the ultimate view of territorial aggrandizement. After the battle of San Jacinto, the U. States recognised the independence of Texas, in conformity with the principle and practice which have always prevailed in their councils of recognizing the government "de facto," without regarding the question de jure. . . .

This narrative shows the present actual condition of Texas, so far as I have information about it. If it be correct, Mexico has not abandoned, but perseveres in the assertion of her rights by actual force of arms, which, if suspended, are intended to be renewed— Under these circumstances, if the government of the United States were to acquire Texas, it would acquire along with it all the incumbrances which Texas is under, and among them the actual or suspended war between Mexico and Texas. Of that consequence there cannot be a doubt. Annexation and war with Mexico are identical. Now, for one, I certainly am not willing to involve this country in a foreign war for the object of acquiring Texas. I know there are those who regard such a war with indifference and as a trifling affair, on account of the weakness of Mexico, and her inability to inflict serious injury upon this country. But I do not look upon it thus lightly. I regard all wars as great calamities, to be avoided, if possible, and honorable peace as the wisest and truest policy of this country. What the United States most need are union, peace, and patience. Nor do I think that the weakness of a power should form a motive, in any case, for inducing us to engage in or to depreciate the evils of war.—Honor and good faith and justice are equally due from this country towards the weak as towards the strong. And, if an act of injustice were to be perpetrated towards any power, it would be more compatible with the dignity of the nation, and, in my judgment, less dishonorable, to inflict it upon a powerful instead of a weak foreign nation. But are we perfectly sure that we should be free from injury in a state of war with Mexico? Have we any security that countless numbers of foreign vessels, under the authority and flag of Mexico, would not prey upon our defenseless commerce in the Mexican gulf, on the Pacific ocean, and on every other sea and ocean? What commerce, on the other hand, does Mexico offer, as an indemnity for our losses, to the gallantry and enterprise of our countrymen? This view of the subject supposes that the war would be confined to the United States and Mexico as the only belligerents. But have we any certain guaranty that Mexico would obtain no allies among the great European powers? Suppose any such powers, jealous of our increasing greatness, and disposed to check our growth and cripple us, were to take part in behalf of Mexico in the war, how would the different belligerents present themselves to Christendom and the enlightened world? We have been seriously charged with an inordinate spirit of territorial aggrandizement; and, without admitting the justice of the charge, it must be owned that we have made vast acquisitions of territory within the last forty years. Suppose Great Britain and France, or one of them, were to take part with Mexico, and, by a manifesto, were to proclaim that their objects were to assist a weak and helpless ally to check the spirit of encroachment and ambition of an already overgrown republic, seeking still further acquisitions of territory, to maintain the independence of Texas, disconnected with the United States and to prevent the further propagation of slavery from the United States, what would be the effect of such allegations upon the judgment of an impartial and enlightened world?

Assuming that the annexation of Texas is war with Mexico, is it competent to the treaty-making power to plunge this country into war, not only without the concurrence of, but without deigning to consult congress, to which, by the constitution, belongs exclusively the power of declaring war? . . .

I do not think that Texas ought to be received into the Union, as an integral part of it, in decided opposition to the wishes of a considerable and respectable portion of the confederacy. I think it far more wise and important to compose and harmonize the present confederacy, as it now exists, than to introduce a new element of discord and distraction into it. In my humble opinion, it should be the constant and earnest endeavor of American states-men to eradicate prejudices, to cultivate and foster concord, and to produce general contentment among all parts of our confederacy. And true wisdom, it seems to me, points to the duty of rendering its present members happy, prosperous, and satisfied with each other, rather than to attempt to introduce alien members, against the common consent and with the certainty of deep dissatisfac-tion. . . .

It is useless to disguise that there are those who espouse and those who oppose the annexation of Texas upon the ground of the influence which it would exert, in the balance of political power, between two great sections of the Union. I conceive that no motive for the acquisition of foreign territory would be more unfortunate, or pregnant with more fatal consequences, than that of obtaining it for the purpose of strengthening one part against another part of the common confederacy. Such a principle, put into practical operation, would menace the existence, if it did not certainly sow the seeds of a dissolution of the Union. It would be to proclaim to the world an insatiable and unquenchable thirst for foreign con-quest or acquisition of territory. For if to-day Texas be acquired to strengthen one part of the confederacy, to-morrow Canada may be required to add strength to another. And, after that might have been obtained, still other and further acquisitions would become necessary to equalize and adjust the balance of political power. Finally, in the progress of this spirit of universal dominion, the part of the confederacy which is now weakest, would find itself still weaker from the impossibility of securing new theaters for those peculiar institutions which it is charged 'with being desirous to extend. . . .

Although I have felt compelled, from the nature of the inquiries addressed to me, to extend this communication to a much greater length than I could have wished, I could not do justice to the subject, and fairly and fully expose my own opinions in a shorter space. In conclusion, they may be stated in a few words to be, that I consider the annexation of Texas, at this time, without the assent of Mexico, as a measure compromising the national character, involving us certainly in war with Mexico, probably with other foreign powers, dangerous to the integrity of the Union, inexpedient in the present financial condition of the country, and not called for by any general expression of public opinion.

I am, respectfully, your obedient servant,

38. Manifest Destiny

THE United States Magazine and Democratic Review, most commonly referred to as the Democratic Review, was founded in 1837 and quickly assumed the role of arbiter for Democrats in matters of politics, society, literature, the arts and almost everything else. John L. O'Sullivan was its editor, and several of his editorials are classic statements of Jacksonian opinion about democracy and American politics. In the expansionist surge of the 1840s it was he who first used the term "manifest destiny" to explain and justify the nation's westward thrust. In the following article he attempted to scotch the argument that annexation meant the extension of slavery into the territories or the strengthening of that "peculiar institution."

It is time now for opposition to the Annexation of Texas to cease, all further agitation of the waters of bitterness and strife, at least in connexion with this question,—even though it may perhaps be required of us as a necessary condition of the freedom of our institutions, that we must live on forever in a state of unpausing struggle and excitement upon some subject of party division or

SOURCE: *United States Magazine and Democratic Review* XVII (July-August, 1845): 5–10.

other. But, in regard to Texas, enough has now been given to Party. It is time for the common duty of Patriotism to the Country to succeed;—or if this claim will not be recognized, it is at least time for common sense to acquiesce with decent grace in the inevitable and the irrevocable.

Texas is now ours. Already, before these words are written, her Convention has undoubtedly ratified the acceptance, by her Congress, of our proffered invitation into the Union; and made the requisite changes in her already republican form of constitution to adopt it to its future federal relations. Her star and her stripe may already be said to have taken their place in the glorious blazon of our common nationality; and the sweep of our eagle's wing already includes within its circuit the wide extent of her fair and fertile land. She is no longer to us a mere geographical space—a certain combination of coast, plain, mountain, valley, forest and stream. She is no longer to us a mere country on the map. She comes within the dear and sacred designation of Our Country. . . .

Why, were other reasoning wanting, in favor of now elevating this question of the reception of Texas into the Union, out of the lower region of our past party dissensions, up to its proper level of a high and broad nationality, it surely is to be found, found abundantly, in the manner in which other nations have undertaken to intrude themselves into it, between us and the proper parties to the case, in a spirit of hostile interference against us, for the avowed object of thwarting our policy and hampering our power, limiting our greatness and checking the fulfilment of our manifest destiny to overspread the continent allotted by Providence for the free development of our yearly multiplying millions. This we have seen done by England, our old rival and enemy; and by France, strangely coupled with her against us, under the influence of the Anglicism strongly tinging the policy of her present prime minister, Guizot. The zealous activity with which this effort to defeat us was pushed by the representatives of those governments, together with the character of intrigue accompanying it, fully constituted that case of foreign interference, which Mr. Clay himself declared should, and would unite us all in maintaining the common cause of our country against the foreigner and the foe. We are only astonished that this effect has not been more fully and strongly produced, and that the burst of indignation against this unauthorized, insolent and hostile interference against us, has not been more general even among the party before opposed to Annexation, and has not rallied the national spirit and national pride unanimously upon that policy. We are very sure that if Mr. Clay himself were now to add another letter to his former Texas correspondence, he would express this sentiment, and carry out the idea already strongly stated in one of them, in a manner which would tax all the powers of blushing belonging to some of his party adherents.

It is wholly untrue, and unjust to ourselves, the pretence that the Annexation has been a measure of spoliation, unrightful and unrighteous—of military conquest under forms of peace and law— of territorial aggrandizement at the expense of justice, and justice due by a double sanctity to the weak. This view of the question is wholly unfounded, and has been before so amply refuted in these pages, as well as in a thousand other modes, that we shall not again dwell upon it. The independence of Texas was complete and absolute. It was an independence, not only in fact but of right. No obligation of duty towards Mexico tended in the least degree to restrain our right to effect the desired recovery of the fair province once our own—whatever motives of policy might have prompted a more deferential consideration of her feelings and her pride, as involved in the question. If Texas became peopled with an American population, it was by no contrivance of our government, but on the express invitation of that of Mexico herself; accompanied with such guaranties of State independence, and the maintenance of a federal system analogous to our own, as constituted a compact fully justifying the strongest measures of redress on the part of those afterwards deceived in this guaranty, and sought to be enslaved under the yoke imposed by its violation. She was released, rightfully and absolutely released, from all Mexican allegiance, or duty of cohesion to the Mexican political body, by the acts and fault of Mexico herself, and Mexico alone. There never was a clearer case. It was not revolution; it was resistance to revolution; and resistance under such circumstances as left independence the necessary resulting state, caused by the abandonment of those with whom her former federal association had existed. What then can be more preposterous than all this clamor by Mexico and the Mexican interest, against Annexation, as a violation of any rights of hers, any duties of ours? . . .

Nor is there any just foundation for the charge that Annexation is a great pro-slavery measure calculated to increase and perpetuate that institution. Slavery had nothing to do with it. Opinions were and are greatly divided, both at the North and South, as to the influence to be exerted by it on Slavery and the Slave States. That it will tend to facilitate and hasten the disappearance of Slavery from all the northern tier of the present Slave States, cannot surely admit of serious question. The greater value in Texas of the slave labor now employed in those States, must soon produce the effect of draining off that labor southwardly, by the same unvarying law that bids water descend the slope that invites it. . . .

Texas has been absorbed into the Union in the inevitable fulfilment of the general law which is rolling our population westward; the connexion of which with the ratio of growth in population which is destined within a hundred years to swell our numbers to the enormous population of two hundred and fifty millions (if not more), is too evident to leave us in doubt of the manifest design of Providence in regard to the occupation of this continent. It was disintegrated from Mexico in the natural course of events, by a process perfectly legitimate on its own part, blameless on ours; and in which all the censures due to wrong, perfidy and folly, rest on Mexico alone. And possessed as it was by a population which was in truth but a colonial detachment from our own, and which was still bound by myriad ties of the very heart-strings to its old relations, domestic and political, their incorporation into the Union was not only inevitable, but the most natural, right and proper thing in the world—and it is only astonishing that there should be any among ourselves to say it nay. . . .

California will, probably, next fall away from the loose adhesion which, in such a country as Mexico, holds a remote province in a slight equivocal kind of dependence on the metropolis. Imbecile and distracted, Mexico never can exert any real governmental authority over such a country. The impotence of the one and the distance of the other, must make the relation one of virtual independence; unless, by stunting the province of all natural growth, and forbidding that immigration which can alone develope its capabilities and fulfil the purposes of its creation, tyranny may retain a military dominion which is no government in the legitimate sense of the term. In the case of California this is now impossible. The Anglo-Saxon foot is already on its borders. Already the advance guard of the irresistible army of Anglo-Saxon emigration has begun to pour down upon it, armed with the plough and the rifle, and marking its trail with schools and colleges, courts and representative halls, mills and meeting-houses. A population will soon be in actual occupation of California, over which it will be idle for Mexico to dream of dominion. They will necessarily become independent. All this without agency of our government, without responsibility of our people—in the natural flow of events, the spontaneous working of principles, and the adaptation of the tendencies and wants of the human race to the elemental circumstances in the midst of which they find themselves placed. . . .

Whether they will then attach themselves to our Union or not, is not to be predicted with any certainty. Unless the projected railroad across the continent to the Pacific be carried into effect, perhaps they may not; though even in that case, the day is not distant when the Empires of the Atlantic and Pacific would again flow together into one, as soon as their inland border should approach each other. But that great work, colossal as appears the plan on its first suggestion, cannot remain long unbuilt. Its necessity for this very purpose of binding and holding together in its iron clasp our fast settling Pacific region with that of the Mississippi valley— the natural facility of the route—the ease with which any amount of labor for the construction can be drawn in from the overcrowded populations of Europe, to be paid in the lands made valuable by the progress of the work itself—and its immense utility to the commerce of the world with the whole eastern coast of Asia, alone almost sufficient for the support of such a road—these considerations give assurance that the day cannot be distant which shall witness the conveyance of the representatives from Oregon and California to Washington within less time than a few years ago was devoted to a similar journey by those from Ohio; while the magnetic telegraph will enable the editors of the "San Francisco Union," the "Astoria Evening Post," or the "Nootka Morning News" to set up in type the first half of the President's Inaugural, before the echoes of the latter half shall have died away beneath the lofty porch of the Capitol, as spoken from his lips.

Away, then, with all idle French talk of *balances of power* on the American Continent. There is no growth in Spanish America! Whatever progress of population there may be in the British Canadas, is only for their own early severance of their present colonial relation to the little island three thousand miles across the

Atlantic; soon to be followed by Annexation, and destined to swell the still accumulating momentum of our progress. And whosoever may hold the balance, though they should cast into the opposite scale all the bayonets and cannon, not only of France and England, but of Europe entire, how would it kick the beam against the simple solid weight of the two hundred and fifty, or three hundred millions—and American millions—destined to gather beneath the flutter of the stripes and stars, in the fast hastening year of the Lord 1945!

39. Oregon: Speech of Thomas Hart Benton

PRESSURE FOR *the annexation of Oregon was belligerently expressed by Democrats in the presidential campaign of 1844 by the cry of "Fifty-Four Forty or Fight." President Polk notified the British of his intention to end joint occupation of the Oregon country; this was interpreted in some quarters as a preliminary statement to a declaration of war unless Oregon was ceded to the United States. In a speech before the Senate on May 28, 1846, Thomas Hart Benton explained the advantages of possessing this vital area. Fortunately, hostilities between Great Britain and the United States were averted when the territory was amicably divided between the two countries at the forty-ninth parallel.*

The value of the country—I mean the Columbia River and its valley—(I must repeat the limitation every time, lest I be carried up to 54°40′)—has been questioned on this floor and elsewhere. It has been supposed to be of little value—hardly worth the possession, much less the acquisition; and treated rather as a burden to be preserved. This is a great error, and one that only prevails on this side of the water; the British know better; and if they held the tithe of our title, they would fight the world for what we depreciate. It is not a worthless country, but one of immense value, and that under many respects, and will be occupied by others, to our injury and annoyance, if not by ourselves for our own benefit and protection. Forty years ago it was written by Humboldt, that the banks of the Columbia presented the only situation on the northwest coast of

SOURCE: U.S., Congress, Senate, *Congressional Globe*, 29th Congress, 1st session, pp. 914–5.

America fit for the residence of a civilized people. Experience has confirmed the truth of this wise remark. All the rest of the coast, from the Straits of Fuca out to New Archangel, (and nothing but a fur trading post there,) remains a vacant waste, abandoned since the quarrel of Nootka Sound, and become the derelict of nations. The Columbia only invites a possessor; and for that possession, sagacious British diplomacy has been weaving its web. It is not a worthless possession; but valuable under many and large aspects; to the consideration of some of which I now proceed.

It is valuable, both as a country to be inhabited, and as a position to be held and defended. I speak of it, first, as a position, commanding the North Pacific ocean, and overlooking the eastern coast of Asia. The North Pacific is a rich sea, and is already the seat of a great commerce: British, French, American, Russian, and ships of other nations, frequent it. Our whaling ships cover it: our ships of war go there to protect our interest; and, great as that interest now is, it is only the beginning. Futurity will develop an immense, and various, commerce on that sea, of which the far greater part will be American. That commerce, neither in the merchant ships which carry it on, nor in the military marine which protects it, can find a port, to call its own, within twenty thousand miles of the field of its operations. The double length of the two Americas has to be run—a stormy and tempestuous cape to be doubled—to find itself in a port of its own country: while here lies one in the very edge of its field, ours by right, ready for use, and ample for every purpose of refuge and repair, protection and domination. Can we turn our back on it? and, in turning the back, deliver it up to the British? Insane, and suicidal would be the fatal act!

To say nothing of the daily want of such a port in time of peace, its want, in time of war, becomes ruinous. Commodore Porter has often told me that, with protection from batteries in the mouth of the Columbia, he never would have put himself in a condition to be attacked under the weak, or collusive guns of a neutral port. He has told me that, with such a port for the reception of his prizes, he would not have sunk in the ocean, or hid in islands where it was often found, the three millions of British property captured in his three years' daring and dauntless cruise. Often has he told me, that, with such a port at his hand, he would never have been driven to spill upon the waters, that oil, for want of which, as a member of the British Parliament said, London had burnt darkly—had been in the dark—for a whole year. What happened to Commodore Porter and his prizes—what happened to all our merchant ships, driven from the North Pacific during the war—all this to happen again, and upon a far larger scale, is but half the evil of turning our backs now upon this commanding position; for, to do so, is to deliver it into the hands of a Power that knows the value of positions—the four quarters of the globe, and our own coasts attest that—and has her eye on this one. The very year after the renewal of the delusive convention of 1818—in the year 1819—a master ship-carpenter was despatched from London to Fort Vancouver, to begin there the repair of vessels, and even the construction of small ones; and this work has been going on ever since. She resists our possession now! If we abandon, she will retain! And here wooden walls, bristling with cannon, and issuing from the mouth of the Columbia, will give the law to the North Pacific, permitting our ships to sneak about in time of peace—sinking, seizing, or chasing them away, in time of war. As a position, then, and if nothing but a rock, or desert point, the possession of the Columbia is invaluable to us; and it becomes our duty to maintain it at all hazards. . . .

The carrying trade between eastern Asia and western America will be another of the advantages belonging to the Columbia. It is the only position between the Isthmus of Darien and Behring's Straits on which a naval power can exist. Mexico has no timber, few ports, and none of the elements of ship building. The Lower California is the same. Northern California, with the Bay of San Francisco, and the magnificent timber of the Sierra Nevada is now shown, by the discoveries of Captain Frémont, to be geographically appurtenant to the Columbia, and in time must obey its destiny. The Columbia river is the seat of a great naval preeminence. . . . The people on the Columbia, then will be the carriers, almost exclusively, between eastern Asia . . . and all Mexico, California and Northwest America . . . and rich will be the profits of such carrying.

40. The Mexican War

THE EXPANSIONIST *ambitions of the nation to take California soon provoked war with Mexico. Polk chose to regard the Rio Grande River as the southern boundary of Texas, rather than the Nueces River, which was the boundary claimed by Mexico. In January, 1846, Polk ordered General Zachary Taylor to occupy the northern bank of the Rio Grande; this was a deliberate act of invasion. Fighting immediately broke out between American and Mexican forces, and in May, 1846, the President asked Congress for a declaration of war. Some Americans, particularly within the Whig party, were appalled by the war and the moral corruption that had precipitated it. Philip Hone, a New York merchant, recorded his horror over one of the most disgraceful acts in the history of the United States.*

Mexico. May 7, 1846—Affairs in this quarter wear an alarming aspect. If the government intended by its measures to bring disaster and defeat upon the insufficient forces sent into that unhappy country, and thereby make popular the war which it is preparing to wage against Mexico, it is likely that it may succeed; but the people will have an awful account to settle with it. A war simultaneously with England and Mexico for Oregon and Texas,—neither of which is worth the blood of a single American soldier,—and without a force adequate to carry out the least of those enterprises, would be pushing the forbearance of the people to a dangerous length. But we have reason to know that the tyranny of party discipline is more absolute in this country than the mandate of the Czar of Moscow, or the will of the Khan of Tartary. . . .

May 9 . . . Mr. Polk and his party have accomplished their object: the war with Mexico is fairly commenced. The President (in violation of the Constitution, which gives to Congress the exclusive power to declare war) announces formally that a state of war exists, calls for volunteers and money, which Congress unhesitatingly grants; and if any old-fashioned legislator presumes to doubt the authority of Pope Polk, or questions the infallibility of

SOURCE: Philip Hone, *The Diary of Philip Hone 1828–1851*, ed. Bayard Tuckerman, Volume II (New York, 1889), pp. 276–8, 283.

his bull, he is stigmatized by some of the ruffians of the West as an enemy to his country, in league with the Mexicans. These charges he must submit to, or, by making a suitable retort, expose himself to the necessity of fighting himself out of his difficulty, or leaving a vacant seat to be filled by some more subservient representative of the magnanimous *American people*.

This war has commenced most disastrously, as might have been expected from the scanty force sent into the disputed territory. My suggestion of Thursday appears uncharitable; but it really looks as if this result was anticipated, and the American blood shed was to excite American feelings, and to make the war popular. . . . Extras were published today, by all the papers, giving further particulars received from New Orleans of the dangerous position of General Taylor's little army on the Rio Grande. He is cut off by Arista from his resources at Point Isabel, at the mouth of the river, and, although within cannon-shot of Metamoras, on the opposite side of the river, he cannot send men to attack it. These disasters will raise the blood of the American people to the war point, and cause them to cease inquiring, What is this war about? What compensation is to be had for the blood shed and the treasures squandered? and, How will the national character be redeemed which we have staked on this dreadful issue? They will thus be compelled to support a cause which their conscience condemns and their judgement disapproves.

May 12—The President's message, announcing a state of war with Mexico, was sent to Congress yesterday, who forthwith granted him power to call out fifty thousand volunteers, and appropriated ten millions of dollars as a small outfit for his military operations. This is a horrible state of things. But a little philosophy can extract grains of comfort even from this. The tariff cannot be touched whilst such expenditures are incurred, nor will the sub-treasury and specie scheme be carried into effect with such a war impending. . . .

August 12—Congress adjourned on Monday night, after a session of nearly eight months; the most corrupt, profligate, and disastrous the United States have ever known. Pliant and sub-servient to a wicked administration, the Constitution has been violated, the industry and enterprise of the people have been sacrificed to foreign influences, the currency disturbed, commerce deprived of its customary facilities, the country plunged into an unjust, unnecessary, and expensive war, and national honour, honesty, and good faith made the sport of party dictation and executive power.

The pestilence is stayed for a brief period; but its victims lie unburied in the sight of the survivors, or linger on paralyzed and mutilated. The storm is abated; but its ravages will long be seen in the shattered ruins of domestic industry. The dark clouds which have overshadowed the land, late so happy and prosperous, are dispersed; but no star of hope is left to cheer the prospects of the future.

VI

American Life and Society

41. Three Impressions

DURING THE 1830s and 1840s American life fell under the concentrated scrutiny of many foreign visitors, particularly the French and British. These visitors traveled to all parts of the nation, recording their impressions and detailing what they admired and what they disliked. In the following three documents Harriet Martineau, Francis Trollope and Tyrone Power describe segments of American life in three widely different places—one the relatively new city of Chicago, the second a remote forest farm and finally the then-southwestern region of the country around Mobile.

A. CHICAGO

Chicago looks raw and bare, standing on the high prairie above the lake-shore. The houses appeared all insignificant, and run up in various directions, without any principle at all. A friend of mine who resides there had told me that we should find the inns intolerable, at the period of the great land sales, which bring a concourse of speculators to the place. It was even so. The very sight of them was intolerable; and there was not room for our party among them all. I do not know what we should have done, (unless to betake ourselves to the vessels in the harbour,) if our coming had not been foreknown, and most kindly provided for. We were divided between three families, who had the art of removing all our scruples about intruding on perfect strangers. None of us will lose the lively and pleasant associations with the place, which were caused by the hospitalities of its inhabitants.

I never saw a busier place than Chicago was at the time of our

SOURCE: Harriet Martineau, *Society in America*, Volume I (New York, 1837), pp. 259–62.

arrival. The streets were crowded with land speculators, hurrying from one sale to another. A negro, dressed up in scarlet, bearing a scarlet flag, and riding a white horse with housings of scarlet, announced the times of sale. At every street-corner where he stopped, the crowd flocked round him; and it seemed as if some prevalent mania infected the whole people. The rage for speculation might fairly be so regarded. As the gentlemen of our party walked the streets, store-keepers hailed them from their doors, with offers of farms, and all manner of land-lots, advising them to speculate before the price of land rose higher. A young lawyer, of my acquaintance there, had realised five hundred dollars per day, the five preceding days, by merely making out titles to land. Another friend had realised, in two years, ten times as much money as he had before fixed upon as a competence for life. Of course, this rapid money-making is a merely temporary evil. A bursting of the bubble must come soon. The absurdity of the speculation is so striking, that the wonder is that the fever should have attained such a height as I witnessed. The immediate occasion of the bustle which prevailed, the week we were at Chicago, was the sale of lots, to the value of two millions of dollars, along the course of a projected canal; and of another set, immediately behind these. Persons not intending to game, and not infected with mania, would endeavour to form some reasonable conjecture as to the ultimate value of the lots, by calculating the cost of the canal, the risks from accident, from the possible competition from other places, &c., and, finally, the possible profits, under the most favourable circumstances, within so many years' purchase. Such a calculation would serve as some sort of guide as to the amount of purchase-money to be risked. Whereas, wild land on the banks of a canal, not yet even marked out, was selling at Chicago for more than rich land, well improved, in the finest part of the valley of the Mohawk, on the banks of a canal which is already the medium of an almost inestimable amount of traffic. If sharpers and gamblers were to be the sufferers by the impending crash at Chicago, no one would feel much concerned: but they, unfortunately, are the people who encourage the delusion, in order to profit by it. Many a high-spirited, but inexperienced, young man; many a simple settler, will be ruined for the advantage of knaves.

Others, besides lawyers and speculators by trade, make a fortune in such extraordinary times. A poor man at Chicago had a preemption right to some land, for which he paid in the morning one hundred and fifty dollars. In the afternoon, he sold it to a friend of mine for five thousand dollars. A poor Frenchman, married to a squaw, had a suit pending, when I was there, which he was likely to gain, for the right of purchasing some land by the lake for one hundred dollars, which would immediately become worth one million dollars.

There was much gaiety going on at Chicago, as well as business. On the evening of our arrival a fancy fair took place. As I was too much fatigued to go, the ladies sent me a bouquet of prairie flowers. There is some allowable pride in the place about its society. It is a remarkable thing to meet such an assemblage of educated, refined, and wealthy persons as may be found there, living in small, inconvenient houses on the edge of a wild prairie. There is a mixture, of course. I heard of a family of half-breeds setting up a carriage, and wearing fine jewellery. When the present intoxication of prosperity passes away, some of the inhabitants will go back to the eastward; there will be an accession of settlers from the mechanic classes; good houses will have been built for the richer families, and the singularity of the place will subside. It will be like all the other new and thriving lake and river ports of America. Meantime, I am glad to have seen it in its strange early days.

B. Forest Farm

We heard on every side, that of all the known places on "the globe called earth," Cincinnati was the most favourable for a young man to settle in; and I only awaited the arrival of Mr. T. to fix our son there, intending to continue with him till he should feel himself sufficiently established. We accordingly determined upon making ourselves as comfortable as possible. I took a larger house which, however, I did not obtain without considerable difficulty, as, notwithstanding fourteen hundred new dwellings had been erected the preceding year, the demand for houses greatly exceeded the supply. We became acquainted with several amiable people, and we beguiled the anxious interval that preceded Mr. T.'s joining us

Source: Francis Trollope, *Domestic Manners of the Americans,* Volume I (London, 1832): 68–71.

by frequent excursions in the neighbourhood, which not only afforded us amusement, but gave us an opportunity of observing the mode of life of the country people.

We visited one farm, which interested us particularly from its wild and lonely situation, and from the entire dependence of the inhabitants upon their own resources. It was a partial clearing in the very heart of the forest. The house was built on the side of a hill, so steep that a high ladder was necessary to enter the front door, while the back one opened against the hill side; at the foot of this sudden eminence ran a clear stream, whose bed had been deepened into a little reservoir, just opposite the house. A noble field of Indian corn stretched away into the forest on one side, and a few half-cleared acres, with a shed or two upon them, occupied the other, giving accommodation to cows, horses, pigs, and chickens innumerable. Immediately before the house was a small potatoe garden, with a few peach and apple trees. The house was built of logs, and consisted of two rooms, besides a little shanty or lean-to, that was used as a kitchen. Both rooms were comfortable furnished with good beds, drawers, &c. The farmer's wife, and a young woman who looked liked her sister, were spinning, and three little children were playing about. The woman told me that they spun and wove all the cotton and woollen garments of the family, and knit all the stockings; her husband, though not a shoemaker by trade, made all the shoes. She manufactured all the soap and candles they used, and prepared her sugar from the sugar trees on their farm. All she wanted with money, she said, was to buy coffee, tea, and whiskey, and she could "get enough any day by sending a batch of butter and chicken to market." They used no wheat, nor sold any of their corn, which, though it appeared a very large quantity, was not more than they required to make their bread and cakes of various kinds, and to feed all their live stock during the winter. She did not look in health, and said they had all had ague in "the fall"; but she seemed contented, and proud of her independence; though it was in somewhat a mournful accent that she said, " 'Tis strange to us to see company: I expect the sun may rise and set a hundred times before I shall see another _human_ that does not belong to the family."

I have been minute in the description of this forest farm, as I think it the best specimen I saw of the back-wood's independence, of which so much is said in America. These people were indeed independent, Robinson Crusoe was hardly more so, and they eat and drink abundantly; but yet it seemed to me that there was something awful and almost unnatural in their loneliness. No village bell ever summoned them to prayer, where they might meet the friendly greeting of their fellow-men. When they die, no spot sacred by ancient reverence will receive their bones—Religion will not breathe her sweet and solemn farewell upon their grave; the husband or the father will dig the pit that is to hold them, beneath the nearest tree; he will himself deposit them within it, and the wind that whispers through the boughs will be their only requiem. But then they pay neither taxes nor tythes, are never expected to pull off a hat or to make a curtsy, and will live and die without hearing or uttering the dreadful words, "God save the king."

C. Mobile

. . . The grounds on which the vast and seemingly extravagant increase of the cotton crop of this State of Alabama may be justified, are to be found, not only in the great fertility of the virgin soil yearly brought under cultivation, but in the unprecedented increase of population. This very year, it is calculated, not less than twenty-five thousand slaves have been brought into this country from the older States on the Atlantic; this amount will, in all probability, be exceeded by the increase of next season, as there are many millions of acres of the most fertile land in the Union yet in the hands of Government for sale, lately conceded in exchange by the Indians of the Creek and Cherokee tribes.

The great cause of emigration from the Atlantic States is to be looked for in the temptation offered the planter by a soil of vastly superior fertility. In South Carolina and in most parts of Georgia, it will appear that a good average crop will give one bale or bag of cotton, weighing 310 lbs. for each working-hand employed on the plantation; now, in Alabama, four or five bales, each weighing 430 lbs. is a fair average for an able-bodied slave engaged in the cultivation; and I have conversed with many planters, holding places upon the bottom-lands of the river, who assured me their crop was yearly ten bales of cotton for each full-grown hand.

When it is considered that this season the value of cotton has

SOURCE: Tyrone Power, *Impressions of America During the Years 1833, 1834 and 1835*, Volume II (Philadelphia, 1836), pp. 135–8.

been ranging from sixpence-halfpenny to ninepence per pound, the enormous receipts of some of these persons, who make from four hundred to three thousand bales of 430 lbs. weight each, may be imagined.

These are the men who have been my companions on all my late steamboat trips, for this is the season that affords them *relâche* and brings them together; and in this city especially, as at Natchez, it is by this singular class I am surrounded: they are not difficult to comprehend, and a slight sketch of their condition and habits may not be uninteresting, as they form the great mass now inhabiting this mighty region, and it is from them a probable future population of one hundred million of souls must receive language, habits, and laws.

We generally associate with the Southern planter ideas of indolence, inertness of disposition, and a love of luxury and idle expense: nothing, however, can be less characteristic of these frontier tamers of the swamp and of the forest: they are hardy, indefatigable, and enterprising to a degree; despising and contemning luxury and refinement, courting labour, and even making a pride of the privations which they, without any necessity, continue to endure with their families. They are prudent without being at all mean or penurious, and are fond of money without having a tittle of avarice. This may at first sight appear stated from a love of parodox, yet nothing can be more strictly and simply true; this is, in fact, a singular race, and they seem especially endowed by Providence to forward the great work in which they are engaged—to clear the wilderness and lay bare the wealth of this rich country with herculean force and restless perseverance, spurred by a spirit of acquisition no extent of possession can satiate.

Most men labour that they may, at some contemplated period, repose on the fruits of their industry: adventurers in unhealthy regions, generally, seek to amass wealth that they may escape from their *pénible* abodes, and recompense themselves by after enjoyment for the perils and privations they have endured. Not so the planters of this south-western region; were their natures moulded after this ordinary fashion, these States, it is true, might long continue mines of wealth, to be wrought by a succession of adventurers; but never would they become what Providence has evidently designed they shall be,—great countries, powerful governments, and the home of millions of freemen yet unborn.

These men seek wealth from the soil to return it back to the soil, with the addition of the sweat of their brows tracking every newly-broken furrow. Their pride does not consist in fine houses, fine raiment, costly services of plate, or refined cookery: they live in humble dwellings of wood, wear the coarsest habits, and live on the plainest fare. It is their pride to have planted an additional acre of cane-brake, to have won a few feet from the river, or cleared a thousand trees from the forest; to have added a couple of slaves to their family, or a horse of high blood to their stable.

It is for these things that they labour from year to year. Unconscious agents in the hands of the Almighty, it is to advance the great cause of civilization, whose pioneers they are, that they endure toil for their lives, without the prospect of reaping any one personal advantage which might not have been attained in the first ten years of their labour.

It is not through ignorance either that they continue in these simple and rude habits of life. Most of these planters visit the Northern States periodically, as well as New Orleans; their wealth, and the necessity the merchant feels to conciliate their good-will, makes them the ready guests at tables where every luxury and refinement abounds; but they view these without evincing the least desire to imitate them, prefer generally the most ordinary liquids to the finest-flavoured wines, and, as guests, are much easier to please than to catch; for not only do they appear indifferent to these luxuries, but they seek to avoid them, condemn their use, and return to their log-houses and the cane-brake to seek in labour for enjoyment.

There must, however, be a great charm in the unrestrained freedom of this sort of life; since I have frequently met women, who were bred in the North, well educated, and accustomed for years to all the agrémens of good society, who yet assure me that they were happiest when living in the solitude of their plantation, and only felt dull whilst wandering about the country or recruiting at some public watering-place.

The great drawback to these frontiers, and one which will, I fear, exist for some time, unless the citizens of the towns take the law into their own hands, and execute it in a summary manner, is to be found in the presence of certain idle ruffians who exist here. The only matter of surprise to me is, that there are so few of the description, and that in such a country crime is so rare, where the facility afforded for escape is great, and where the laws view with such reverence the liberty of the subject.

42. Literature and Newspapers

ONE OF THE most important factors of American life in the Jacksonian period—a factor that cannot be emphasized too much—was the existence of a great number of newspapers in virtually every community in the country. In 1828 there were approximately six hundred newspapers in the United States, and that number increased to over a thousand in the next twenty years; as the cost of newspapers was reduced to a penny a copy, a greater number of people could afford to buy them. To the ordinary citizen the newspaper was an essential part of his life; to political parties it was the sine qua non for efficient organization. In the following selection an English traveler commented about this phenomenon at the same time as he discoursed briefly on American literature. It is interesting that he was apparently not yet aware of some of the most distinguished literary figures of the period, such men as Hawthorne, Melville, Emerson and Lowell.

In a country of whose people it may be said that they all read, it is but natural that we should look for a national literature. For this we do not look in vain to America. Like its commerce, its literature is as yet comparatively young, but like it in its development it has been rapid and progressive. There is scarcely a department of literature in which the Americans do not now occupy a respectable and prominent position. The branch in which they have least excelled, perhaps, is the drama. In poetry they have been prolific, notwithstanding the practical nature of their pursuits as a people. A great deal of what they have produced in this form is valueless, to say nothing else; but some of their poets have deservedly a reputation extending far beyond their country's bounds. Of the novels of Cooper it is not necessary here to speak. There is an originality in the productions of Pierpoint, and a vigour in those of Halleck, a truthfulness as well as force in the verses of Duna, and a soothing influence in the sweet strains of Bryant, which recommend them to

SOURCE: Alexander Mackay, *The Western World, or, Travels in the United States in 1846–47*, Volume III (London, 1849), pp. 238–46.

all speaking or reading the glorious language in which they are written. In the bright galaxy of historical authors, no names stand higher than do those of some of the American historians. The fame of Prescott has already spread, even beyond the wide limits of Anglo-Saxon-dom. The name of Bancroft is as widely and as favourably known; his history of the United States, of which only a portion has as yet appeared, combining the interest of a romance with fidelity to sober realities. In biographical literature, and in essays of a sketchy character, none can excel Washington Irving; whilst in descriptive writing, and in detailing "incidents of travel," Stevens has certainly no superior. Many medical works of great eminence are from American pens; and there is not a good law library in this country but is indebted for some of its most valuable treasures to the jurisprudential literature of America. Prominent amongst the names which English as well as American lawyers revere, is that of Mr. Justice Story. Nor have American theologians been idle, whilst jurists and physicians have been busy with their pens. Dwight, Edwards, and Barnes, are known elsewhere as well as in America as eminent controversialists. Nor is the country behind in regard to science, for not only have many valuable scientific discoveries been made and problems solved in it, but many useful works of a scientific character have appeared, to say nothing of the periodicals which are conducted in the interest of science. The important science of Economy has also been illustrated and promoted by the works of American economists, whilst Americans have likewise contributed their share to the political and philological literature of the world. The American brain is as active as American hands are busy. It has already produced a literature far above mediocrity, a literature which will be greatly extended, diversified, and enriched, as by the greater spread of wealth the classes who can most conveniently devote themselves to its pursuit increase.

It is but natural that a government which does so much for the promotion of education should seek to make an ally of literature. Literary men in America, like literary men in France, have the avenue of political preferment much more accessible to them than literary men in England. There is in this respect, however, this difference between France and America, that whilst in the former the literary man is simply left to push his way to place; in the latter, he is very often sought for and dragged into it. In France he must combine the violent partisan with the literateur ere he realises a position in connexion with his government. In America the literateur is frequently converted into the politician, without ever having been the mere partisan. It was thus that Paulding was placed by President Van Buren at the head of the navy department, that Washington Irving was sent as minister to Spain, and Stevens despatched on a political mission to Central America. It was chiefly on account of his literary qualities that Mr. Everett was sent as minister to London, and that Mr. Bancroft was also sent thither by the cabinet of Mr. Polk. Like Paulding, this last-mentioned gentleman was for some time at the head of a department in Washington, previously to his undertaking the embassy to London. The historian exhibited administrative capacity, as soon as he was called upon to exercise it; whilst in this country he has earned for himself the character of an accomplished diplomatist, a finished scholar, and a perfect gentleman. But Mr. Bancroft's future fame will not depend upon his proved aptitude for administration or diplomacy. As in Mr. Macaulay's case, so with him, the historian will eclipse the politician.

As is the case in this country, the periodical and newspaper press occupies a very prominent position in the literature of America. Periodicals, that is to say, quarterlies, monthlies, and serials of all kinds, issue from it in abundance; the reviews and magazines being chiefly confined to Boston, Philadelphia, and New York.

In connexion with American newspapers, the first thing that strikes the stranger is their extraordinary number. They meet him at every turn, of all sizes, shapes, characters, prices, and appellations. On board the steamer and on the rail, in the counting-house and the hotel, in the street and in the private dwelling, in the crowded thoroughfare and in the remotest rural district, he is ever sure of finding the newspaper. There are daily, tri-weekly, bi-weekly, and weekly papers, as with us; papers purely political, others of a literary cast, and others again simply professional; whilst there are many of no particular character, combining everything in their columns. The proportion of daily papers is enormous. Almost every town, down to communities of two thousand in number, has not only one but several daily papers. The city of Rochester, for instance, with a population a little exceeding 30,000, has five; to say nothing of the bi-weekly and weekly papers which are issued in it. I was at first, with nothing but my European experience to guide me, at a loss to understand how they were all supported. But I found that, in addition to the extent of their advertising patronage, which is very great, advertisements being free of duty in America, the number of their readers is almost co-extensive with that of the population. There are few in America who do not both take in and read their newspapers. English newspapers are, in the first place, read but by a few; and in the next, the number of papers read is small in comparison with the number that read them. The chief circulation of English papers is in exchanges, news-rooms, reading-rooms, hotels, taverns, coffeehouses, and pot-houses, but a fraction of those who read them taking them in for themselves. Their high price may have much to do with this. In America the case is totally different. Not only are places of public resort well supplied with the journals of the day, but most families take in their paper, or papers. With us it is chiefly the inhabitants of towns that read the journals; in America the vast body of the rural population peruse them with the same avidity and universality as do their brethren in the towns. Were it otherwise it would be impossible for the number, which now appear, to exist. But as newspapers are multiplied, so are readers, every one reading and most subscribing to a newspaper. Many families, even in the rural districts, are not contented with one, but must have two or more, adding some metropolitan paper to the one or two local papers to which they subscribe.

The character of the American press is, in many points of view, not as elevated as it might be. But in this respect it is rapidly improving, and, as compared to what it was some years ago, there is now a marked change in it for the better. There may be as much violence, but there is less scurrility than heretofore in its columns; it is also rapidly improving in a literary point of view. There are several journals in some of the great metropolitan cities, which, whether we take into account the ability with which they are conducted, or the dignity of attitude which they assume, as favourably contrast with the great bulk of the American press, as do the best conducted journals of this country. . . .

43. General View of American Society

IN THE following selections two visitors summed up their general impressions of American society. Alexander Mackay was a journalist who worked for the London Morning Chronicle when he was sent on assignment to America in 1846–47. He spent a considerable amount of time learning about the United States, and his published account of his tour has been judged the most penetrating account of American institutions written by an Englishman up to that time. Captain Frederick Marryat, on the other hand, was a novelist and former naval officer. He visited the United States in 1837 and came away with fairly favorable opinions about American society, although he was less than enthusiastic about the country's climate and government. Whatever the differences in their background and perspectives, the views of both men complement each other in detailing general characteristics of Americans during the Age of Jackson.

A. ALEXANDER MACKAY

If there is much in the social development of America that strikes an European as different from that to which he has been accustomed, he should recollect that society, in the two hemispheres, rests upon very different bases. In the old world, where the feudal relations are still permitted so largely to influence the arrangement of the social system, society presents an agglomeration of distinct parts, each having its determinate relation to the rest, and the members of each having the range of their sympathies confined to their own particular sphere. European society, in its different manifestations, is constituted, as it were, of a series of different layers, which, though in close contact, only partially fuse into each other. . . .

Very different from this are both the basis and the manifestation of society in America. There social inequality has never been a recognised principle, moulding the social fabric into arbitrary forms, and tyrannically influencing each person's position in the general scheme. Society in America started from the point to which society in Europe is only yet tending. The equality of man is, to this moment, its corner-stone. As often as it has exhibited any

SOURCE: Mackay, The Western World, I: 192–208.

tendency to aberration, has it been brought back again to this intelligible and essential principle. . . .

The ease, and sincerity of manner, which spring from this social manifestation, are so marked, as immediately to strike even the most apathetic observer. There is very little in America of what we understand by acquaintanceship. Intercourse leads to friendship, or it leads to nothing, it being contrary to an American's nature to feel indifferent, and yet look cordial. Having none of the sympathies, he has none of the antipathies of class; his circle is his country; and in that circle, admitting of no superiors, he sees none but equals. Not but that there are in America many who are superior, in the share which they possess of all the conventional ingredients of a gentleman, to the great bulk of their countrymen, and to whom cultivated society is more grateful than that which is rude and undisciplined. The distinction of polish and refinement is all the difference that is discernible on the surface of American society, there being no exclusiveness of feeling, or isolation of sympathy concealed beneath a polished exterior. The American is first and essentially an American, and then a gentleman: with him refinement is not the enamel which conceals what is beneath, but the polish which brings out the real grain, exhibiting him in a better light, but ever in the same character. . . .

It is obvious, however, that to retain this ease and accessibility of manner, it is very necessary to guard the equality of condition which is at their very foundation. Americans are all equal, not only in the eye of the law, but in social position, there being no rank to which one man is born and from which another is excluded, any more than there is political status, which, instead of being gained by personal effort, is a mere matter of inheritance. In European society, the superior ranks have every advantage in the cultivation of manner, for when not with equals, they are with inferiors, and thus learn ease and acquire self-possession. So it is with all Americans, who have no superiors to put, by their presence, an awkward, constrained, and artificial cast upon their actions. But let this equality of condition be invaded, and let a distinct class arise in America, with distinct interests and views of its own, and let that class take form and obtain an organized footing in the community, and the natural and unaffected manner, which marks the intercourse of society in that country, will give place to the artificial traits which indicate its European manifestations; and against this danger American society has constantly to struggle. It is difficult, where there are vast accumulations of wealth, to adhere to a horizontal scale in social conditions. In America wealth has great influence, and the circle of its possessors is daily being enlarged, a state of things which would bode no good to the social equilibrium, were it not for the presence of other and counteracting influences. If there is a very wealthy class in America, there is not a very poor class, by whose co-operation the wealthy class might act with effect upon the mass intervening between the two extremes. Indeed, so far as competence involves the absence of poverty, there is in America no class which can strictly be denominated poor; that is to say, there is no class whose condition is incompatible with their independence. It is evident, therefore, that although wealth has undoubtedly its influence, and invests its possessor with a certain share of adventitious consideration; it has, as yet, no power in America to alter the essential characteristic of society—that universal equality which is based on universal independence. In the political equality of the people is also to be found another of the counteracting influences which check the social tendencies of wealth. . . . With so many, and frequently such rough competitors, to deal with in the political race, the wealthy, to whom life has other attractions, retire from the scramble, leaving the ring in the possession of the energetic, the needy, and the adventurous. Thus it is, that if the rich man has a political object of his own to subserve, he cannot afford to lose the aid of his less wealthy neighbour, but frequently more influential politician. The consequence is, that between the political footing of the one and the wealth of the other, they meet on neutral ground, where they find themselves restored to that equality which, but for the circumstances in which they are placed, might have been permanently disturbed. . . . The political arena is filled with those who plunge into it from the very depths of society, as affording them a shorter road to consideration than that which they would have to pursue in the accumulation of property. Daily accessions being made to the wealthy class itself, whilst there is no definite section of society from which it is known that they will spring; and daily transmutations going on from obscurity to political importance, whilst political aspirations are limited to no class, and political aid may be received from an individual, emanating from the humblest sphere,—render it impossible, without the presence of a poor and absolutely dependent class, for wealth, at least in its present development, to over-ride the social order of things established in America. Keeping this in view, it need surprise no one to find a free and unreserved intercourse subsisting externally amongst all the members of the community. The man of leisure, the professional man, and the merchant, the mechanic, the artizan, and the trades-man, meet each other on equal terms, the only obstacle that can arise between them being, on the part of any of them, impropriety of behaviour or infamy of character. So long as the ballot-box is in the hands of those with whom the suffrage is universal, so long will the poorer classes have it in their power to check any social aberrations in the more wealthy, should the latter be inclined to substitute for the general easy intercourse which prevails, an exclusive social and political regime. . . .

The exclusive feature of American society is no where brought so broadly out as it is in the city of Philadelphia. It is, of course, readily discernible in Boston, New York, and Baltimore; but the line drawn in these places is not so distinctive or so difficult to transcend as it is in Philadelphia. The fashionables there are more particular in their inquiries, than are their neighbours, before they give admittance to the stranger knocking at their gates. As a general rule, an unexceptional recommendation is all that is necessary in America to secure the stranger a ready acceptance by those to whom he is presented. The presumptions are all in favour of his fitness for the sphere which he aspires to adorn. To this, however, society in Philadelphia forms the most notable exception; a recommendation there only operating to put the new comer on his probation, and if found wanting, his recommendation goes for no more than it is worth; being estimated more from the proved qualities of the party receiving, than from the standing or authority of the party giving it. Once admitted, however, society in Philadelphia will be found amply to compensate for any delays and uncertainties with which the preliminary ordeal may have been accompanied. It is intellectual without being pedantic, and sprightly without being boisterous. It seems to be a happy blending of the chief characteristics of Boston and New York society. In both society is more accessible than in Philadelphia. In Boston the nucleus on which it turns is the literary circle of the place, which, comprising individuals and families of all grades of wealth, gives to society there a more democratic cast than it possesses either in New York or Philadelphia. It must be confessed, however, that there is a literary affectation about it, which is easier to be accounted for than endured, Bostonians always appearing to best advantage when they are farthest from home. In New York, again, the commercial spirit predominates over every other, and largely infuses itself into the society of the city. There is a permanent class of wealthy residents, who form the centre of it; its great bulk being composed of those who, by themselves or friends, are still actively engaged in the pursuits of commerce. With a few exceptions it is, therefore, in a state of constant fluctuation, in accordance with the fluctuating fortunes of commercial life. Its doors are guarded, but they seem never to be closed, and you have a constant stream flowing in and out. The consequence is, that there is much more heart than refinement about it. It is gay to a degree, sprightly and cordial, but far less conventional than the corresponding circle in Philadelphia. Society in the latter has all the advantages incident to a large community, in which the commercial spirit does not overbear every thing else, and in which literature is cultivated as an ornament, more than pursued as a business. . . .

In a social point of view, there is this difference in America between the north and the south; that in the former, society, in its narrower sense, takes its chief development in towns, whereas, in the latter, it is more generally confined to the rural districts. This difference is chiefly attributable to the different systems which obtain in the distribution of property, and to other causes, social and political, which will be presently adverted to. As a general rule, in the north and west there is no such thing as a country society, in the ordinary acceptation of the term. The land is divided into small lots, each man, generally speaking, occupying only as much as he can cultivate. The whole country is thus divided into farms; there are few or no estates. The rural population is almost, without exception, a working population, with little leisure, if they had otherwise the means, to cultivate the graces of life. As you travel through the country you see multitudes of comfortable houses and good farming establishments, but no mansions. There is not, in fact, such a class in existence there as is here known as the country gentry. . . .

In the south, on the other hand, things assume a very different aspect. In the States of Maryland, Virginia, the two Carolinas, Georgia, and Florida, as indeed in all the Southern States, land is possessed, as with us, in larger quantities; the owners, as in England, generally living on their estates. It is thus that, although

Baltimore has its social circle, the chief society of Maryland is to be found in the counties; whilst, in the same way, the capital of Virginia affords but a faint type of the society of the State. In the rural life of these two States, and in that of South Carolina, are to be found many of the habits and predilections of colonial times, and a nearer approach to English country life than is discernible in any other portion of the republic. The country is divided into large plantations, containing, in many instances, many thousands of acres; on which reside the different families, in large and commodious mansion-houses, surrounded by multitudes of slaves and by all the appliances of rural luxury. It is thus that, removed as they are from the necessity of labour, and being interrupted in their retirement only by the occasional visits of their friends and neighbours, the opportunity is afforded them of cultivating all those social qualities which enter into our estimate of a country gentry. In the society of the Southern Atlantic States, but particularly in that of the three last mentioned, there is a purity of tone and an elevation of sentiment, together with an ease of manner and a general social applomb, which are only to be found united in a truly leisure class. Any general picture of American society would be very incomplete, into which was not prominently introduced the phase which it exhibits in the rural life of the South. . . .

B. Captain Frederick Marryat

The character of the Americans is that of a restless, uneasy people—they cannot sit still, they cannot listen attentively, unless the theme be politics or dollars, they must do something, and, like children, if they cannot do anything else, they will do mischief— their curiosity is unbounded, and they are very capricious. Acting upon impulse, they are very generous at one moment and without a spark of charity the next. They are good-tempered and possess great energy, ingenuity, bravery, and presence of mind. Such is the estimate I have formed of their general character, independent of the demoralizing effects of their institutions, which renders it so anomalous. . . .

Source: Captain Frederick Marryat, *A Diary in America With Remarks on its Institutions*, Volume II (London, 1839), pp. 120–141.

The Americans have few amusements; they are too busy. Athletic sports they are indifferent to; they look only to those entertainments which feed their passion for excitement. The theatre is almost their only resort, and even that is not so well attended as it might be, considering their means. There are some very good and well-conducted theatres in America: the best are the Park and National at New York, the Tremont at Boston, and the Chestnut Street Theatre at Philadelphia. . . .

The love of excitement must of course produce a love of gambling, which may be considered as one of the American amusements; it is, however, carried on very quietly in the cities. In the south, and on the Mississippi, it is as open as the noon day; and the gamblers may be said to have there become a professional people. I have already mentioned them, and the attempts which have been made to get rid of them. Indeed, they are not only gamesters who practise on the unwary, but they combine with gambling the professions of forgery, and uttering of base money. If they lose, they only lose forged notes. There is no part of the world where forgery is carried on to such an extent as it is in the United States, chiefly in the western country. The American banks are particularly careful to guard against this evil, but the ingenuity of these miscreants is surprising, and they will imitate so closely as almost to escape detection at the banks themselves. Bank-note engraving is certainly carried to the highest state of perfection in the United States. . . .

There is one very remarkable point in the American character, which is that they constantly change their professions. I know not whether it proceeds simply from their love of change or from their embracing professions at so early a period that they have not discovered the line in which from natural talents they are best calculated to succeed. I have heard it said that it is seldom that an American succeeds in the profession which he had first taken up at the commencement of his career. An American will set up as a lawyer, quit, and go to sea for a year or two; come back, set up in another profession; get tired again, go as clerk or steward in a steamboat, merely because he wishes to travel; then apply himself to something else and begin to amass money. It is of very little consequence what he does; the American is really a jack of all trades and master of any to which he feels at last inclined to apply himself. . . .

It is true that they prefer broad humor and delight in the

hyperbole, but this is to be expected in a young nation, especially as their education is, generally speaking, not of a kind to make them sensible to very refined wit, which, I acknowledge, is thrown away upon the majority. What is termed the undercurrent of humor, as delicate raillery, for instance, is certainly not understood. . . .

If there required any proof of the dishonest feeling so prevalent in the United States, arising from the desire of gain, it would be in the fact that almost every good story which you hear of an American is an instance of great ingenuity and very little principle. . . .

It is singular to observe human nature peeping out in the Americans, and how tacitly they acknowledge by their conduct how uncomfortable a feeling there is in perfect equality. The respect they pay to a title is much greater than that which is paid to it in England, and naturally so; we set a higher value upon that which we *cannot* obtain. I have been often amused at the variance on this point between their words and their feelings, which is shown in their eagerness for rank of some sort among themselves. Every man who has served in the militia carries his title until the day of his death. There is no end to generals, and colonels, and judges; they keep taverns and grog shops, especially in the western states; indeed, there are very few who have not brevet rank of some kind; and I, being only a captain, was looked upon as a very small personage, so far as rank went. . . .

The Americans possess courage, presence of mind, perseverance, and energy, but these may be considered rather as endowments than as virtues. They are propelling powers which will advance them as a people and, were they regulated and tempered by religious and moral feeling, would make them great and good, but without these adjuncts they can only become great and vicious. . . .

I have said that the people of the United States, at the time of the Declaration of Independence, were perhaps the most moral people existing, and I now assert that they are the least so; to what cause can this change be ascribed? Certainly not wholly to the spirit of gain, for it exists everywhere, although perhaps nowhere so strongly developed as it is under a form of government which admits of no other claim to superiority. I consider that it arises from the total extinction, or if not extinction, absolute bondage, of the aristocracy of the country, both politically as well as socially. There was an aristocracy at the time of the independence—not an aristocracy of title, but a much superior one: an aristocracy of great,

The Age of Jackson

Printed by offset lithography by Halliday Lithograph Corporation
on 55# Warren's University Text. This acid-free paper, noted for
its longevity, has been watermarked with the University of South
Carolina Press colophon. Binding by Halliday Lithograph Corporation in Scott Graphics' Corinthian Kivar 9.

powerful, and leading men, who were looked up to and imitated; there was, politically speaking, an aristocracy in the Senate, which was elected by those who were then independent of the popular will; but although a portion of it remains, it may be said to have been almost altogether smothered, and in society it no longer exists. It is the want of this aristocracy that has so lowered the standard of morals in America, and it is the revival of it that must restore to the people of the United States the morality they have lost. The loss of the aristocracy has sunk the republic into a democracy; the renewal of it will again restore them to their former condition.